AF553588

CORPORATE PROFITABILITY ANALYSIS

CORPORATE PROFITABILITY ANALYSIS

By

Dr. A. Vijayakumar
Associate Professor in Commerce
Erode Arts and Science College (Autonomous)
Erode

Dr. P. Tamizhselvan
Associate Professor in Financial Management
Tamil Nadu Institute of Urban Studies
Coimbatore

DISCOVERY PUBLISHING HOUSE PVT. LTD.
NEW DELHI-110 002

Published by:
Tilak Wasan
DISCOVERY PUBLISHING HOUSE PVT. LTD.
4831/24, Ansari Road, Prahlad Street
Darya Ganj, New Delhi-110002 (India)
Phone: +91-11-23279245, 43764432
Fax: +91-11-23253475
E-mail: parul.wasan@gmail.com
info@discoverypublishinggroup.com
web: www.discoverypublishinggroup.com

First Edition: **2011**
ISBN: 978-81-8356-760-2

Corporate Profitability Analysis

Printed at:
Shree Balaji Art Press
Delhi

Preface

Financial management of resources in terms of profitability constitutes, by far, to be the most important element of their operational efficiency. The profit test is more than whether the resources are gainfully employed or not and whether the business enterprise is operating competitively or not. It has a direct bearing on the ability to function as a successful business firm. Further, their ability to tap the capital market by issuing equity shares and bonds/debentures would depend on their financial viability. Profit is the engine that drives the business enterprises. Profit and profitability play the same role in business as 'Blood' and 'Pulse' in the human body. The survival of a human being is not possible in the absence of adequate blood and ability to generate blood. Similarly, a business needs profits not only for its existence but for expansion and diversification.

The growth of the corporate sector in India has been rapid. The economic growth of a nation largely depends upon the growth and development of its corporate sector. The corporate sector is not only an institution for the maximization of shareholder's wealth, but also an administrative and social organization possessing the capacity for initiating its own growth and thereby contributing to the economic growth of the country. The growth of an enterprise is based on its success and profit is the primary test of the success of an enterprise. The greater the profit, the greater will be the entrepreneurial activity; greater the profit, larger is the accumulation of capital; and greater the profit more will be the technological innovations and thereby higher will be the economic growth.

The growth of a company can be measured in terms of changing investment, sales, profit or profitability. Thus, growth in the profitability means all round growth of a business enterprise. No doubt, a change is observed in profitability trend of corporate sector. But, it is not uniform in all the companies working in the country. While companies functioning in the advanced region prospered remarkably, but the companies working in the relatively backward region were found lagging behind. In the same region again the trends of profitability were different depending upon the size, age and nature of industrial activity of companies. Viewed in this perspective, the study devoted to profitability analysis may be rewarding one.

The sugar industry is the second largest industry in India next to cotton textile, playing an important role in the national economy. The sugar industry has a great significance which cannot be devalued in its relation to agricultural and industrial economy of the rural region of India. It is an agro-based industry. Therefore, the expansion of sugar industry in India is an indispensable factor for the uplift of socio-economic life in India. Located in rural India, sugar industry has provided the most effective instrument for carrying progressive trends into the country side. The most outstanding feature of the industry is the vital link between the factory and the cultivators whose interest and well being are interdependent. Further, they have an intrinsic symbiotic relationship between rural masses and same as nerve center for rural development. It also provides employment to quite a large number of people at national and State level. Sugar industry has been wide spread and has attained almost its stature. But the industry cannot said to be well-established, as it has to solve number of problems. A serious problem for the industry has been its chronic instability. There has been an alteration of increases and decreases in production and prices over short period, resulting in wide spread difficulties for consumers and producers. Therefore, the present study was undertaken for a proper insight in to the profitability analysis in the sugar industry.

This book contains various aspects of profitability in the Indian sugar industry. Further, in order to cater to the needs of research scholars, teachers and financial executive, the subject matter in the book has been treated in a conceptual-cum-analytical manner. The book is intended to be useful for practising managers, financial executives working in the service sectors, students of M.Com, MBA, MFC and other banking professional examinations. Further, this book is of special interest of Ph-D. and M.Phil. scholars of various universities, colleges and research institutions. The contents of the book may be much useful to researchers pursuing research in the field of profitability analysis.

We earnestly hope that it would serve its purpose and meet the market needs. However, we would gratefully welcome suggestions and feedback from colleagues, students and practitioners. Any constructive criticism will undoubtedly help us greatly to enhance our research capability.

A. Vijayakumar

P. Tamizhselvan

Acknowledgements

We express our heartfelt gratitude to God Almighty whose blessings guided us in carrying out the research successfully. The work presented in this book could be possible only because of the co-operation, guidance and assistance given by a number of persons and a few institutions. It is difficult to recount them all and we tender due apologies to all those contributions we have not been able to recount. However, we cannot afford not to mention a few.

In the preparation of this book, We have received help and encouragement from different sources. We shall forever cherish the kind permission and encouragement given to us by *Thiru. K.M. Dhandapani,* President, The Mudaliar Educational Trust. We are grateful to *Thiru. K.K. Balusamy,* our most beloved Secretary and Correspondent, Erode Arts College, for his encouragement and inspiration given to use. I would like to thank *Thiru. K.N.Murugesan,* Vice-President, *Thiru. U.N.Murugesan,* Vice-President, *Thiru. L. Kumaravel,* Treasurer and other management committee members for their encouragement.

We would like to thank *Dr. V. Venkateswaran,* Principal, Erode Arts College, Erode for the necessary help we required in completing this work. We also express our deep sense of gratitude to faculty members of Department of Commerce, Erode Arts College, Erode for their co-operation and assistance for completing this task. We are grateful to our colleagues and friends for their help and support in the completion of this book.

We also extend our profound thanks to Discovery Publishing House Private Limited, New Delhi, for giving shape to our ideas by publishing this book in a record time.

A. Vijayakumar
P. Tamizhselvan

Contents

CHAPTER 1

Introduction

Corporate sectors have to play a predominant role in the economic life of almost all countries, irrespective of their ideological moorings. The corporate sector has been recognized as a model and democratic form of business organization. It occupies a pivotal place not only in the industrially advanced countries, but also in the developing countries such as India. Corporate sector is the backbone of Indian economy so far as it provides a vital, effective and organized system for the growth of the industrial as well as non-industrial sector of the economy. The contribution of corporate sector towards the balanced development of various areas of an organized economic activity can be seen in the combined efforts of various companies in achieving the goal of industrialization and increased production.

Corporate sectors have short-term goals such as improving annual profits and value-added as well as long-term goals in terms of contribution to national wealth, creation of more employment, building up infrastructure facilities, building up a broad-based and healthy capital structure, operating of essential services, creating export potential and thus participating actively in the overall economic growth of a country and improving the standard of living of its people. Ultimately, the Gross Domestic Products

(GDP) and the tax revenue to the government in the form of both direct and indirect taxes are maximized. The rapid growth of the corporate sector in India and the increasing scale of its operations and investments have turned it into the most dominant form of economic organization.

The ever increasing importance and role of corporate sector in the economic growth of a country, particularly in the developing country such as India, have attracted several academicians, professional institutions, researchers, administrators to conduct diversified studies in this area. There is a need to study the industries internal efficiencies which ultimately shall determine the overall industrial development in future. The present study is a small endeavour to update our knowledge in this aspect.

Meaning and Concept of Profit

The word 'profit' has got different meanings for businessmen, accountant, tax collectors, workers and economist. The term 'profit' is an absolute term. Profit may be defined as the excess of total revenue over total cost during the specified period of time. There is almost universal agreement with general definition that profit is "primarily a residue or surplus of prices over expenses of production or leaving above cost".[1] Therefore, profit is necessarily a residual sum. It is the payment received by a factor of production called the organizer. He organizes land, labour and capital, produces goods, sells them and bears uninsurable risks which others unwilling to bear, and if he is successfully bears a risk he receives reward called profit. Thus, profits are non-contractual income and therefore, there may be positive or negative, whereas, the contractual income of other factors of production is always positive and never negative. This may be called as the functional definition of profit. The concept of profit has been divided into three broad categories, viz.: (1) Accounting Concept, (2) Economic Concept and (3) Social Concept.

According to Accounting Concept, profit is known as excess of total revenues over their total cost during a given period. Thus, accounting profit lies in the difference between current value of sales and historic cost of expenses.[2] Further, the meaning of accounting profit varied according to the purpose for which it is used. For example, the owners are interested in net profit whereas, creditors are interested in Earnings Before Interest and Tax.

There is no complete agreement among the economists about the true nature and origin of profits. Economic profit is a profit over and above what could be earned in the best alternative use of resources. Economic profit equals accounting profit minus the opportunity cost of the resources used in the business. Thus, what is meant by accounting concept, labeled, as profit is not profit as the economist view them. In this sense economic profit is the residue of income after all the contractual and non-contractual payment have been made from the revenue realized during a given period of time.

Social profit may be defined as the difference between social benefits and social costs. Moreover, the chief executive of a large corporation has the problem of reconciling the demands of employees for more wages and improved benefit plans, customers for lower prices and greater values; shareholders for higher dividends and greater capital appreciation – all within a framework that will be constructive and acceptable to society.

Meaning and Concept of Profitability

The concept of profit refers to the absolute quantum of profit. It does not speak what the reason for profit is, how it is scattered, and what the relationship of one figure is with another. All these questions can be answered by the concept of profitability. Profitability is a relative measure. It refers to the ability to earn profit. The profitability of a company is the net result of a large number of policies and decisions taken by an enterprise. Profitability is composed of two words 'profit' and 'ability'. On this basis, the concept of profitability may be defined as the ability of a given investment to earn a return from its value.[3] This ability is also referred to as 'earning power' or the operating performance of the concerned investment. Increase in profit does not necessarily increase the profitability of the concern.

One striking feature of the concept of profitability is its varying nature. Profitability is not a constant and static phenomenon that remains unaffected by changes in its determinants but to a great extent, a changing and varying one. Changes in its determinants result in change of profitability. It is reasonable as well as convincing to compare profitability with weather. The comparison of profitability with weather strengthened by these arguments as follows:

First the state of profitability is variable phenomenon like the weather of a day. The weather can change or will change according to change in humidity, temperature and other relevant factors. Similarly, profitability will change owing to change in its determinants. Second the study of the weather on a particular day makes it possible to forecast the weather on the following day. In the same manner, analytical study of profitability in a concern or business provides us with the base of forecast possible future trends of profitability. Third, the study of the determinants of profitability by an accountant/financial advisor/analyst can also be linked to temperature reading and study of humidity by a meteorologist.

The concept of profitability has been divided into two broad categories: (1) Commercial or accounting profitability and (2) Social profitability.

Commercial or Accounting Profitability

Commercial profitability is the traditional measure of the performance. By measuring the output as a proportion of the input and comparing with the results of other similar firms or periods, the relative changes in its profitability can be measured. The output indicates the profitability of a firm.

This is known as return on investment. This return on investment acts as a measure of overall profitability which has two components: (*i*) Profit margin and (*ii*) Investment turnover ratio. If the management wants to improve its profitability, it can do so by improving profit margin or investment turnover ratio or both.

Social Profitability

From the point of view of the society, social profitability is a much better measure of performance as compared to the other forms of profitability. It is also referred to as the national economic profitability. The measurement of social profitability is undertaken within the framework of social cost-benefit analysis. In other words, when all outputs and inputs are evaluated at their social opportunity costs, and when all external effects of the domestic economy are given social valuation and included in the measure, one gets a measure of net social profitability. The measurement of social profitability poses a number of problems such as estimation of social opportunity cost, valuation of tangible and intangible benefits etc. Therefore, in this study, accounting profitability has been used.

Significance of Profitability

The objectives of business are to provide goods and services which the society needs at a price and can afford to pay. Profit is merely a measure of the approval of the society for the work being done for them. Profits are necessary for existence of business. Lord Keynes has rightly marked, "Profit is the engine that drives the business enterprises", and profits and profitability play the same role in business as "blood" as "pulse" in the human body. The survival of a human being is not possible in the absence of adequate blood and ability to generate blood. The same may be applied to business. A business needs profits not only for its existence but for expansion and diversification. Profit and profitability are, therefore, the nerve-knot of a business and without it the existence of a firm is likely a body without the backbone.

A business enterprise can discharge its obligations to the various segments of the society only through earning profit. But, at the same time one should distinguish profit earning from profiteering. Where the amount of profit made exceeds a socially acceptable limit by questionable methods, it is a case of profiteering.[4] We are talking about profit-earning only and not-profiteering. Thus, profits are a useful measure of overall efficiency of a firm or business. "Profits to the management are the test of efficiency and a measure of control; to the owners, a measure of worth of their investments; to the creditors, the margin of safety; to employees, a source of fringe benefits; to the government, a measure of tax-paying capacity and the basis of legislative action; to customers, a hint to demand for better quality and price-cuts; to an enterprise, less cumbersome some source of finance for growth and existence and finally to the country, profits are an index of economic progress."[5] There must be not only enough profits to yield the capital market rate of return on money which is already sunk in business but also to provide additional capital needed to cover the cost of staying in business. Therefore, profit is indeed a magic eye that mirrors all aspects of entire business operations including the quality of output.[6] If an enterprise fails to earn profit, invested capital is eroded and if this situation prolongs, the enterprise may ultimately cease to exist.

Therefore, the overall objective of a business is to earn atleast a satisfactory return on the fund invested in it consistent with a sound financial position.

Tools and Techniques for Analysis of Profitability

There are many techniques which may be used for analyzing profitability. These techniques may be classified as (*a*) Accounting techniques, (*b*) Statistical techniques and (*c*) Mathematical techniques. Accounting techniques or tools which may be used for profitability analysis are many such as ratio analysis, common-size statement analysis, trend analysis, comparative statement analysis, value added analysis etc. The users pick up the techniques to suit their requirements and also on the basis of data available to them. Further, use of statistical techniques has become a normal phenomenon in any type of analysis. The statistical techniques which are proposed to be used in financial statement analysis consists of measures of central tendency like mean, median, mode, measures of dispersion, such as range, mean deviation and standard deviation, correlation and regression analysis, analysis of time series, analysis of variance, chi-square test etc. Further, the use of various mathematical techniques is also made frequently for profitability analysis. The mathematical tools generally applied are Programme Evaluation and Review Techniques (PERT), Critical Path Method (CPM), Linear programming etc. However, in this study various accounting and statistical techniques have been applied for analyzing the financial statements. The mathematical techniques could not be applied in the present study for want of necessary data.

Need for the Study

The growth of the corporate sector in India has been rapid. The economic growth of a nation largely depends upon the growth and development of its corporate sector. The corporate sector is not only an institution for the maximization of shareholder's wealth, but also an administrative and social organization possessing the capacity for initiating its own growth and thereby contributing to the economic growth of the country. The growth of an enterprise is based on its success and profit is the primary test of the success of an enterprise. The greater the profit, the greater will be the entrepreneurial activity; greater the profit, larger is the accumulation of capital; and greater the profit more will be the technological innovations and thereby higher will be the economic growth.

The growth of a company can be measured in terms of changing investment, sales, profit or profitability. Thus growth in the profitability means all round growth of a business enterprise. No doubt, a change is observed in profitability trend of corporate sector. But, it is not uniform in all the companies working in the country. While companies functioning in the advanced region prospered remarkably, but the companies working in the relatively backward region were found lagging behind. In the same region again the trends of profitability were different depending upon the size, age and nature of industrial activity of companies. Hence, at this juncture an analysis of profitability in the Indian corporate sector is felt relevant.

Selection of Sugar Industry

The sugar industry is the second largest industry in India next to cotton textile, playing an important role in the national economy. The sugar industry has a great significance which cannot be devalued in its relation to agricultural and industrial economy of the rural region of India. It is an agro-based industry. Therefore, the expansion of sugar industry in India is an indispensable factor for the uplift of socio-economic life in India. Located in rural India, sugar industry has provided the most effective instrument for carrying progressive trends into the country side. The most outstanding feature of the industry is the vital link between the factory and the cultivators whose interest and well being are interdependent. Further, they have an intrinsic symbiotic relationship between rural masses and same as nerve center for rural development. It also provides employment to quite a large number of people at national and state level.

Sugar industry has been wide spread and has attained almost its stature. But the industry cannot said to be well established, as it has to solve number of problems. A serious problem for the industry has been its chronic instability. There has been an alteration of increases and decreases in production and prices over short period, resulting in wide spread difficulties for consumers and producers. India's dual pricing policy of subsidizing levy sugar procured by the government from the industry at prices 20 per cent below cost of production. Based on the hypothesis that higher prices of levy-free sugar in open market will compensate its losses has lost focus and has been driven to illogical ends. Indian producers are fleeced by making their part with 40 per cent of their output towards levy at far below production cost for sales through the Public Distribution System (PDS). The resultant losses contribute to the mounting of sugarcane arrears to farmers.

The Central Government declares the Statutory Minimum Price (SMP) for sugarcane every year in lieu of the Minimum Support Price (MSP) that it declares for food grains and other essential commodities. But several State governments have rashly promised to raise cane prices in an effort to win farmers loyalty due to political compulsion. In effect the prices of sugarcane are increased every year by the centre and further by each State. The unrealistic high State dictated cane prices have been made most of the sugar mills unviable and they turned sick. With mill declaring losses, lakhs of farmers have gone unremunerative for their cane. In such a situation, farmers who sell canes to the *gur* and *khandasari* unit get their payment, but the price is unremunerative.

Sugar prices in India in retail have remained low and continued to be the lowest among almost all countries. This has caused uneconomic working over long period and all pervading sickness in all sector. Although wide fluctuations in production are not new for the agro-based industry, which depend solely on the supply of the perishable crop like sugarcane, some of them are due to lower sugarcane production arising out of lower acres under sugarcane and unfavourable weather conditions. Further, sugarcane cropping has not received due attention in the hands of central government like such other food crops as wheat and paddy. The above said major problems faced by the sugar industry left sugar industry in the lurch. But it was left to fend for itself. This has encouraged the researcher to analyze the profitability of sugar industry. Some research studies have been undertaken on Indian sugar industry at the national level. But the sugar industry operated in the South India has received only second attention. Thus an attempt was made by the researcher to analyze the profitability performance of selected South Indian sugar industry.

Statement of the Problem

The efficiency of the business is measured by the amount of profit earned. The greater the profit, the more efficient is the business considered to be. The profit of a business may be measured by studying the profitability of investment in it. Profitability is referred to as lending power or operating performance of the concerned investment. Profitability is a relative term and its relation with the other factor by which the profit is affected. It is the test of efficiency, powerful motivational factor and the measure of control in any business. Hence, an attempt has been made to study the profitability of selected South Indian sugar industry by using vital profitability ratios.

In the financial statement analysis literature, a lot of importance has been attached to financial ratios for assessing a firm's financial performance and condition. Items of the income statement alone or along with the balance sheet items also can generate a number of profitability ratios. But, many ratios reveal the similar things. The analyst is always at a loss to find out which ratios to use to determine profitability of a firm. An attempt to determine inter-relationships between and among the profitability ratios, in order to select a few ratios which can possibly give maximum information about the profitability of a firm is an empirical issue.

Rate of profit is an indicator and sources of and a need for the expansion of the business through reinvestment and through attracting and absorbing new capital in the industry. Hence, investors and lenders are interested in knowing the profitability of a concern and industry over time or at a point of time. The celebrated tendency of rates of profit to fall over a long period of time had been theoretically developed by classical economists such as Adam Smith, David Ricardo, etc., their critic Karl Marx and also be neo-classical writers such as Alfred Marshal. The study therefore, indents to empirically examine whether the rates of profit in South Indian private sector sugar industry have a tendency to rise or fall over a long period of 15 years. The objective here is not to test the validity of classical hypothesis as the economic conditions as assumed by classical writers do not prevail in India. However, knowledge about whether the profitability is rising or falling over the period from 1991-92 to 2005-06 would throw interesting results for formulation of future policies.

With the recognition of the concept of economies of scales the question of size of firm has assumed special importance in industrial economics. In this context, issue of the relationship of size of firm and profitability and concept of efficiency in relation to size has undergone a change. It is behind that larger the size of the firm, greater the efficiency in terms of costs and therefore, higher the profits. This can be possibly achieved by producing the particular level of output. However, the output has to be of optimum size where firms' per unit cost is at the minimum level. This indicates that firms can not expand their output beyond this limit and would not continue to make excess profits for long. However, over a period of time the concept of optimum size of firms has also become a controversial issue. Baumol[7] has hypothesized that there is a positive relationship between firm size and profits. A counter argument is that size breaths inefficiencies and that, accordingly, large firms cannot undertake the option open to a small firm as efficiently as small firms and hence profitability may decline with the size of firm. It is in view of this contradictory suggestion, that it becomes necessary to study the relationship between size and profitability of firms in India. The present study, in this context, fulfils the requirement and attempts to study the issue of size and profitability.

It is felt that there is a need to study important role of working capital in profit generating process. If a company desires to take a greater risk for bigger profit or losses it reduces the size of working capital in relation to its sales. If it is interested in improving its liquidity, it increases the level of its working capital. However, this policy is likely to result in a reduction of the sales volume, therefore of profitability. Hence, a company should strike a balance between liquidity and profitability. Hence, an attempt has been made in this study to analyze the relationship between liquidity and profitability of South Indian private sector sugar industry.

The relationship between growth and profitability of the firm in an industry has attracted the attention of many economists in the world. Many empirical studies have been conducted about relationship between growth and profitability. This has led to an inconclusive debate. It is evident from the previous study in general we can expect a positive or negative association between growth and profitability. Furthermore, the nature and form of this relationship may between firms of different sizes, between industries and over time for the same industry. This is the reason the present study has made an attempt to analyze the relationship between growth and profitability of South Indian private sector sugar industry.

Actually profitability is highly sensitive economic variable which is affected by a host of factors operating through a variety of ways. Some of them affect product prices and quantities; some affect cost of production while others make changes in capital stock, size, market share and growth of the firm. Further, corporate policy relating to various functions will affect profitability. Some of them are relevant in the short run while others have impact in the long run. It is difficult to build a theory of profitability, which accounts for all such factors. Because of these difficulties, it is quite natural to analyze the variation in profitability by taking the partial approach *i.e.,* to find the effect of certain major variables, ignoring the implications of other left out independent variables at a time. Hence, in this study an attempt has been made to analyse about the determinants of profitability of South Indian private sector sugar industry during the study period. Further, an attempt has been made to assess the financial health of selected South Indian private sector sugar industry using Altman Z-Score model.

Thus, the present study attempts to answer the following questions:

1. What is the quantum of profit earned by the selected sugar industry? Is there any significant change taking place over a period of time?
2. What is the variability in profit rates in various industries?
3. Is investment in fixed assets and current assets utilized effectively?
4. What is the trend of profit rate of the selected industry over a period of time?
5. Is there any systematic relationship between size and profitability?
6. Is there any relationship between growth and profitability?
7. What are the factors that influence profitability of selected industry?

NOTES

1. Drucker, Peter F., *The Practice of Management*, Allied Publishers, New Delhi, 1970, pp. 46-47.
2. Most Kenneth, S. (1982). *Accounting Theory*, Grid Publishing Inc., Columbus, Ohio, p. 207.

3. Howard, B. Bion and Upton Miller, *Introduction to Business Finance*, McGraw-Hill Book Company Inc., New York, 1953, p. 147.

4. Varshney, R.L. and Maheswari, K.L., *Managerial Economics*, Sultan Chand and Sons, New Delhi, 1977, p. 297.

5. Sharma, R.K. and Gupta, Shashi K., *Management Accounting-Principles and Practice,* Kalyani Publishers, New Delhi, 1986, p. 150.

6. Kulshrestha, N.K., *Theory and Practice of Management Accounting,* Novman Prakashan, Aligarh, 1976, p. 265.

7. See, Baumol, W. J. (1967), *Business Behaviour, Value and Growth*, Harcourt Brace and World, New York.

CHAPTER 2

Approaches to the Study of Profitability Analysis

This chapter presents the review of literature relating to the study undertaken. The collection of reviews has been made from various studies undertaken by the academicians, practitioners, researchers, etc., from time to time. These reviews will enlighten the existing knowledge of the researcher. Besides this, the reviews of empirical studies explore the avenues for present and future research related to the subject-matter. In order to understand the research problem the earlier attempts made by the academicians, economist, socialist, etc., are needed to be studied. The review of literature guides the researchers for getting better understanding of methodology used, limitations of various available estimation procedures, database, lucid interpretation and reconciliation of the conflicting results. In case of conflicting and unexpected results, the researcher can take the advantage of knowledge of other researchers simply through the medium of their published works.

A large number of research studies had been carried out on different aspects of the profitability analysis by the researchers, economists and academicians in India and abroad. Different authors had analysed profitability performance in different perspective. A review of these analysis is important in order to develop an approach that can be employed in the context of the study of sugar industry in south India. Therefore, the present chapter reviews the various approaches to the study of profitability analysis.

Stekler (1964)[1] in his research study entitled 'The Variability of Profitability with Size of Firms 1947-1958', tested several hypotheses about the relative profitability and growth possibility of firms of various sizes. Each hypothesis was designed to perform a specific task. Interest was added to profit to avoid bias that could result due to variations in the ratio of equity to debt financing. The study concluded that variation over a period of time of average profitability for small firms was less than that of medium size firms.

Baumol (1967)[2] in his study "Business Behaviour, Value and Growth" had emphasized that there was a positive relationship between firm size and profits. He stated that increased money capital will not only increase the total profits of the firm but because it puts the firm in a higher echelon of imperfectly computing capital groups, it may also increase its earning per dollar of investment. Besides large firms have as they can enter in variety of product lines give them the benefits of both the scale and the size. Generally these firms are in a position to take full advantage of technical and pecuniary economies in manufacturing, marketing, supervision and in raising capital.

Samuels and Smyth (1968)[3] in "Profits, Variability of Profits and Firm Size" took the cross-section data of annual observation (1959 to 1963) of profits and net assets for 186 United Kingdom companies. These companies engaged in manufacturing distribution and mining were classified, into ten size classes according to their assets in 1954. Net assets were used as measure of firm size and the ratio of profits (after depreciation but before taxation) to net assets, was the measure of profitability. There was some evidence that firm's size was a significant factor in the determination of its mean profits over the ten-year period. The analysis did not indicate whether the higher profit rates were associated with large or small firms. But the mean rate of return for each size group for each year and also the average for the whole ten-year period, suggested that the higher the profit rates were associated with the smaller firms. Further, it was observed that the difference in the profit rates of large and small firms were becoming more marked over time. In order to examine the variability of profit rates, the hypothesis tested was that large companies are more able to withstand fluctuations in the level of activity against profits in another. Time variability of profit rates was thus inversely related to firm size. There was greater variability among profit rates of firms of the same size for small firms than for large size.

Singh and Whittington (1968)[4] in "Growth profitability and Valuation" conducted an empirical study of the relationship between the growth, size and profitability of the firm, growth being the main dependent variable, for 450 UK Public quoted companies, existing over the period 1948-60. The book value of the "net assets" was used as a measure of size of the firm and the difference between the values of net assets had represented differences in size of firm. The results exhibited that the average growth rate measured in terms of net assets was independent of the opening size of the firm. The same was also true of profitability. But the variability of the growth rates and the profit rates as between firms did change with the size to a significant extent. In both cases it tended to decrease as size increased. Large firms had a more predictable rate of profits, but not a higher one.

Marcus (1969)[5] in "Profitability and Size of the Firm: Some Further Evidence" tried to re-evaluate the hypothesis that the rate of return increases with the size of the firm, against new data within an improved analytical framework. His conclusion was that the hypothesis did not perform uniformly in all the industries and that it cannot therefore be viewed for having general validity.

Gale (1972)[6] in his study "Market Share and Rate of Return" stated that the effect of market share on the rate of return of selected firms which operating in different environment using data of high market share was associated with high rates of return and that the effect of share on profitability depends on other firm and industry characteristics such as degree of concentration and rate of growth in the industries in which the firm completes and on the absolute size of the firm. He also found that the relation between rate of return on equity and the equity to capital ratio to be positive and significant.

Mancke (1974)[7] in the study entitled 'Causes of Inter Firm Profit Differences: A New Interpretation of the Evidence', probed from a sample of 226 large firms observed from 1956 through 1962 tried to answer if the causes of inter firm profitability differences were the differences in firm size, market share and growth. In the model, measures of firm profit rates, market share and growth were positively correlated with profit rates. Other conclusions of the study included that empirical relationship between market share and profitability was stronger than the empirical relationship between firm size and profitability, monopoly power was found to be an important determinant of inter-firm profitability differences, more concentrated industries tended to earn higher profit rates and firm profit rates were positively related with the absolute volume of firm advertising expenditure.

Barthwal (1976)[8] in his study on 'The Determinants of Profitability in Indian Textile Industry' had identified the factors that cause variation in the profitability. The explanatory variables used by him were profitability, size of the firm, age of the firm, past growth, capital-output ratio and change in average cost of production. Among them, past profitability and changes in the average cost of production over the previous years had been found to be significant determinants of profitability of the firms in the industry, in different regions of the country.

Agarwal (1978)[9] in his study entitled "Size, Profitability and Growth of some Manufacturing Industries" highlighted relationship between profitability measured as profit/net worth and net profit/net assets and size expressed as total sales for seven Indian Manufacturing Industries viz., cotton spinning and weaving, cotton ginning, cement, jute textiles, paper and pulp, sugar and aluminum for the period 1962-1972. The relationship between size and profitability was observed in cotton spinning industry, jute textiles industry, sugar and brewing industry and aluminium industry, while in case of cement and cotton spinning and ginning industry no such relationship was observed.

Steer and Cable (1978)[10] in 'Internal Organisation and Profit: An Empirical Analysis of Large U.K. Companies', selected a sample of 82 large U.K. companies, for which organisational form classifications were available. These companies were drawn from the food, brewing, electrical engineering and mechanical engineering industries for the period 1967-71, to isolate the effects of internal organisation on profitability. They found that owner-controlled firms outperformed manager-controlled firms in terms of both profitability and growth. The owner-controlled firms were operating comparatively close to the region of maximum profits, with growth rates that were high, but not sufficiently so to be at the expense of profit. The manager-controlled firms exhibited unambiguous managerial slack, failing to grow as fast as they might at the profitability levels.

Neumann, et al. (1979)[11] in their study entitled "Profitability, Risk and Market Structure in West German Industries", explained mean rates of return of the period from 1965 to 1973 of 334 West German joint stock companies by risk and market structure. The results suggested that investors were risk averters and that risk bearing was accordingly compensated by a higher rate of return. Degrees of concentration and product differentiation were positively related to profitability while export and import ratio exerted an adverse impact on profitability. As regards size and profitability, smaller firms tended to be more flexible, tended to take chances of growth more easily than the bigger ones.

So there was inverse relationship between growth and profitability.

Whittington (1980)[12] in 'The Profitability and Size of United Kingdom Companies: 1960-1964' extended his investigation further covering the period from 1960 to 1974 and found that average profitability was largely independent of firm size. The relationships between inter company dispersion of profitability and variability of profits through time tended to decline with firm size. He also found that the average profitability margins and sales/assets ratio did not vary systematically with firm size and also profitability margins of large firms tended to be relatively stable through time whereas their sales/assets ratio did not. Thus, the relative stability through time of the rates of return of large firms was due to relative stability of their profits, rather than the stability of their capacity utilisation. Profitability was not an incentive for large firms to grow at a relatively higher rate.

Jain (1981)[13] in "Price-Cost Margin in Indian Manufacturing industries: An Econometric Analysis" analyzed the price cost margin over time in the two digit industries. Price-cost margin was used as a measure of profitability. Cost factors emerged as significant determinants of profitability while the structural variables like concentration ratio, capacity utilization, and growth and capital intensity showed mixed pattern. Results varied among the industries.

Bothwell, et al. (1982)[14] in their research "A new view of Market Structure - Performance Debate" used a sample of 156 large U.S. manufacturing firms over a period 1960-67 for determining the relationship between profit rate and other variables like seller concentration, advertising intensity, economics of scale, absolute capital requirements, leverage, profit variability, firm growth, firm size and market share etc. Positive correlation between seller concentration, market share and growth of demand, business risk, advertisement expenses and profit rate was found. Profit rates were negatively related with the extent of economics and capital requirements.

Gangadhar (1982)[15] in 'Cement Industry - Some Aspects of profitability' examined and made comment on the profitability of large public limited cement companies in India in order to bring out fluctuations, if any, and to offer possible causes for such fluctuations. The study revealed that the profitability in cement industry had fluctuated very widely with low rate during the period under review. The profit margin in the cement industry had shown declining trend whereas the asset turnover showed an increasing trend. The profit margin accounted to a great extent for lower rate of ROI in the industry as compared to asset turnover.

Rao (1985)[16] in his work entitled 'Impact of Debt-Equity Ratio on Profitability - An Exploratory Study of Engineering Industry' observed whether the earning ability i.e., profitability, had any impact on the debt-equity ratio in engineering companies. The study based on the impact of profitability on the debt-equity ratio had revealed a negative association i.e., high debt-equity ratios meant low profitability due to large interest payments, whereas low debt-equity ratio caused high profitability because of low interest payments. The operating efficiency of the firm and reasonable rate of return on owner's capital ultimately depend on the profits earned by it. Thus, profits are necessary to run the firm in a healthy atmosphere of present day cut throat competitions and defend it from business rivalry.

Chalam and Dakshinamurthy (1985)[17] in 'Performance of Public Enterprises in India: Impact of Heavy External Financing', had made a study on the performance of public sector enterprises in India and they had attributed the poor financial performance to the excessive use of external sources in their capital structure. They had evaluated the effects of heavy external finances on net incomes and on short-term liquidity position, in turn affecting the working funds available for successful operation. They had suggested for allowing more private equity participation, increasing the operational efficiency through controlling costs and improving the capacity utilisation and factors such alike for improving the performance of Public Enterprises in India.

Kumar (1985)[18] examined the Corporate Growth and profitability in the Large Indian Companies. To meet the objectives of the study, 100 largest non-banking, non-financial, non-government joint stock companies in India ranked on the basis of their total net assets in 1979 were selected from the *Economic Times* directory of Private Sector Giants. The study covers the period from 1969-70 to 1978-79. The growth of the firm was measured by the growth of total net assets at current prices. From the analysis, the profitability explained a very small part of the growth and the ability to perceive growth opportunities and exploit them fully exert an important influence on the finance growth seems to have been provided by the sector institutions like IDBI, ICICI, IFC and SFC.

Chawola (1986)[19] studied an empirical analysis of the profitability of the Indian man-made fibres industry. This study examined and explains the trends in the profitability of the Indian man-made fibers industry. The relevant data for the study was obtained from 17 firms found in *BSE Official Directory* for the period 1963-64 to 1977-78. An increase in the excise duty of man-made fibers seems to be associated with the decline in profitability of the industry. Both concentration and vertical integration influence the profitability. However, their impact differs for cellulose and petro-chemical based group of fibers.

Manasan, Rosario G. et al. (1988)[20] had made a study of The Public Enterprise Sector in the Philippines: Economic Contribution and Performance, 1975-1984. The public enterprise sector in the Philippines had grown at a tremendous pace in the last decade. It had contributed a large proportion of gross domestic capital formation but its impact on production, employment and savings was by no means significant. At the same time, estimates of financial profitability ratios and factor productivity measures suggested that the public sector enterprises are generally inefficient.

Chattopadhayay (1989)[21] in 'Central Government Enterprises: An Eighteen Years Profile', had brought an evaluation work on the performance of Central Government Enterprises covering a period of 18 years from 1969-70 to 1986-87. He presented the criticisms leveled against the performance of public sector enterprises and evaluated that the public sector units do have the potential to record much better results, provided they are run on business lines by maximising the rate of return on capital employed. He had put forward a number of suggestions to improve the working of these units, including the application of principles of sound management.

Sankar et al. (1990)[22] in a study sponsored by Planning Commission, Government of India highlighted that the financial performance of State level public enterprises was not satisfactory. The findings of the study were that the State level public enterprises had a long way to go in order to earn optimum rates of return on investment. About one-third of these enterprises were in the red at the gross margin level, other one-third incurred losses at the operating margin level and about one-third of the enterprises showed small amount of surplus. The study showed that the financial performance was unsound and there was poor record in respect of the finalisation of accounts.

Nagarajan and Burthwal (1990)[23] in their research work entitled "Profitability and Structure: A Firm Level Study of Indian Pharmaceutical Industry", intensively examined the relationship between profitability and structure, using a sample of 38 pharmaceutical firms in India for the period 1970-1982. The analysis demonstrated that under the condition of price controls the most significant determinant of the profitability of the firms in this industry was vertical integration. Size and advertising intensity did not appear to be major determinants. This was perhaps due to the inability of firms to translate their market power into prices, because of controls. The coefficient of growth rate of sales was positive and significant, suggesting that factors on the demand side of a firm had a greater impact on profitability than on the supply side.

Pant (1991)[24] had sought to identify factors which influence corporate economic performance. Important industrial characteristics such as concentration, market share, industry growth, research and development expenditure, advertisement intensity, and size of firms in the industry which influenced corporate economic performance. These characteristics may allow firms to be in a better position to implement their strategies successfully and profitably. Consequently, firms may reflect better performance on account of favourable industrial characteristics.

Conyon and Machin (1991)[25] in 'The Determinants of Profit Margins in U.K. Manufacturing' made an attempt to find the causes of inter-industry variations in profit margins for 90 U.K. Manufacturing Industries over the period 1983 to 1986. Labour-market characteristics (such as trade union coverage and unemployment), import intensity, concentration and capital stock were taken as independent variables. The study revealed that the union coverage and unemployment had a negative impact on profit margins. On the other hand, import intensity concentration and capital stock were significant in explaining inter-firm variations in profit margins.

Krishnaveni (1991)[26] in her study evaluated the impact of policy changes since 1982-92 on profitability and growth of firms in the industry using Tobin's q as a measure of profitability. The study finds no evidence to show that firms had made supernormal profits. Profitability was found to be explained mainly by age of the firms, vertical integration, diversification and industry policy dummy variables. Important determinants of the growth of firms are found as diversification, industry policy dummy variable, gross retained profits and expansion of capacities. Results also reveal differences in performance between car and non-car sectors as well as within the sectors of the industry.

Bharatwaj et al. David (1993)[27] attempted to estimate the impact of growth on market share of a sample of 276 Indian firms. The variables considered for the study were profitability, return on sales, return on capital employed, advertising intensity, market growth rate, intangibles and research and development expenditure. The study showed that the profitability, research and development, intangibles were positively and significantly associated with growth in market share.

Chandrasekaran (1993)[28] in his study entitled 'Determinants of Profitability in Cement Industry' had studied the determinants of profitability in cement industry. The study aims at drawing inference on impact of policy measures which led to change in price and distribution polices relevant for cement industry. Determinants of profitability are analysed using the technique of ordinary least squares. Based on existing theories and relevant econometric empirical works, variables are selected. The study concluded that efficiency in inventory management and efficient management of current assets were important to improve profitability.

Cleveland and Frederick (1993)[29] in their study 'Profitability, Uncertainty and Firm Size', examined the connections between variations in profit and loss rates among firms in small-firm and large-firm size classes as reflections of uncertainty. They found that, within industries, such variations are particularly great for firms in small-firm size classes, leading to operating policies for small firms best characterized as entrepreneurial. Large firms, in contrast, faced with less uncertainty in earning profit, appear to adopt policies that manifest an emphasis on strategic planning.

Kallu Rao (1993)[30] had made a study of inter company financial analysis of tea industry-retrospect and prospect. An attempt had been made in this study to analyse the important variables of tea industry and projected future trends regarding sales and profit for the next 10-year periods, with a view to help the policy makers to take appropriate decisions. Various financial ratios had been calculated for analyzing the financial health of the industry. The forecast of sales and profits of tea manufacturing companies showed that the Indian tea industry had bright prospects. The recent changes in the Indian economic policies will boost up the foreign exchange earnings, which will benefit those companies, which are exporting to hard currency areas.

Eisenberg and Sundgren (1993)[31] in 'Larger Board Size, Decreasing Firm Value and Increasing Firm Solvency', finds significant correlations between board size and profitability and between board size and solvency in a sample of small and mid-size firms. They found that a negative correlation between board size and profitability in small and mid-size Finish firms. Finding a board-size effect for a new and different class of firms points towards the influence of group size on risk-taking behavior as a source of the board-size effect. A new board-size effect, a positive correlation between board size and firm solvency, further supports the hypothesis that board-size effects result from distortions of risk-taking behaviour.

Pai et al. (1995)[32] studied about the financial performance of the diversified companies. An effort was made to study the relationship between diversified firms and their financial performance. Seven large firms having different products - both related and otherwise - in their portfolio and operating in diverse industries were analyzed. A set of performance measures/ratios was employed to determine the level of financial performance. The results revealed that the diversified firms studied had been healthy financial performance. However, variation in performance from one firm to another had been observed and statistically established.

In RBI study (1995),[33] an attempt was made to study the financial performance of private corporate business sector during the period 1994-95. Of the 1030 companies covered in this study, 925 were non-financial companies and 105 were financial companies. The results of the non-financial and financial companies were also analyzed size-wise apart from the analysis of the consolidated results for the entire sector. The good corporate performance during 1994-95 reflected in major profitability ratios registering distinct improvement in the year under review as compared to the previous year.

Vijayakumar and Venkatachalam (1995)[34] in 'Working Capital and Profitability - An Empirical Analysis' studied the impact of working capital on profitability in sugar industry of Tamil Nadu by selecting a sample of 13 companies; 6 companies in co-operative sector and 7 companies in private sector over the period 1982-83 to 1991-92. They applied simple correlation and multiple regression analysis on working capital and profitability ratios. They concluded through correlation and regression analysis that liquid ratio, inventory turnover ratio, receivables turnover ratio and cash turnover ratio had influenced the profitability of sugar industry in Tamil Nadu.

Vijayakumar (1996)[35] in 'Assessment of Corporate Liquidity - A Discriminant Analysis Approach' had revealed that the growth rate of sales, leverage, current ratio, operating expenses to sales and vertical integration are the important variables which determine the profitability of companies in the sugar industry. Further, the author had studied the short-term liquidity position in twenty-eight selected sugar factories in co-operative and private sectors. A discriminant analysis had been undertaken to distinguish the good risk companies from poor risk companies based on current and liquidity ratios. Discriminating 'Z' scores have been calculated with the help of discriminant function and according to the 'Z' scores the companies are ranked in the order of liquidity.

Kim and Kunchul (1996)[36] studied the relationship between profitability, growth and risk. An attempt was made to understand the profitability differentials in terms of simultaneously determined inter-relationships among profitability, growth and risk. The authors focused on the process of production and investment decision-making, which was the main activity for a firm's profits maximization. The major objective of the investment and production decision was to simultaneously choose optimum levels of profitability, growth and risk. Therefore, these variables were endogenous in a firm's profit maximization and simultaneously inter-related.

McDonald (1997)[37] in the study entitled 'The Determinants of Firm Profitability in Australian Manufacturing' provides new evidence on the determinants of the profitability of Australian manufacturing firms by analyzing a unique firm level data set of firm performance over the period 1983-1993. From estimations based on an adaptation of a standard oligopoly model, econometric results suggest that lagged profitability is a significant determinant of current profit margins, and that industry concentration is positively related to firm profit margin. As well, both union density and real wage inflation are found to be negatively associated with firm profits. Finally, the cyclicality of profit margins depends on industry concentration - firm margins are pro-cyclical in concentrated industries and are counter-cyclical in less concentrated industries.

Chhibber and Majumdhar (1997)[38] in their study examined the influence of foreign ownership on the performance of firms operating in India. Firm's performance was measured as return on sales and return on assets. The results show that, foreign ownership did not affect firm performance. But different categories of ownership had varying influences on return on sales and return on assets. Further, the concentration of domestic ownership, which could influence the ability of foreign investors to exercise control over a firm, did not have any significant influence on performance. The study suggested that the foreign ownership had a position and significant on various dimensions of firm performance, but only when it crosses a certain threshold, one that was defined by the property rights regime.

Geroski et al. (1997)[39] in their study argued that current period corporate growth rates reflect changes in current expectations about the long-run profitability of a firm. This means growth rates are likely to vary randomly over time. Using data from 271 large sized U.K. firms over the period 1976-82, the authors reported the existence of a positive, statistically significant and robust correlation between expectations about long-run profitability, namely changes in the stock market valuation of the firm. Nevertheless, they find that variations in corporate growth rates are difficult to predict.

Nugent (1998)[40] tried to determine the range of likely factors such as exchange rates and the degree of monopoly power which influence movements in profitability. Correlation analysis suggests that demand side variables such as economic activity and, to a lesser extent, the exchange rate play an important role. There was also evidence that supply–side variables such as relative ULCs also explain profits.

Sidhu and Bhatia (1998)[41] studied the factors affecting profitability in Indian textile industry. In this study an attempt was made to identify the major determinants of profitability in Indian textile industry with the help of empirical data taken from *Bombay Stock Exchange Directory* for the year 1983. To find out the factors affecting profitability, regression analysis had been applied. From the analysis, there was no clear-cut relationship between current profitability and capital intensity. The age of the firm was having generally negative but statistically insignificant relationship with current profitability which points towards the fact firms in Indian textile industry are absolute and need modernization.

Kaur (1998)[42] studied size, growth and profitability of firms in India. It was in this context that the study of various facets of 235 firms of India had been undertaken, covering the period from 1970-71 to 1989-90. Growth pattern of the firms showed that majority of the firms recorded growth rate from 10 to 20 per cent. Two measures of profitability such as profitability margins and profitability rate had been used in the study. The analysis of the study in case of Indian firms showed that there was no systematic tendency for average profitability to increase/ decrease as the size of the firm changed.

Mallick and Debasish (1998)[43] examined the Working capital and Profitability: a case study in inter-relation. The study explored the correlation between ROI and several ratios relating to working capital management. In this study an effort had been made to make an empirical study of AFT Industries Ltd., a tea producing enterprise in Assam, for assessing the impact of working capital on profitability by computing simple correlation co-efficient between ROI and each of some selected important ratios relating to working capital management and to test the significance of such coefficients. The study on the inter-relation between the selected ratios in the areas of working capital management and profitability of the company revealed both negative and positive association.

Feeny and Rogers (1998)[44] in their research work entitled 'Profitability in Australian Enterprises' analysed profitability in a sample of large Australian companies over the period 1985 to 1996. Various measures of profitability are used and the paper provides a discussion of the theoretical basis for these measures. The key issues investigated are a comparison of the profitability measures, the distribution of profitability between firms, and the persistence of firm profitability. The results are compared to previous studies on firm profitability.

Vijayakumar (1998)[45] had examined the determinants of corporate size, growth and profitability - of Indian industries. To meet the objectives of the study, Indian public sector industries were selected. The data relating to size, growth and profitability were collected from their annual reports published by the Bureau of Public Enterprises (BPE), Government of India. The technique of average, correlation and linear and multiple regression analysis had been used in this study. Inter-industry analysis revealed that the growth was positively and significantly associated with the size in all the industry groups except textiles.

Purohit (1998)[46] in 'Profitability in Indian Industries: An Analysis of Firm Size and Profitability' examined the relation between size and profitability in Indian industries. The study highlighted the following two common conclusions. Firstly, though the average profitability of firms did not seem to vary significantly with their size and the variability of profit rates declines with size. Secondly, the average growth rates of firms did not seem to vary significantly with their size but the variability of growth rates only. The study further explored the factors that determine profitability. Besides the size, the model also tests for the impact of age of the firm and growth in sales on profitability at both micro and macro levels. The study concluded that the selected industries and firms have made efforts to increase profitability through various means including increase in size through diversification and moving into higher technology.

Glancey (1998)[47] in his study "Determinants of growth and profitability in small entrepreneurial firm" investigated the relationship between company characteristics including size, age, location and industry group and profitability and growth. The trade-off between the possibly conflicting objectives of profit and growth was considered primarily from the entrepreneurial rather than the managerial standpoint which previous econometric studies of small firm performance have concentrated on. It was argued that a firm size measure based on employment was more appropriate than one based on sales or assets which previous studies have used. Firm characteristics are found to be of limited value in explaining profitability. However, larger firms are found to grow faster than smaller, and younger firms are found to grow faster than older. There was also some evidence that growth was stronger in urban than in suburban or rural locations.

Pandey and Bhat (1998)[48] in their study entitled 'Financial Ratio Patterns in Indian Manufacturing Companies - A Multivariate Analysis', identified three groups of financial ratios which contain the maximum amount of information about profitability, with available data for 612 companies on R.B.I. data type for 1965-66 to 1984-85 period. They confined their analysis to only those companies which belonged to manufacturing and processing industries and for which sales data were available. These three groups of financial ratios are (1) Return on investment (profit before depreciation interest and tax to total tangible assets), (2) Sales efficiency (Profit after tax to Net Sales) and (3) Equity Intensiveness (Retained cash flow from operations to tangible net worth). They further observed a declining trend in profitability in relation to shareholder's equity and total investment, whose impact has been deepened by the increasing interest burden. A consistent downward trend in the above three groups of ratios covering the profitability aspect was also marked across most of the firms.

Ahuja and Majumdar (1998)[49] examined the determinants of performance of 68 Indian State-owned enterprises in the manufacturing sector for a five-year period: 1987 to 1991. Relative performance was determined using data envelopment analysis, with variations performance patterns subsequently explained using regression analysis. The study revealed that the size was positively associated and age negatively associated with efficiency. Further, economic liberalization and reforms aimed at improving the performance of State-owned firms induces efficiency gains over time.

Agarwal (1999)[50] studied the Profitability and Growth in Indian Automobile Manufacturing Industry. The objective of this study was to evaluate the impact of policy changes since 1981-82 on profitability and growth of firms in the industry using Tobin's Square as a measure of profitability. The study finds no evidence to show that firms have made super normal profits. Profitability was found to be explained mainly by the age of the firms, vertical integration, diversification and industry policy dummy variable. Important determinants of the growth of firms are found as diversification, industry policy dummy variables, gross retained profits and expansion of capacities. Results also revealed differences in performance between car and non-car sectors as well as with in the sectors of the industry.

Rogers (1999)[51] provided and overview of the performance of Small and Medium Private Enterprises (SMEs) using the growth and performances survey. Three aspects of performance such as profitability, productivity and innovation are considered. The results of the study highlighted that SMEs as a group tend to had higher median profitability than large firms in manufacturing. Furthers, SMEs tend had lower median labour productivity and higher median capital productivity than large firms. This reflects the act that SMEs had lower capital to labour ratios, this was contradiction to the traditional theory any would suggest that large firms should be more profitable.

Dutta (1999)[52] examined an analysis of profitability trend in the Indian Cotton Mill industry. The disadvantage situations of a large number of mills are reflected in the haphazard movement of the mill sector's profitability ratio.

Loss of market share of mill made cotton cloth to synthetic substitutes, burden of unfavorable excise duty, uncertainty in supply of raw cotton, untoward labour legislation, under utilization of capital and high capital cost added to the aforesaid fluctuations in profitability. Lower base of the profitability ratios and the warning financial position of the majority of the mills had left them with resources to undertake renovation and modernization.

Feeny and Rogers (1999)[53] in their research work entitled 'Market Share, Concentration and Diversification in Firm Profitability' reviewed the role of market share, concentration and diversification in firm performance. An empirical analysis of the profitability of 722 Large Australian firms for the period 1993 to 1996 was undertaken. Using simple regression techniques, the analysis suggested that industry concentration (as proxies by the 4-firm concentration ratio) had a positive influence on profitability. The market share of a firm did not appear to have any significant linear association with profitability; however, a non-monotonic relationship was found to be significant.

Govinda Rao and Mohana Rao (1999)[54] in 'Impact of working capital on profitability in cement industry - a correlation analysis', analysed the impact of profitability on working capital in cement industrial units in India. Ten variables on working capital ratios have a close interaction with profitability measures viz., current ratio, debt-equity ratio, cash position ratio, working capital turnover ratio, inventory turnover ratio, debtors turnover ratio, cash turnover ratio, current assets turnover ratio and average collection period are selected for analysis. The inter-relationship are to be studied with the help of Karl-Pearson's co-efficient of correlation technique, by arranging the correlation of one variable with each other variable in the form of matrices which are a triangular and symmetrical about the principal diagonal. On overall basis out of 10 variables with PBDIT, three variables showed a significant co-efficient and seven exhibited insignificant relationships. Out of the 10 variables, five variables showed negative association while the others showed positive relationships.

Raghunathan and Das (1999)[55] have made a study of the corporate performance of post-Liberalization. In this study, they analyzed the performance of Indian manufacturing sector in the last 8 years since liberalization on the parameters of profitability, liquidity, leverage and solvency. While the solvency and profitability ratios were encouraging till 1996 they had been gradually diminishing after that. This problem gets more pronounced when the EVA is calculated which shows that the Indian Manufacturing sector had destroyed wealth, while the MNCs had generated wealth for their shareholders. The study points that poor corporate performance had led to an economic slowdown and not the other way round. Corporate raised funds during the blacken days of equity markets and ended up investing these funds at below their cost of capital. The outcome has been a prolonged economic slowdown.

D'Souza and Megginson (1999)[56] had studied the financial and operating performance of privatized firms during the 1990s. This study compares the pre- and post-privatization financial and operating performance of 85 companies from 28 industrialized countries that were privatized through public share offerings for the period from 1990 through 1996. The significant increases in profitability, output, operating efficiency, dividend payments and significant decreases in leverage ratios for the full sample of firms after privatization were noticed. Capital expenditures increase significantly in absolute terms, but not relative to sales. Employment declines, but insignificantly. The findings of the study strongly suggested that privatization yields significant performance improvements.

Sur (1999)[57] studied inter-company profitability analysis of Indian General Insurance industry. The main objective was to measure the profitability of general insurance companies in India by computing four important profitability ratios, namely, return on operating assets employed, return on gross capital employed, return on net capital employed and return on net worth and to study the variations of these ratios during the period under study by calculating standard deviation and co-efficient of variations of each ratios. It confirmed the satisfactory performance of the management of companies regarding their financial management. All the companies under study could enjoy the benefit of financial leverage. The differences between the estimated and the computed operating profits were highly significant in all the enterprises under the study.

Feeny and Rogers (1999)[58] studied on overview of the performance of large Australian based private companies using a data set of 653 companies for the period 1993-1996. Four aspects of performance such as profitability, growth of revenue, export intensity and innovation had been considered in this study. In addition, two important company characteristics-the debt to equity ratio and Tobin's Q are considered. The study concluded that manufacturing firms tend to have higher profitability than non-manufacturing firm. Another finding was that the distribution of profitability for non-listed firms tends to be more dispersed than listed firms.

Islam (2000)[59] studied the profitability of Fertilizer Industry in Bangladesh from 1985-86 to 1994-95. The sample included five fertilizer enterprises of the seven fertilizer enterprises in Bangladesh under the control of Bangladesh Chemical Industries Corporation (BCIC). The findings of the study indicated that none of the selected units were consistent and all the units were plagued with declining profits. The study concluded with suggestions for improvement of the profitability of fertilizer industry in Bangladesh.

Feeny (2000)[60] in his research study entitled "Determinants of Profitability" an empirical investigation was made using Australian tax entities. Using simple regression techniques the analysis suggested that size of entity was positively related to profitability but industry characteristics had limited importance in explaining entity profitability. Concentration, defined at a four digit level, was positively and significantly related to entity profitability in 27 per cent of Australian three digit industries, while a significant negative association was found in 8 per cent of the industries. There was some evidence that barriers to entry had the positive relationship with entity profitability as dictated by theory when proxies by the industry capital intensity but not when proxies by the minimum efficient scale or industry trademark intensity. There was strong evidence that the market share of an entity had a U-shaped relationship with profitability.

Sahu (2000)[61] analysed the corporate profitability in multivariate approach. This was an empirical based study on the secondary data from a sample of 100 non-financial, non-government, public limited companies in Eastern India for a span of ten years and the study attempted to measure the composite profitability of a firm by a single index, thereby facilitating case of comparison and ranking. The main objectives of the study were to study the degree of relationship between the ratios included under each of the main category in order to identify the ratios, which overlap in the information they provide about profitability, and to integrate the selected ratios into a single of the ratios.

Sur et al. (2001)[62] studied the Liquidity Management in Indian Private Sector Enterprises - A Case Study of Indian Primary Aluminum industry. From the analysis, it may be summarized that the overall performance regarding liquidity management at INDAL was better in terms of efficient utilization of short term funds, whereas HINDALCO was unable to do so. A very high degree of positive correlation between liquidity and profitability in case of both the companies was a notable feature, reflecting the favourable effect of liquidity on profitability.

Aggarwal and Singla (2001)[63] in their study developed a single index of financial performance through the technique of Multiple Discriminant Analysis (MDA), They attempt to identify from among the 11 ratios, used as inputs, those ratios, which are relevant in distinguish between profit making units and loss making units in Indian paper industry. The study indicated that model has correctly classified 82.14 per cent of units selected as profit making and loss marking. The study also showed that inventory turnover ratio, interest coverage ratio, net profit to total assets and earning per share are the most important indicators of financial performance. The study also suggests that the results of MDA can be used as predictor of future profitability/sickness.

Loundes (2001)[64] examined whether there has been any change in the financial performance of government trading enterprises operating in electricity, gas, water, railways and ports industries as a result of several measures introduced during 1990 to improve the efficiency and financial performance of government trading enterprises in Australia. The study empirically viewed that there does not appear to have been noticeable enhancement in the financial performance of most of these business, although railways have improved slightly, from a 1000 base points.

Rogers (2001)[65] in his research the effect of diversification on firm performance analyses the association between diversification and firm performance in a sample of up to 1449 Large Australian firms (1994 to 1997). Firm performance was measured by profitability and, for quoted firms, market value. Results from the full sample showed that more focused firms had higher profitability. This result controls for firm's specific effects and other determinants of profitability. However, this association was not found in sub-sample regressions for listed firms. This was true both when either profitability or market value was used as a performance measure. The results may indicated that listed firms may be under closer scrutiny and competitive pressures that ensure, on average, that these firms are at their optimal degree of diversification.

Sur (2001)[66] studied the Liquidity Management: An Overview of Four Companies in Indian Power Sector. In this study a comparative analysis regarding the liquidity management in Electricity generation and distribution industry had been made for the period 1987-88 to 1996-97. The study revealed that the overall liquidity should be managed in such a way that not only it should not hamper profitability but also its contribution towards increase in profitability should be positive.

Rei and Sur (2001)[67] studied the profitability analysis of Indian food products industry: A case study of Cadbury India Ltd. The study attempted to measure the profitability scenario of Cadbury India Ltd. and analysed the relationship among various profitability ratios and their joint impact using multiple correlation co-efficient and multiple regression method. The study on the inter-relation between the selected ratios regarding the company's position and performance and profitability of the company revealed both negative and positive association.

Vijayakumar (2002)[68] in "Determinants of Profitability- A firm level study of the Sugar Industry of Tamil Nadu", delved into the various determinants of profitability viz., growth rate of sales, vertical integration and leverage. Apart from these three variables, he had selected current ratio, operating expenses to sales ratio and inventory turnover ratio. Econometric models were used to test the various hypotheses relating to profitability with other variables. The researcher noted in his conclusion that efficiency in inventory management and current assets are important to improve the profitability.

Bosworth and Loundes (2002)[69] in their study entitled the Dynamic performance of Australian Enterprises investigate the interaction of discretionary investments (R&D, capital investment, training and advertising), innovation, productivity and profitability within a dynamic framework of firm performance. A dynamic and closed model of firm performance was set up, and the resulting empirical model was tested as a series of recursive equations, using a four-year balanced panel data set of Australian firms drawn from the Business Longitudinal Survey. The results indicated that current economic profit has an important role to play in enabling firms to invest, and the findings indicate which of these investments are complements and which are substitutes.

Mulla (2002)[70] in 'Use of 'Z' score analysis for evaluation of financial health of textile mills - A case study' had been made an insight into the financial health of Shri Venkatesh Co-operative Textile Mills Ltd., Arunageri of Dharwad District. The 'Z' score analysis had been applied to evaluate the general trend in financial health of a firm over a period by using many of the accounting ratios. From the study it was concluded that the textiles mill under study was just on the verge of financial collapse. On the one hand, current assets declined because of the negative profitability performance, whereas on the other hand, the current liabilities were on the increase because of poor liquidity performance of the mill.

Aussenegg and Jelic (2002)[71] examined the operating performance of 154 Polish, Hungarian and Czech companies that were fully or partially privatized between January 1990 and December 1998. The study revealed that privatized firms in the sample did not manage to increase profitability, and significantly reduced efficiency and output in the post privatization period. Enterprises privatized through mass privatization programs (Czech SOEs) achieved lower profitability in the post-privatization period compared to their counterparts privatized through case-by-case method. The study further revealed that private sector IPOs under performs their privatization counterparts in terms of profitability, efficiency, capital investments and output. Finally firm's size did not seem to influence key performance measures in selected countries.

Glen et al. (2002)[72] in their study presents time-series analyses of corporate profitability in seven leading Developing Countries (DC_s) using the common methodology as the persistence of profitability (PP) studies and systematically compare the results with those for Advanced Countries (AC_s). Surprisingly, both short and long term persistence of profitability for DC_S was found to be lower than those for AC_s. The paper concentrated on economic explanation for these findings. It also reports the results on the persistence of the two components as profitability-capital-output ratios and profit margins. These two raise important general issues of economic interpretation for persistence of profitability studies, which are outlined.

Shanmugam and Bhaduri Saumitra (2002)[73] in their study analysed growth of the Indian manufacturing companies taking a sample of 390 companies during 1990-93. The age and size of the companies were taken as independent variables and growth in sales as dependent variable. The statistical techniques such as mean, standard deviation and regression analysis were used to study the growth of the companies. The study showed that the age was positively influenced the growth and size had negative and significant impact on growth.

Vijayakumar (2002a)[74] in his study 'Financial appraisal of Salem Co-operative Sugar Mills Ltd, Mohanur' analysed the various aspects of the working of Salem Co-operative Sugar Mills Ltd, Mohanur. Financial appraisal had been studied with respect to profitability, capital structure, fixed assets and working capital. The researcher's main finding was about the Mill's over reliance on external funds which results in interest burden. It was certain that the Mill had better scope to function in an efficient manner if the owner's funds are increased and the borrowings are reduced.

Vijayakumar (2002b)[75] studied the Assessment of Corporate Liquidity – A Discriminant Analysis Approach. There are 28 firms in the sugar industry operating in Tamil Nadu of which 14 are under co-operative sector and 14 under private sector. In order to select the units for the purpose of the study, only those units which were established before 1984 and were having a crushing capacity of 2000MT (per day) have been considered. There were 10 such units of which 5 are under co-operative sector and 5 are under the private sector. The study concluded that the co-operative sector classified as poor risk in all the selected years as per current and liquid ratio, have become good risk in the year 1986-87 and 87-89 as per discriminating 'z' score. The way of discrimination analysis employed was a useful exercise to determine the combined effects of the ratios. The study revealed that the overall liquidity position of the industry was satisfactory.

Fu et al. (2002)[76] examined the relationship between profitability and financial capital for 1276 small firms in Taiwan over the period 1992-97. The results indicated a statistically positive relationship between profitability and capital growth. When financial capital was further divided into debt and equity, the results indicate a significantly positive relationship between profitability and equity financing, but a significantly negative relationship between profitability and debt financing. Moreover, the profitability of small firm was positively related to both the external economic conditions and the firms' previous profitability.

Yucel el al. (2002)[77] investigated the relationship of cash conversion cycle with profitability, liquidity and debt structure. The findings of the study suggested that cash conversion cycle was positively related to liquidity ratios and negatively related to return on asset and return on equity. High leverage ratios affect adversely the liquidity and profitability of the company. There was no statistically significant relationship between the cash conversion cycle and the basis of period, but it differed on the basis of sector and firm size.

Kaen and Hans (2003)[78] in their study measured the profitability of US companies with a sample of 64 selected randomly. They had taken sales, EBITDA, EBIT, EBITDA margin, EBIT margin, total assets and number of employees as independent variables and return on assets as dependent variable for the study. Using regression and correlation techniques their study resulted that about half of industry, firms profitability increases at decreasing rate and eventually declines as the firms become larger, for the remaining half, no relationship between profitability and size was found.

Ray (2003)[79] in his study investigated the effect of economic reforms on the efficiency of Indian manufacturing firms. The efficiency of a cross-section of firms belonging to 27 industry groups of the capital in O/E' database has been estimated. Regressions have been run for each year in period 1991 to 2001, in order to estimate the impact of various policy reforms on efficiency and outline their friends over the years. The results highlighted the positive impact of important liberalization on the efficiency of firms thorough import of capital goods and import of technology.

Vijayakumar and Kadirvel (2003a)[80] studied the determinants of profitability of Indian Public Sector Manufacturing Industries. It was evident from the results that age was the strongest determinant of profitability followed by the variables vertical integration, leverage, size, current ratio, inventory turnover ratio, operating expenses to sales ratio and growth rate. The selected variables had both positive and negative contribution in variation of profit rate. In a nutshell, it can be concluded that firms should consider all these possible determinants while considering its profitability.

Vijayakumar and Kadirvel (2003b)[81] studied the profitability and size of firm in Indian Minerals and Metals industry. Generally, it was suggested that the larger the firm may be in a position to earn a higher rate of return on its investment than the smaller firm. Similarly, a counter argument was that size breed's inefficiency and hence profitability may decline with size of firms. Thus, they found that some theoretical arguments suggest that profitability should increase with the firm size, others suggest a negative relationship. It was in view of these contradictory suggestions, that it becomes necessary to study the relationship between size and profitability of the firms. For this purpose, Indian public sector minerals and metals industry has been selected. The study revealed that size was found to be significantly associated with the profitability during the study period. It was also evident from the analysis that size was positively associated with the profitability. Thus, larger firm may be in a position to earn higher rate of return on investment through diversification and moving into higher technology.

Wei (2003)[82] in 'The financial and operating performance of China's newly privatized firms', examined the pre- and post-privatization financial and operating performance of 208 firms privatized in China during the period 1990-97. The full sample results showed significant improvements in real output, real assets and sales efficiency, and significant declines in leverage following privatization, but no significant change in profitability. Further, analysis showed that privatized firms experience significant improvements in profitability compared to fully state-owned enterprises during the same period. Firms in which more than 50 per cent voting control was conveyed to private investors via privatization experience significantly greater improvements in profitability, employment, and sales efficiency compared to those that remain under the state's control.

Reddy (2003)[83] studied the financial performance of paper industry in Andhra Pradesh. The main objectives set for the study are to evaluate the financing methods and practices to analyze the investment pattern and utilization of fixed assets, to ascertain the working capital condition, to review the profitability performance and to suggest measures to improve the profitability. The data collected have been examined through ratios, trend, common size, comparative financial statement analysis and statistical tests have been applied in appropriate context. The main findings of the study are that A.P. Paper Industry needs the introduction of additional funds along with restructuring of finances and modernization of technology for better operating performance.

RBI Corporate Studies Division (2003)[84] had made an attempt to study the performance of corporate business sector during the first half of 2002-03. The results of 146 private companies of various sectors were analyzed on the various parameters of performance. Aggregation and comparison of the results of the first two quarters were done on these performance parameters. It was concluded that the performance of the private sector was better when compared with the first half of the previous year (2001-02).This was indicated by the following parameters viz., higher sales, reduced interest payments and ultimately improved profitability. Sector-industry wise analysis of performance had been done to highlight those areas where the performance had been better vis-à-vis sectors, which had lagged behind in performance.

Ghosh and Maji (2003)[85] in 'Utilisation of current assets and operating profitability: An empirical study on cement and tea industries in India', made an empirical study on utilisation of current assets and operating profitability data for 11 firms of cement and tea industries were collected for the period 1992-93 to 2001-02. The study concluded that the degree of current assets was positively associated with the operating profitability of the firm.

Liu and Hsu (2004)[86] identified the determinants of growth of Taiwan manufacturing firms taking a sample of 280 listed Taiwan firms. The variables taken into account for the study were independent variables viz., size, age, capital intensity, Research and Development, export ratio, investment ratio, debt equity ratio and retention ratio as independent variables and dependent variable as growth in net sales. In their study correlation and regression techniques were used. The study showed that the growth was positively and significantly related to firms' size, age, and capital intensity, Research and Development, export ratio, investment ratio and profitability.

Sarkaria and Shergil (2004)[87] aimed to test how market structure may affect performance. The study had employed model consulting determinants of both structure and profits. In order to decompose the variation performance variables like industry effect, seller concentration, market share, capacity utilization, size, leverage, skill, risk, age and capital intensity had been included in the regression models as the determinants as performance. The study results suggested that market share was positively and concentration was negatively related to performance. The industry membership had turned up to be an important determinant of firm growth.

Lima and Resende (2004)[88] in their work entitled profit margins and business cycles in the Brazilian industry: a panel data study investigated the relationship between profit margins and business cycle in the Brazilian industry during the 1992-1998 period, taking as reference a dynamic panel data model founded around a conjectural variation framework. The empirical results indicated pro-cyclical behavior of profit margins for the aggregate business cycle but are less clear in the case of sector-specific business cycle variables. Among the most robust results, one can highlight the roles of lagged profitability and import intensity and the negligible role of union density.

Patel (2004)[89] in his study made an attempt to examine the profitability of Colour-Chem Limited during the period

1981-99. The multiple correlation coefficient technique was used for analyzing the impact of net fixed assets, sales and net worth on the profitability. The result of the study showed that sales and net fixed assets, sales and net worth, and net fixed assets and net worth had significant effect on net profit of Colour-Chem limited. The analysis of profitability ratios showed that the company was in a round position.

Weill (2004)[90] in his study leverage and corporate performance-a frontier efficiency analysis provided new empirical evidence on a major corporate governance issue: the relationship between leverage and corporate performance. His study provides two major importance's to this literature by applying frontier efficiency techniques to obtain performance measures for companies from several countries (France, Germany and Italy). The study proceeds to regressions of corporate performance on a various set of variables including leverage. The study found mixed evidence depending on the country; while significantly negative in Italy, the relationship between leverage and corporate performance was significantly positive in France and Germany. This tends to support the influence of some institution characteristics on this link.

Leahy (2004)[91] tested the proposition that profitability was related to the functions performed and risks assumed by a company. The three measures of profitability such as gross margin, operating margin and Berry ratio are examined and related to proxies for the functions performed and/or risks assumed by those manufacturers. The results showed that SGA/Sales, Inv/COGs and AP/COGs variables are significant determinants of profitability. The results vary according to the measure of profitability employed i.e., the significance of the independent variable may depend on the profitability measure employed.

Bhanu (2005)[92] in his study "The Structural Adjustment Programmes and the New Industrial Policy Adopted by the

Indian Government" has enabled business houses to undertake the programme of expansion either by entering into a new market or through expansion in an existing market. In this context, it was found that in order to expand and grow companies in India, they are increasingly resorting to mergers and acquisitions. In this regard, this study had identified twelve companies and examined the growth of the merged company's *vis-à-vis* select 134 companies in terms of net fixed assets and paid-up capital for the period 1990-91 to 1997-98. The study also examined the trends in profitability of the merged and selected companies for the above-mentioned period. The study concluded that the merged companies had been more successful and profitability under all the heads examined, were higher for these companies as compared to the selected companies.

Hamsalakshmi and Manickam (2005)[93] had made a study of the financial performance analysis of selected software companies. In this study, they examined the management of finance playing a crucial role in the growth. It was concerned with examining the structure of liquidity position, leverage position and profitability position of selected thirty four software companies in India for a period of five years (1997-98 to 2001-2002). The study revealed that the liquidity position and working capital were favourable during the period of study. The result indicated that the overall profitability position of selected software companies had been increasing at a moderate rate. The development will create large domestic demand over the next few years.

Niskanen and Niskanen (2005)[94] examined the determinants of growth of small and micro firms with a sample of 100 Finland firms. The period of the study was between 1994 and 1997. In order to examine the growth independent variables such as age, size, profitability, location, financial status and financial structure and dependent variable such as average annual growth in sales were taken in to account for the study. The study revealed that the location, financial status, financial structure, and firm size were positively and significantly associated with growth.

Patra (2005)[95] in his study the impact of liquidity on profitability was analysed in the case of Tata Iron & Steel Company Limited. The study of the impact of liquidity ratios on profitability showed both negative and positive association. Out of seven liquidity ratios selected for this study, four ratios namely current ratio, acid test ratio, current assets to total assets ratio and inventory turnover ratio showed negative correlation with profitability ratio. However, these correlation co-efficient were not statistically significant. The remaining three ratios namely working capital turnover ratio, receivable turnover ratio and cash turnover ratio had shown positive association with the profitability ratio, all of which are statistically significant at 5 per cent level of significance. The result of all the correlation co-efficient was as desirable except correlation co-efficient between inventory turnover ratio and ROI. However, this undesirable sign between ITR and ROI was not supported by the multiple regression analysis, which shows the positive association between these two variables. There was increasing profitability that depends upon many factors including liquidity.

Fitzsimmons et al. (2005)[96] in their study, investigated the longitudinal behaviour of growth rates and profitability for a large sample of Australian firms. Using a regression equation with lagged profit and growth variables, the study found no evidence of a consistent relationship between growth and profitability. The longitudinal behaviour of the growth profitability relationship was also investigated. Consistent with previous research higher growth firms were on average younger and high and low profit firms were found to be younger on average. The study also found that a higher proportion of firms pursuing the profitability pathway were much more likely to achieve high growth and profitability in following years.

Agiomirgianakis et al. (2006)[97] examined financial determinants of firm profitability and employment growth are identified by using a panel of 3094 Greek manufacturing firms for 1995 and 1999, just before the country's accession to the European Monetary Union. The analysis includes stepwise regression models. The independent variables used are size, age, location and exports, as well as a number of financial ratios describing the asset structure, capital structure, reliance on debt, employee productivity and managerial efficiency. The results show that size, age, exports, debt structure, investment in fixed assets and profitability assets and sales contribute significantly to firm growth. Econometric results also reveal that firm size, age, exports, sales growth, reliance on debt on fixed assets and investment growth, as well as efficient management of assets, influence profitability.

Mallik and Mukherjee (2006)[98] had studied the performance of leasing industry in West Bengal. This empirical study conducted covering fourteen leasing financing companies in West Benagal. An attempt was made to ascertain the profitability and to make a comparative analysis of profitability of the selected companies. With the help of ratio analysis performance of the selected units was evaluated. The findings of the study indicated good performance of leasing industry in West Bengal over the period of the study.

Raja and Kumar (2006)[99] had studied the impact of firm age and size on firm performance. The main purpose of this study was to find out whether firm age and size can behave in similar fashion across industries particularly in manufacturing and service industries. The results showed that manufacturing firms are older and slightly better profitable than service firms. The age of the firm was significant but negatively related to service firms and not related with firm performance of manufacturing firms. The size of the manufacturing firms was significantly related to firm performance, but it produced negative relationship between firm size and firm performance. The firm size did not yield any results for service firms. It was concluded that the age and size of the firm behave differently according to the industry characteristics.

Luthra et al. (2006)[100] had made a study "Profitability and size: A study of small-scale industries in Uttar Pradesh". The objective of this study was to assess the importance of certain structural variables for determining the profitability of firms in small-scale business in India. A single equation regression framework had been chosen as the method of analysis. The relationship between profitability and different determinants of size such as total assets, scale of operation, etc., was studied by regressing the profitability on each of these variables. In this study, the hypothesis that profitability of a small business firm was a function of its size was tested. A preliminary cross-section analysis of the concerned relationship was also done.

Vishnani and Shah (2006)[101] had studied the role of working capital in profit generating process. If a company desires to take a greater risk for bigger profits and losses, it reduces the size of its working capital in relation to its sales. If it was interested in improving its liquidity, it increases the level of its working capital. However, this policy was likely to result in a reduction of the sales volume, therefore of profitability. Hence, a company should strike a balance between liquidity and profitability. In this study an effort had been made to make an empirical study of Indian Consumer Electronics Industry for assessing the impact of working capital on profitability during the period 1994-95 to 2004-05. The impact of working capital on profitability had been examined by computing co-efficient of correlation and regression analysis between profitability and working capital ratio.

Thirumavalavan (2006)[102] in his study entitled 'Determinants of Earnings Before Interest and Tax (EBIT) of Aluminium companies', intensively measured the profitability and performance of a corporate entity either internally or externally. Earnings before interest and tax was the major variable used to measure the internal performance of a business entity. Earnings before interest and tax could be mainly influenced by internal as well as external variables. External variables of economic and industry are too large and highly dynamic. In this paper an attempt had been made to find out the internal variables, which influence the earnings before interest and tax of Aluminium companies through multiple regression. The results were Hindalco's EBIT was mostly influenced by fixed assets and net worth and Indalco's EBIT was mostly influenced by cost of sales and profits retained.

Singh (2007)[103] in his study made an attempt to assess the performance of the sugar mills of Uttar Pradesh, the largest sugarcane producing state in India. Data envelopment analysis models have been applied on the input-output data of 36 sugar mills for the period 1996-97 to 2002-03. The study found that during the period, the average overall technical efficiency (OTE) in the sugar mills of the state had been 93 per cent. This implied that an average mill can make radial reduction in all its cost by seven per cent without detriment to its output levels. The OTE showed a cyclical pattern mainly due to fluctuations in the scale efficiency. The performance of the mills was found to vary significantly across sector, plant size, and region. The private sector mills achieved the highest efficiency scores, followed by the cooperative sector. It had also been observed that the mills with bigger plant size attained relatively higher efficiency scores. Labour and energy inputs are found highly under utilized in almost all the inefficient mills. Targets set for relatively inefficient mills suggested that an average, these mills can become as efficient as the mills reference set, if they could adjust their operation to the associated target point determined by the efficient mills that define their reference set.

Ghosh (2007)[104] studied the working capital management practices in some selected industries in India. A study on working capital management efficiency had been conducted on the leading pharmaceutical companies. Top fifty pharmaceutical companies had been taken up for the study and the companies had been ranked in the descending order of their sales turnover. The main objective of the study was to understand the relationship between credit period given by companies and their actual performance in terms of sales and profitability. The author found out that there was an increase in the average profits and working capital of the top fifty pharmaceutical companies. The result signifies that increase in profits results in increase in working capital. Exposure was needed by companies as an industrial practice to improve profitability.

Sam Luther (2007)[105] in his study, made an attempt to study the Liquidity, profitability and risk trade off of Madras Cement Ltd (MCL). The study concluded that there was a linear relationship between liquidity and profitability. The study further revealed that the high degree of aggressive police adopted by MCL had made a negative impact on its profitability. The study suggested that MCL was to formulate certain policies to control the working capital so as to meet any sort of financial distress that may occur in future.

Manor Selvi and Vijayakumar (2007)[106] in their study entitled "Structure of Profit rates in Indian Automobile Industries – A Comparison", an attempt had been made to examine the trends in rates of profit of selected Indian Automobile Industries over the period 1991-92 to 2003-04. Further an effort had also been made to capture the industry wise variations in the series of profit rates, which reveals the dispersion of the series for each industry over the study period. Findings of the study showed that the declining trend of profitability was proof of adverse effect of various controls on prices, output, expansion and investment etc., exerted by government on these industries over time.

Chander and Aggarwal (2007)[107] in their study identified the determinants of growth of selected companies in drugs and pharmaceutical industry in India. It was based on a sample of 50 firms drawn from the list of companies in drugs and pharmaceutical industry given in the PROWESS database developed by Centre for Monitoring Indian Economy (CMIE). Multiple regression analysis was used to develop a model to identify the determinants of growth of firms in this industry. The results revealed that size, advertising expenditure, age, efficiency ratio, profitability, and research and development were statistically significant in determining the growth of firms in drugs and pharmaceutical industry.

Conclusion

From the above reviews of empirical work, it is clear that different authors have approached profitability analysis in different ways in varying level of analysis. These different approaches helped in the emergence of more and more literature on the subject over the time. It gives an idea on extensive and diverse works on profitability. It has been noticed that the studies on profitability analysis in various sectors provide divergent results to the study period. The main reason for diversion in the results is the difference in the methods used for the measurement of the factors like profitability, liquidity, etc.

All the studies aimed at analysing profitability performance with number of factors. It facilitates to understand the various structural and non-structural variables that determine profitability. It has been noticed that the study on the profitability analysis in various industries used the variables such as seller's concentration, advertising intensity, economics of scale, leverage, profit variability, firm growth and size. Similarly few studies approached which used the quantum of sales, return on investment and appropriation of profit to explore the profit variation of the industries.

Survey of the existing literature indicates that so far no specific study has been carried on to examine the profitability analysis of South Indian private sector Sugar Industry after liberalization in the manufacturing sector. The present study is an attempt towards this direction and therefore, aims to enrich the literature of profitability performance relating to South Indian private sector Sugar Industry. Further, the study is intended to employ different sophisticated statistical techniques, before qualifying any aspects of profitability analysis for wider acceptability and appreciation.

NOTES

1. Stekler, H.O. (1964), "The Variability of Profitability with Size of Firms 1947-1958", *Journal of American Statistical Association*, Vol. 59, pp. 1183-1193.
2. Baumol, W.J. (1967), *Business Behaviour, Value and Growth* (Revised Ed.,), NewYork: Harcourt Brace and World.
3. Samuels, J.M. and Smyth, D.J (1968), "Profits, Variability of Profits and Firm size," *Economica*, Vol. 35, pp. 127-139.
4. Singh, Ajith and Whittington, G. (1968), "Growth, Profitability and Valuation", *E.A.E Occasion paper 7*, Cambridge: Cambridge University Press.
5. Marcus, M. (1969), "Profitability and Size of firm: some further evidence" *Review of Economics and Statistics*, Vol. 51, pp. 104-107.
6. Gale, B.T. (1972), "Market Share and Rate of Return", *Review of Economics and Statistics,* Vol. 54, pp. 412-423.
7. Mancke, R.B. (1974), "Causes of Inter-Firm Profit Differences: A New Interpretation of the Evidence", *Quarterly Journal of Economics*, Vol. 83, pp. 181-193.
8. Barthwal, R.R. (1976), "The Determinants of profitability in Indian Textile Industry", *Economica,* Vol. 43, pp. 267-274.
9. Agarwal, V.K. (1978), "Size, Profitability and growth of some Manufacturing Industries", Unpublished Thesis, IIM, Ahmedabad.
10. John, Steer Peter and Cable. (1978), "Internal Organisation and Profit : An Empirical Analysis of Large U.K. Companies", *The Journal of Industrial Economics,* Vol. 27, pp. 13-26.

11. Neumann, Bobel and Haid (1979), Profitability, Risk and Market Structure in West German industries, *The Journal of Industrial Economics*, Vol. 27, pp. 227-242.

12. Whittington, G. (1980), "The Profitability and Size of United Kingdom Companies 1960-1964", *The Journal of Industrial Economics,* Vol. 28, pp. 335-342.

13. Jain, Asha (1981), Price-Cost Margin in Indian Manufacturing Industries: An Econometric Analysis, Ph.D. thesis, IIT, Kanpur.

14. Bothwell, Cooley and Hall, (1982), A new view of Market Structure-Performance Debate, *The Journal of Industrial Economics and Statistics,* Vol. 64, pp. 635-645.

15. Gangadhar, V. (1982), Cement Industry - Some Aspects of Profitability, *The Management Accountant*, p. 477.

16. Rao, M.P. (1985), Impact of Debt Equity Ratio on Profitability - An Exploratory study of Engineering Industry, *Lok Udyog*, Vol. 19(5), pp. 29-34.

17. Chalam, G.V. and Dakshinamurthy, D. (1985), Performance of Public Enterprises in India: Impact of Heavy External Financing, *Public Enterprises,* Vol. 6, No. 2, pp. 16-20.

18. Kumar, P. (1985), Corporate growth and Profitability of firms in India, *Margin*, pp. 32-36.

19. Chawola, Deepak (1986), An empirical analysis of the profitability of the Indian man-made fibres industry, *Decision*, pp. 106-115.

20. Manasan, Rosario G., Junaita Amatong and Gil Beltran, (1988), The public enterprise sector in the Philippines: economic contribution and performance: 1975-1984, *Public Enterprise,* Vol. 8, No. 4, pp. 339-351.

21. Chattopadhayay, P. (1989), Central Government Enterprises: An Eighteen Years Profile, *Facts for You,* Vol. 10, No. 9, pp. 11-19.

22. Sankar, T.L, Mishra, R.K. and Nandagopal, R.N. (1990). State Level Public Enterprises in India: An Overview, *Economic and Political Weekly,* Bombay, pp. 1-37.

23. Nagarajan and Burthwal, (1990), Profitability and Structure: A Firm Level Study of Indian Pharmaceutical Industry. *The Indian Economic Journal,* Vol. 38, No. 2, pp. 70-84.

24. Pant, L.W. (1991), An Investigation of Industry and Firm Structural characteristics in Corporate Turnaround, *Journal of Management Studies,* Vol. 28, No. 12, pp. 623-643.

25. Conyon, N. and Machin, S. (1991), The Determinants of Profit Margins in U.K.Manufacturing, *The Journal of Economics,* Vol.34, No. 4, pp. 369-382.

26. Krishnaveni, (1991), Profitability and growth in Indian Automobile manufacturing industry, *Indian Journal of Economic Growth,* Vol. 26, pp. 81-97.

27. Bharatwaj, Sunder, G., Varadarajan, Rajan, P., and Szymanski David,M. (1993), "An Analysis of Market Share and Profitability relationship", *Journal of Marketing,* Vol. 57, pp. 1-18.

28. Chandrasekaran, N. (1993), Determinants of profitability in Cement Industry, *Decision,* Vol. 20, No. 4, pp. 235-244.

29. Cleveland and Frederick, W. (1993), Profitability, Uncertainty and Firm Size, *Small Business Economics*, Vol. 5, pp. 87-100.

30. Kallu Rao, P. (1993), Inter Company Financial Analysis of Tea Industry - Retrospect and Prospect, *Finance India,* Vol. VII, No. 3, pp. 587-602.

31. Eisenberg, Theodore and Sundgren, Stefan (1993), "Profitability, Uncertainty and Firm Size", *Small Business Economics,* Vol. 55, pp. 87-100.

32. Pai, V.S, Vadivel,V. and Kamala, K.H. (1995), "Diversified companies and financial performance: A study, *Finance India,* Vol. IX, No. 4, pp. 977-988.

33. *RBI Bulletin* (1995), Financial performance of private corporate business sector, *Finance India,* Vol. IX, No. 4, pp. 901-908.

34. Vijayakumar, A. and Venkatachalam, A. (1995), Working Capital and Profitability—An Empirical Analysis, *The Management Accountant,* Vol. 15, No. 3, pp. 748-750.

35. Vijayakumar, A. (1996), Assessment of Corporate Liquidity—A Discriminant Analysis approach, *The Management Accountant,* Vol. 31, No. 8, pp. 589-591.

36. Kim and Kunchul, (1996), "Profitabilty, Growth and Risk (Optmisation)", *Austaralian Economic Papers,* Vol. 33, pp. 65-88.

37. McDonald James Ted (1997), The Determinants of Firm Profitability in Australian Manufacturing, Melbourne Institute of Applied Economic and Social Research, The University of Melbourne, *Working paper No. 17/97.*

38. Chhibber, Pradeep K. and Sumit K.Majumdhar (1997), Foreign Ownership and Proftability: Property Rights, Strategic Control and Corporate Performance in Indian Industry, *Working Paper No. 64,*

The William Davidson Institute, University of Michigan Business School.

39. Geroski, Paul A., Stephen Machin and Christopher F. Walters (1997), *Journal of Industrial Economics,* Vol. 45, No. 2, pp. 171-189.
40. Nugent, Jim (1998), Corporate profitability in Ireland; Overview and Determinants, *Journal of the statistical and social inquiry, Society of Ireland,* Vol. XXVIII, Part-I, pp. 35-70.
41. Sidhu, H.S. and Gurpreet Bhatia, (1998), Factors affecting profitability in Indian Textile Industry, *The Indian Economic Journal,* pp. 137-143.
42. Kaur, Kuldip (1998), Size, Growth and Profitability of Firms in India-An Empirical Investigation. *Finance India,* Vol. XII, No. 2, pp. 455-457.
43. Mallick, Amit and Debasish Sur, (1998). Working Capital and Profitability: A Case Study in Inter relation, *The Management Accountant,* pp. 805-809.
44. Feeny, Simon and Mark Rogers, (1998), Profitability in Australian Enterprises, Melbourne Institute of Applied Economic and Social Research, The University of Melbourne, *Working paper No: 21/98.*
45. Vijayakumar, A. (1998), Determinants of corporate size, growth and profitability, *The Management Accountant,* Vol. X, No. 4, pp. 925-932.
46. Purohit, Vishnu Kanta (1998), *Profitability in Indian Industries,* New Delhi : Gayatri Publications.
47. Glancey, K. (1998), Determinants of growth and profitability in small entrepreneurial firms, *International Journal of Entrepreneurial Behaviour and Research,* Vol. 4, No. 1, pp. 18-27.
48. Pandey, I.M., and Bhat, R. (1998), "Financial Ratio Patterns in Indian Manufacturing Companies : A Multivariate Analysis", *Working Papers No. 764*, Ahmedabad: Indian Institute of Management.
49. Ahuja,Gautam and Sumit K. Majumdar (1998), An Assessment of the Performance of Indian State-owned Enterprises, *Journal of Productivity Analysis,* Vol. 9. No. 2, pp. 113-132.
50. Agarwal, R.N. (1999), Profitability and Growth in Indian Automobile Manufacturing Industry, *Indian Economic Review,* Vol. 26, No. 1, pp. 81-84.
51. Rogers, Mark, (1999), "The Performance of Small and Medium Enterprises: An overview using the growth and performance survey", Melbourne Institute of Applied Economic and Social Research, The University of Melbourne, *Working paper No. 1/99.*

52. Dutta, Soumyendra Kishore (1999), An Analysis of Profitability trend in the Indian Cotton Mill Industry, *Asian Economic Review*, Vol. 41, No. 2, pp. 294-307.

53. Feeny, Simon and Mark Rogers (1999), Market Share, Concentration and Diversification in Firm Profitability, Melbourne Institute of Applied Economic and Social Research, The University of Melbourne, *Working paper No: 20/1999.*

54. Govindan Rao, D. and Mohana Rao, P. (1999), *Impact of working capital on profitability in cement industry - A correlation analysis*, New Delhi: Deep and Deep Publications.

55. Raghunathan, V. and Prabina Das, (1999), Corporate Performance: Post- Liberalization, *The ICFAI Journal of Applied Finance,* Vol. 5, No. 2, pp. 6-29.

56. D'Souza, Juliet and William L.Megginson, (1999), Financial and operating performance of privatized firms during the 1990s, *The Journal of Finance,* Vol. LIV, No. 4, pp. 1397-1434.

57. Sur, Debasish (1999), " Working Capital Profitability: A case study in inter-relation", *The Management Accountant,* Vol. 33, No. 1, pp. 805-809.

58. Feeny, Simon and Mark Rogers (1999), The performance of large private Australian enterprises, Melbourne Institute of Applied Economic and Social Research, the University of Melbourne, Working paper No. 2/99.

59. Islam, Mohammed Rafiqul (2000), Profitability of Fertilizer Industry in Bangladesh. *The Management Accountant,* pp. 338-345.

60. Simon Feeny (2000), Determinants of profitability: an empirical investigation using Australian tax entities, Melbourne Institute of Applied Economic and Social Research, The University of Melbourne, Working paper.

61. Sahu,S.K. (Aug.2000), "Analysis of corporate profitability: a multivariate approach, *The Management Accountant,* Vol. 35, No. 8, pp. 571-577.

62. Sur, Dabasish, Joydeep Biswas and Prasenjit Ganguly, (2001), Liquidity Management in Indian Private Sector Enterprises -A case study of Indian Primary Aluminum industry, *Indian Journal of Accounting,* Vol. XXXII, pp. 8-14.

63. Aggarwal, N. and Singla, S.K. (2001), How to develop a single index for financial performance, *Indian Management,* Vol. 12, No. 5, pp. 59-62.

64. Loundes, Joanne (2001), "The Financial Performance of Australian Government Trading Enterprises pre-and post-reform, Melbourn Institute of Applied Economic and Social Research, The University of Melbourne, Working paper No. 5/01.

65. Rogers, Mark (2001), The Effect of Diversification on Firm Performance, Melbourne Institute of Applied Economic and Social Research, The University of Melbourne, Working paper No: 02/2001.

66. Sur, Dabasish (2001), Liquidity Management: An overview of four companies in Indian Power Sector, *The Management Accountant,* pp. 407-412.

67. Rei, Debashish and Debashish, Sur, (2001), Profitability Analysis of Indian Food Products Industry: A case study of Cadbury India Ltd, *The Management Accountant,* Vol. 36, No. 6, pp. 407-412.

68. Vijayakumar, A. (2002), Determinants of Profitability-A Firm Level study of the Sugar Industry of Tamil Nadu, *The Management Accountant,* pp. 458-465.

69. Bosworth, Derek and Joanne Loundes, (2002), The Dynamic Performance of Australian Enterprises. Melbourne Institute of Applied Economic and Social Research, The University of Melbourne, Working Paper No: 03/2002.

70. Mulla, Mansur A. (2002), Use of 'Z' score analysis for evaluation of financial health of textile mills— A case study, *Abhigyan,* Vol. XIX, No. 4, pp. 37-40.

71. Aussenegg, Wolfgang and Ranko Jelic, (2002), Operating performance of privatized companies in transition economies- the case of Poland, Hungary and the Czech Republic.

72. Glen, Jack, Kevin Lee and Ajit Singh, (2002), Corporate profitability and the dynamics of competition in emerging markets- A time series analysis, ESRC Center for Business Research, University of Cambridge, *Working paper No. 248.*

73. Shanmugam, K.R. and Bhaduri Saumitra N. (2002), "Size, Age and Firm Growth in the Indian Manufacturing Sector", *Applied Economics Letters,* pp. 607-613.

74. Vijayakumar, A. (2002a), *Financial appraisal of Salem Co-operative Sugar Mills Ltd., Mohanur:* Research studies in Commerce and Management, Delhi: Classical Publishing Company, pp. 51-65.

75. Vijayakumar, A. (2002b), Assessment of corporate liquidity – A Discriminant Analysis approach, *The Management Accountant,* Vol. 14, pp. 50-62.

76. Fu, Tze-Wei, Mei-Chiu ke and Yen-Sheng Huang (2002). Capital Growth, financing source and Profitability of Small Business: Evidene from Taiwan Small Enterprises, *Small Business Economics,* Vol. 18, No. 4, pp. 257-267.

77. Yucel, Tulay, Kurt and Guluzar, (2002), Cash conversion Cycle, Cash Management and Profitability; An empirical study on the ISE Traded companies, *Istambul Stock Exchange Review,* Vol. 6, No. 2, pp. 1-15.

78. Kaen, Fred, R and Baumann Hans (2003), "Firm Size, Employees and Profitability in US Manufacturing Industries".

79. Ray, Saon (2003), Economic Reforms and Efficiency of firms; the Indian Manufacturing sector during the nineties, Institute of Economic Growth, University of Delhi Enclave, New Delhi.

80. Vijayakumar, A. and Kadirvel, S. (2003a), Determinants of profitability in Indian Public Sector Manufacturing Industries—An Econometric Analysis, *The Journal of Institute of Public Enterprises,* Vol. 26, pp. 1-2.

81. Vijayakumar, A and Kadirvel, S. (2003b), Profitability and Size of the firm in Indian Minerals and Metals industry, *The Management Accountant,* pp. 816-821.

82. Wei, Zuobao, Oscar Varela, Juliet D'Souza and Kabir Hassan.M. (2003), The financial and operating performance of China's newly privatized firms, *Financial Management,* Vol. 32, No. 2, pp. 107-126.

83. Sudarsana Reddy, G. (2003), Financial Performance of Paper industry in A.P, *Finance India,* Vol. XVII, No. 3, pp. 1027-1033.

84. RBI Corporate Studies Division (2003), Performance of corporate business sector during the first half of 2002-2003, *Finance India,* Vol. XVII, No. 3, pp. 987-1002.

85. Ghosh, Santany Kumar and Santi Gopal Maji (2003), "Utilisation of current assets and operating profitability: An empirical study on cement and tea industries in India", *Indian Journal of Accounting,* Vol. xxxiv, pp. 52-60.

86. Liu, Wan-Chun and Hsu, Chan-Min (2004), "Financial Structure, Corporate Finance and Growth of Taiwan's manufacturing firms".

87. Sarkaria, Maninder S. and Shergil U.S. (2004), Market Structure and Financial Performance-An Indian Evidence with Enhanced Controls, Ph.D. Thesis Submitted to the Guru Nanak Dev University.

88. Marcos, A.M.Lima and Marcelo Resende, (2004), Profit margins and business cycles in the Brazilian industry: a panel data study, *Taylor and Francis Journal in Applied Economics,* pp. 923-930.

89. Patel, D.M.(2004), "Proft and Profitability (A case study of Colour-Chem Limited)", *ACCST Research Journal,* Vol. ii, No. 2, pp. 89-95.

90. Weill, Laurent (2004), Leverage and corporate performance - A frontier efficiency. University Robert Schuman, instituted detudes politiques, 47 avenue de la Foret-Noire, 67082 Strasbourg cedex, France. e-mail: Laurent. Weill @ urs.G-strasbg.fr.

91. Leahy, Arthar S. (2004).; The determinants of profitability in the Liquor Industry, Briefing Notes in Economics, No. 61, pp. 1-6.

92. Bhanu, V. (2005), Merged companies-their profitability performance, *Indian Journal of Accounting,* Vol. XXXV (2), pp. 19-38.

93. Hamsalakshmi and Manickam (2005), Financial performance analysis of selected software companies, *Finance India,* Vol.xix, No. 3, pp. 915-935.

94. Niskanen, Mervi and Niskanen Jyrki (2005), "The determinants of Firm Growth in Small and Micro Firms. Evidence on relationship Lending effects".

95. Patra, Santimoy (2005), Liquidity Vs. Profitability, *Indian Journal of Accounting,* Vol. XXXV(2), pp. 39-43.

96. Fitzsimmons, J.R, Steffens. P.R, and Douglas.E.J (2005), "Growth and Profitability in small and medium sized Australian Firms". AGSE Entrepreneurship Exchange, Melbourne.

97. Agiomirgianakis, G, Voulgaris, F. and Papadogonas,T. (2006), Financial factors affecting profitability and employment growth: the case of Greek manaufacturing, *International Journal of Financial Service Management,* Vol. 1 Nos. 2/3, pp. 232-242.

98. Mallik and Debasish Mukherjee (2006), Performance of leasing industry in West Bengal, *The Management Accountant,* pp. 393-398.

99. Raja and Suresh Kumar, A. (2006), Is Age or Size Influences Corporate Performance?, *PSG Journal of Management,* Vol. 1, No. 4, pp. 51-62.

100. Luthra, Renu, Vaishampayan and Dheeraj Misra (2006). Profitability and Size: A study of small-scale industries in Uttar Pradesh, *The ICFAIAN Journal of Management Research,* pp. 28-37.

101. Vishnani, Sushma and Bhupesh Kr Shah (2006), Liquidity Vs Profitability – A detailed study in perspective of Indian consumer electronics industry, *Pranjana,* Vol. 9, No. 2, pp. 13-20.

102. Thirumavalavan, P. (2006), Determinants of Earnings Before Interest and Taxation (EBIT) of Aluminium Companies, *PSG Journal of Management Research,* Vol. 1, No. 2, pp. 33-37.

103. Singh, S.P. (2007), Performance of sugar mills in Uttar Pradesh by Ownership, size and location, *Prajnan,* Vol. XXXV, No. 4, pp. 233-359.

104. Ghosh, Arindam (2007), Working Capital Management practices in some selected industries in India, *The Management Accountant,* pp. 60-68.

105. Sam Luther, C.T. (2007), Liquidity, Risk and Profitability analysis—A case study of Madras Cements Ltd., *The Management Accountant,* Vol. 42, No. 10, pp. 784-789.

106. Manor Selvi, A. and Vijayakumar, A. (2007), "Structure of profit rates in Indian Automobile Industries—A comparision", *The Management Accountant,* Vol. 42, No. 10, pp. 784-789.

107. Chander, Subhash and Priyanka Aggarwal (2007), Determinants of Corporate Growth: An Empirical Study of Indian Drugs and Pharmaceutical Industry, *The Icfaian Journal of Management Research,* Vol. VI, No. 10, pp. 50-70.

CHAPTER 3

Method of Analysis

In research, the methodology needs to be cautiously designed to capitulate results that are as objective as realistic. An able-bodied comprehensible *modus operandi* empowers the new-fangled research investigator to re-examine the study milieu. Good methodology follows the standards of the established conventions. For the present study, a number of indispensable inimitabilities of the research methodology skirmishing the application magnitude and research rationalisation of each one are defined here in this chapter.

The ensuing paragraphs in this chapter deal with the methodology adopted in selection of sample and analysis of data for this study. It outlines the objectives and scope of the study, procedure followed for selection of the sample and the collection of data, classification of the sample and the techniques followed in analyzing the data for the period of study. Further, the hypotheses set and limitations of the study have also been dealt herein.

The Problem

The title of the study is *Corporate Profitability Analysis.*

Objectives of the Study

The present study in general aims at to obtain a true insight into the profitability performance of the selected South Indian private sector sugar industry. An appraisal of profitability performance is made from the accounting point of view to assess the effectiveness of plans, policies and objectives of the industry by measuring the efficiency of the South Indian private sector sugar industry under the study, in various areas of profitability. The specific objectives of the study are:

1. To analyze the profitability of selected South Indian private sector sugar industry.
2. To examine and explain the trends in profitability of selected South Indian private sector sugar industry.
3. To study the relationship between size and profitability of selected South Indian private sector sugar industry.
4. To study the relationship between profitability and liquidity, growth as well as working capital of selected South Indian private sector sugar industry.
5. To determine the factors those influence the profitability of selected South Indian private sector sugar industry.
6. To make suggestions for improvement for successful survival of the selected South Indian private sector sugar industry.

Scope of the Study

The present study includes the empirical analysis of profitability in the South Indian private sector sugar industry. The scope of profitability is very wide and broad-based. For the theoretical understanding, the meaning and definition of profit and profitability and various concepts come under the purview of the study. The second part of the study is confined to the review of literature relating to various aspects of profitability. For the analytical and technical study, tools and techniques, such as ratios, mean, co-efficient of variation, compound annual growth rate, t-test, ANOVA, and linear and multiple regression and their interpretation are included in the study.

It also contains the analysis of relationship between profitability and size as well as liquidity and growth. The present study has analyzed only the accounting profitability and analysis of social and value-added profitability and economic value added profitability is beyond the scope of this study. The period of study has been confined to the years between 1991-92 and 2005-06. The year 1991-92 has been selected as the beginning year of the study period because the tempo of liberalization has actually been started from the year 1990-91.

Hypotheses

Hypotheses mean the researchers must select from the intricacy of observed events such considerable and pertinent facts that would most effectively elucidate the problem under study. It gives us an idea about indispensable associations, which exist between the different fundamentals within the complexity. Therefore, the hypotheses of the present study are:

Hypotheses for Profitability Analysis

(*i*) There is no significant difference in the mean percentage of profitability ratios between initial, growth and maturity phases of liberalization in South Indian private sector sugar industry.

(*ii*) There is no significant difference in the mean percentage of profitability ratios between years and between the sectors in South Indian private sector sugar industry.

Hypothesis for Trend Analysis

(*i*) There is no significant difference between actual and trend values of profitability among different years in the selected sectors of South Indian private sector sugar industry.

Hypotheses for Determinants of Profitability

(*i*) There is a positive relationship between size as well as growth rate of assets and profitability.

(*ii*) Profitability is negatively correlated with leverage and current ratio.

(*iii*) There is a positive relationship between inventory turnover ratio and profitability.

(*iv*) Fixed assets turnover ratio, vertical integration and past profitability are positively correlated with the profitability.

(*v*) Profitability is negatively correlated with operating expenses to sales ratio.

Research Design

It is not possible in practice for an individual research worker to approach all the bits and pieces in the universe. Researchers selects only a small amount of bits and pieces from the universe for the purpose of the study on the basis of stratified sampling. The sample so selected constitutes the sample design for the purpose. A research design is a definite plan for obtaining a sample from a given population. Research design means a sketch or a drawing of a research project's structure. It comprises a series of prior pronouncements that, taken together, provide a roadmap for carrying out a research project. The research design of the present study is outlined hereunder.

Sample Design

Keeping in view of the scope of the study, the private sector sugar industries operated in South India (in the States of Tamil Nadu, Kerala, Karnataka, Andhra Pradhesh, Maharashtra, Goa and Union Territory namely Puducherry were considered for the study. It is decided to include all the industries working under private sector in the South India working before or from the year 1991-92. But owing to several constraints such as non-availability of financial statements or non-working of the company in particular year etc., it is compelled to restrict the numbers of sample industries to fifteen.

Therefore, this study is *exposed facto*-based on survey method making a survey of 15 private sector sugar industries operated in South India. The number of industries operated in the different States of South India is presented in Table 3.1.

Table 3.1. Sector-wise number of industries operated in South India

State	Public Sector	Private Sector	Co-operative Sector	Total
Andhra Pradhesh	1	26	15	42
Goa	-	-	1	1
Karnataka	-	1	1	2
Kerala	3	25	23	51
Maharashtra	-	23	165	188
Puducherry	-	1	1	2
Tamil Nadu	3	19	16	38
Total	**7**	**95**	**222**	**324**

Source: *Indian Sugar Year Book, 2007-08.*

It is evident from the above table that there are 324 sugar industries operating in the South India. Out of which seven industries are under public sector, 95 under private sector and 222 industries under co-operative sector. Since majority of the industries under public sector and co-operative sector were inoperative and sick and also due to non-availability of data, it is decided to include only private sector sugar industries in the sample.

The Capitaline and CMIE database published key financial data of Indian corporate sector systematically. Hence, Capitaline and CMIE databases proved to be complimentary to finalize the sample for the study. The exhaustive list of private sector sugar industry from Capitaline is cross checked with CMIE database to short out industry to make up the sample for the study. The comprehensive list of industries prepared from the database was modified by deleting the firms :

- which were not in operation for any year during the period under study.
- which were in operation but for which financial data were not available for any of the 15-year period under study.
- which were described as sick unit for any year during the period under study.

For the purpose of the study the selected sugar industries were classified as large-sized, medium-sized and small-sized industries based on crushing capacity. The industries having a crushing capacity of 5000 MT (per day) or more have been considered as large-sized, 2501 to 5000 MT (per day) as medium-sized and up to 2500 MT (per day) as small-sized

Table 3.2. Sample Classification

Sl. No.	Sectors	No. of Industries available in database	No. of Industries with 15 years data
1.	**Large-sized** [above 5000 MT per day crushing capacity	10	7
2.	**Medium-sized** [2501 to 5000 MT per day crushing capacity]	7	4
3.	**Small-sized** [up to 2500 MT per day crushing capacity]	13	4
	Total	30	15

Source: *Prowess Database,* 2007

sugar industry. Out of the 95 private sector sugar industries operated in south India, only for 30 industries data are available in the databases. Out of 30 industries, only 15 industries have been included in the study because financial statements for the last 15 continuous years could be obtained for these industries only.

The sector-wise number of industries with consecutive fifteen-year financial data available are presented in Table 3.2.

Further the list of industries selected and included in the present study along with the year of incorporation, ownership and registered office is presented in Table 3.3.

Table 3.3. List of sample industries included in the present study

Sl. No.	Sectors/ Industries	Year of Incor-poration	Owner-ship	Registered office
	Large-sized (7):			
1.	Bannari Amman Sugars Ltd	1983	Sakthi	Coimbatore
2.	EID Parry Ltd	1975	Murugappa	Chennai
3.	Jeypore Sugars and Chemicals Ltd	1985	KCP	Chennai
4.	Rajshree Sugars and Chemicals Ltd	1985	LMW	Coimbatore
5.	Sakthi Sugars Ltd	1961	Sakthi	Erode
6.	Thiru Arooran Sugars Ltd	1954	Private	Chennai
7.	Ugar Sugar Works Ltd	1939	Private	Sangli
	Medium-sized (4):			
8.	Kothari Sugars & Chemicals Ltd	1959	Kothari H C	Chennai

...(Contd.)

Sl. No.	Sectors/ Industries	Year of Incor- poration	Owner- ship	Registered office
9.	Sri Chamundeswari Sugars Ltd	1970	Sakthi	Bangalore
10.	Sri Sarvaraya Sugars Ltd	1956	Private	Chennai
11.	Kakatiya Cements Sugar and Industries Ltd	1979	Private	Hyderabad
	Small-sized (4):			
12.	Dharani Sugars and Chemicals Ltd	1987	Dharani	Chennai
13.	Empee Sugars and Chemicals Ltd	1988	Private	Nellore
14.	India Sugars and Refineries Ltd	1933	Private	Bellary
15.	Ponni Sugars Ltd	1982	Esvin	Chennai

Period of Study

The period 1991-92 to 2005-06 is selected for this study of South Indian private sector sugar industry. This 15-year period is chosen in order to have a fairly long, cyclically well-balanced period, for which reasonably homogeneous, reliable and uptodate financial data would be available. Further, the span chosen for the study is the period of the beginning of liberalization measures introduced by the Government of India. Hence, the period 1991-92 to 2005-06 is an era of growth of corporate performance in the manufacturing sector and has got genuine economic significance of its own.

Source of Data

The study is mainly based on secondary data. The data analysed and interpreted in this study related to all those industries selected are collected from "Capitaline" and "PROWESS" databases, which are the most reliable on the empowered corporate database of Bombay Stock Exchange and Centre for Monitoring Indian Economy (CMIE) respectively. They contain highly normalized databases built on a sound understanding of disclosure in India more than 12,000 companies, which include public, private, co-operative and joint-sector companies. The databases provide financial statements, ratio analysis, funds flow, cash flow, product profiles, returns and risk on the stock market etc.

Beside Capitaline and PROWESS databases, relevant secondary data have also been collected from BSE Stock Exchange Official Directory, CMIE Publications, Annual Survey of Industry, Business newspapers, Reports on Currency and Finance, Libraries of various Research Institutions, through Internet etc.

Data Editing

For this study, major part of data comes from secondary sources. Data have been collected in raw form and then it is made suitable for analysis as per the methodology defined for the purpose.

Selection of Variables

In this study at hand, a number of key financial variables have been identified for the purpose of analysis. The computation of these variables has been made for a period of 15 years. An epigrammatic explanation of the selected variable is outlined below.

Profitability

Return on assets and return on sales are widely used measures of profitability. It is assumed that management may be concerned with effective utilisation of all resources and these two measures could be proper in this line of arguments. The review includes Stkeler (1964), Samuels and

Smyth (1968), Neumann, Bobel and Haid (1979), Deepak Chawala (1986), Narayanan and Barthwal (1990), Amit Mallick and Debasish Sur (1998), Agarwal (1999), Mohammed Rafiqul Islam (2000) and Vijayakumar (2002) which provide direct evidence of using return on assets and return on sales as a measure of profitability. The profit rates measured by sales will give a short-term perspective of profitability because sales are annual flows. On the other hand, the return on assets will give us long-term perspective of profitability. In this study, ratio of profit margin on sales is used as dependent variable.

Size

One of the very important structural characteristics of the industry which is commonly used to explain profitability in applied research is the size of the firm. Many researchers have employed firm size as a variable in their study of determinants of profitability. The big firms have been considered to be endowed with certain advantages such as lower costs and higher returns on accounts of access to capital market (Hall and Weiss, 1967)[1] and economies of scale (Sidhu and Bhatia, 1993)[2]. Hence, generally a positive hypothesis is set for size-profitability relationship. The size - profitability relationship is more likely to be curvi-linear and after reaching a certain stage, the advantage of scale economies may cease and beyond that the relationship may even reverse due to the problems of large scale. Due to the expected curvi-linear size performance relationship, size variable is generally employed in long term. Though the positive relationship between size and profitability has been found to be significant, after a point of time, profitability increases at a rate with proposed increase in size. This could arise when (*i*) other firms in the market follow similar strategies (*ii*) diseconomies and inefficiency due to in manageable size, and (*iii*) increased possibility of public criticism of excessive profits as firm becomes larger. Therefore, impact of firm size on profitability can not be determined apriori.

Generally two size measures are employed, they are assets and sales turnover. Assets express amount of resources utilised for producing output whereas sales turnover is an output variable. Sales are annual flow depending upon output produced and sold in the market. Further sales needs to be adjusted for excise payment to more meaningful comparison. Therefore, in this study the logarithm value of total assets as the measure of size has been employed.

Leverage

A firm with high leverage ratio represents greater financial risk than a firm with relatively less risk. If competition equalises earnings, then high debt should result in higher return on net worth. It is argued that firms have low debt because they operate industries with high degree of business risk and thus expect a negative relation between leverage and profitability, if owners are risk averse. It seems that the relationship between leverage and rate of return is indeterminate apriori. In an intra industry study, business risk is assumed to be same and leverage must be a better measure of risk. The debt-equity ratio as the measure of leverage has been employed in this study.

Current Ratio

The management of working capital involves decisions about the amount and composition of current assets and how they are financed. Such decisions involve a trade off between solvency and profitability. In inter-firm comparison, the firm with higher current ratio has better liquidity. A high ratio of current assets to current liabilities may be indicative of slack management practices, as it might signal poor credit management in terms of over-extended accounts receivables. A low ratio is also not desirous since there will be an inadequate margin of safety. Therefore, current ratio is used to explain profitability of south Indian Private sector sugar industry.

Inventory Turnover Ratio

Another variable that can influence the profitability is the inventory turnover ratio. It is the ratio of sales to inventory which indicates the number of times inventory is replaced during the year. Instead of taking year end stock of inventory, an average of the opening and closing stock of inventory is considered. A high ratio implies good inventory management. But low inventory will adversely affect the ability of a firm to meet customer demand and in turn will affect profitability. On the other hand, a very low inventory turnover ratio signifies excessive inventory or over investment in inventory and high carrying cost. The sign of inventory coefficient is ambiguous.

Fixed Assets Turnover Ratio

Another variable influencing the profitability of the industry is fixed assets turnover ratio which is defined as the ratio of sales to fixed assets. It indicates the relationship between the amount invested in fixed assets and the results in accruing in terms of the sales. It is expected that an increase in this ratio would result in increase in profitability. The capital employed of a firm includes both current and fixed assets. The fixed assets provide the productive base and earning capacity for the firm. But an efficient utilisation of the earning capacity calls for an optimum use of working capital.

Operating Expenses to Sales Ratio

Apart from the above discussed factors operating expenses ratio is included as an explanatory variable in this study. A low operating ratio is by and large a test of operational efficiency. The implication of low operating expenses ratio is that relatively a high percentage share of sales is available for meeting financial liabilities such as interest, taxes and dividends. Therefore, a negative relationship is expected with operating expenses and profitability.

Vertical Integration

Firm-specific vertical integration motivated by considerations such as the avoidance of costs incurred in using the market of organise production, government policies and also consideration of market power is an important determinant of profitability. The costs of using the market alternatively known as transaction costs include search cost, cost of drawing up contracts, monitoring costs, etc. In our context government polices assume an important role in determining vertical integration. The degree of vertical integration is sought to be measured by the value added to sales ratio in the analysis. Value added is defined as total sales revenue less costs of purchased inputs, repair charges and customs and excise duty.

Growth Rate of Assets

The other variable, which is considered, is growth of firm. Growth is essential to a firm even if it is not among the firm's major objectives. The reason is that growth helps in providing the firm finances for attaining its objective by increasing the size of its profit growth, by providing room for initiatives and exercise managerial ability, stimulates managerial efficiency leading to a lower capital output ratio and consequently higher profit rate. It is thus, likely to have positive association with profitability. Growth rate is measured in this study by the ratio of simple growth rate of assets.

Data Analysis

The financial and statistical analysis approach play a vital role in the financial environment. To enjoy the benefit of financial and statistical analysis researcher has collected, assembled and correlated the data, classified the data appropriately and condensed them in to a related data series, stated the resultant information in a comprehensive form, text, tables and analysed and interpreted the reported data. The financial and statistical techniques applied in the study are given below:

It is well-known that management is concerned with efficient performance, profitability and solvency. For this purpose it has to study certain specific ratios, because investors look upon certain ratios, which are concerned with an organization's operating and financial performance. For the purpose of this study, researcher has used ratios namely, operating profit margin, gross profit margin, return on capital employed, interest coverage ratio, net profit margin, return on assets, return on net worth, earnings per share, dividend per share, dividend payout ratio, total assets turnover ratio, fixed assets turnover ratio, current assets turnover ratio and inventory turnover ratio. In order to study the profitability cycle of the selected sectors during the post liberalization period the whole period of 15 years was divided equally into three phases viz., growth phase (1991-92 to 1995-96), medium phase (1996-97 to 2000-01) and maturity phase (2001-02 to 2005-06).

The role of statistical tools is important in analysing the data and drawing inferences therefrom. In order to derive the open handed results from the information collected through secondary data, various statistical tools like mean, standard deviation, variance, compound annual growth rate, regression, tests of hypotheses both parametric and non-parametric have been accomplished through EXCEL, SX and SPSS software. Some of the statistical techniques particularly t-test, Durbin-Watson test, ANOVA and trend analysis have been used to interpret the sense of mathematical relationship amongst values of different variables so computed in the study.

In the present study regression models have also been used to analyse the influence of independent variables on dependent variables in case of determinants of profitability. The hypothesis has been tested separately on the sample. This can be done via the mechanism of the F-test and t-test.

Limitations of the Study

However, there are some limitations of the study, which are generally inherent in all such studies conducted at human being level. The most important among them are:

(*i*) The study is based on secondary data obtained from the published annual reports and as such its finding depends entirely on the accuracy of such data.

(*ii*) Non-availability of the required fifteen consecutive year's financial data for the whole period of study has restricted the size of the sample. Therefore, the limitation of the small sample is also prevalent in this study.

(*iii*) The present study is largely based on ratio analysis which has its own limitations.

(*iv*) Statistical test used in the study to interpret the analysed data to generalize the findings of the study for the entire population has got their own limitations and result in the analysis is subject to same constraints as are applicable to statistical tools.

(*v*) The analysis of financial statement of business enterprise gives diagnostic indicators. Researcher being outside external analyst obviously has no access to internal data. Therefore, inside view of the organization cannot be characterized in the study.

(*vi*) The financial statement does not keep pace with the changing price level.

However, all these limitations, do not, in any way, affect the worth of this research work.

Chapter Scheme

In order to present this research work in a lucid way, it has been divided into six chapters. The layout of these chapters is delineated below:

Chapter 1 This is conceptual in nature and has been divided into eight sub-parts, which include introduction, meaning and concept of profit and profitability, significance of profitability, tools and techniques for analysis of profitability, need for the study, selection of sugar industry and statement of the problem.

Chapter 2 This presents a brief review of related literatures on the subject.

Chapter 3 It encompasses the research methodology of the study. This chapter contains twelve parts that include the problem, objectives of the study, scope of the study, hypotheses, sample design, period of study, sources of data, data editing, selection of variables, data analysis, limitations of the study and chapter scheme.

Chapter 4 This chapter brings out profitability analysis from the view point of financial management, profitability analysis from the view point of shareholders, profitability analysis from the view point of asset utilization and profitability trend of the selected sectors of South Indian private sector Sugar Industry.

Chapter 5 This is committed to the study of relationship between size and profitability, growth and profitability, liquidity and profitability, impact of working capital on profitability and determinants of profitability of the selected sectors of South Indian private sector Sugar Industry.

Chapter 6 It embodies the summary of conclusion and some workable recommendations for the smooth and efficient functioning of South Indian private sector Sugar Industry.

Towards the end of this research work, comprehensive bibliographies on the subject and some appendices have also been added.

NOTES

1. Hall, M. and Weiss, L. (1967). Firm size and profitability, *Review of Economics and Statistics,* Vol. 49, pp. 319-331.
2. Sidhu, H.S. and Bhatia G. (1993). Factors affecting profitability in Indian Textile Industry, *The Indian Economic Journal*, Vol. 41, No. 2, pp. 137-143.

CHAPTER 4

Profitability Analysis and its Trend

ANALYSIS OF PROFITABILITY

The "profit" is the golden egg, the centre of the attraction of all those that are interested in the corporate unit. Therefore, it is necessary to analyse and interpret the profitability in the corporate sector as a whole. The business firms are generally established with a view of earning profit from the business operations. But under different situation the object of the business firms may be changed to survival, growth stability etc., Business firms are to survive in dynamic and expanding environment. It has to go on expanding the scale of its operation on a regular and continuing basis by generating sufficient profit. Profits are useful intermediate beacon towards which a firm's capital should be directed.[1] It is difficult for a business to breathe well without profit. It may be regarded as a mirror of the operating performance of the business activities. But in the real business environment of today, profit is thus, not the sole objective but one among the most important objectives, which normally guide and direct business operations.

Indeed, profits are the test of efficiency and a measure of control; to the owners, a measure of worth of their investment; to the creditor, the margin of safety; to the employees, source of fringe benefits; to the governments, measure of taxable capacity and the basis of legislative action; to the customer, demand for price cut. It is the criterion of judging the efficient operation. In short, profit is the legitimate object of an enterprise from the investor. According to economic thinkers, profits are the report card of the past, incentive gold star for the future and also stake for the new venture. Accountant ascertain profits, is not only a reliable measure of efficient performance in using production resources. But also, means of measuring the progress of the business or "testing its pulse" and of indicating when and whole remedial action, if necessary shall be taken[2].

In the era of economic development, the profit and the profitability are two different concepts. Although both of them are controversial, even then both are inter-related and mutually inter-dependent. Profit is the absolute term and profitability is a relative concept. Notably, while profit is the residue of income, profitability is the profit-making ability of the enterprise. It may be remarked that the profit making ability might denote a constant or improved or deteriorated state of affairs during a given period. Thus, profit is an absolute connotation, whereas profitability is a relative concept, despite being closely related to and mutually interdependent, as they are, profit and profitability are two different concepts. In other words, in spite of their generic nature, each one of them has a distinct role in business concerns might be the same and get more often than note their profitability could differ when measured in terms of the size of investment.[3] An analysis of the profitability reveals as to how the position of profits stands as a result of total transactions made during the year.

Measurement of Profitability

Profitability is the main indicator of the efficiency and effectiveness of a business enterprise in achieving its goal of earning profit. Profitability of a firm can be measured by its profitability ratios. In the process of performance appraisal of a business, profitability ratios can be calculated to measure the operating efficiency. The profitability ratios can be determined on the basis of either investment or sales and for this purpose a quantitative relationship between the profit and the investment or the sales is established. In the words of James C. Van Horne, "Profitability ratios are of two types: those showing profitability in relation to sales, and those showing profitability in relation to investment".[4] He further added "with all of the profitability ratios, comparisons of a company with similar companies are extremely valuable. Only by comparison are we to judge whether the profitability of a particular company is good or bad, and why. Absolute figures give same insight, but it is relative performance which is the most important".[5] The profitability of the company should be evaluated in terms of its investment in assets and in terms of capital contributed by creditors and owners, as such if a company is unable to earn a satisfactory return on investments, its survival is threatened.

The profitability of selected South Indian private sector sugar industry has been analyzed from the point of view of financial management, shareholders and utilization of assets. The following profitability ratios have been computed and analyzed for the selected South Indian private sector sugar industry during the study period.

Profitability from the view Point of Financial Management

1. Operating profit margin ratio
2. Gross profit margin ratio
3. Return on capital employed
4. Interest coverage ratio

Profitability from the view point of Shareholders

1. Net profit margin ratio
2. Return on total assets
3. Return on shareholders funds
4. Earnings per share
5. Dividend pay out ratio

Profitability from the view Point of Utilization of Assets

1. Total assets turnover
2. Fixed assets turnover
3. Current assets turnover
4. Inventory turnover

In order to test the significance of variation in the mean percentage of profitability ratios between the sectors, between the industries and the years, the following hypotheses are framed and tested.

1. H_0 - There is no significant difference in the mean percentages of profitability ratios between the sectors and years.
2. H_0 - There is no significant difference in the mean percentages of profitability ratios between the industry and years.
3. H_0 - There is no significant difference in the mean percentages of profitability ratios of different phases among the sectors and industry.

PROFITABILITY FROM THE VIEW POINT OF FINANCIAL MANAGEMENT

A financial manager is very much interested to locate and pinpoint the causes which are responsible for low or high profitability. The financial manager should continuously evaluate efficiency of his company in terms of profit. The profit margin ratio is a profitability ratio which measures the relationship between the profit and sales. It indicates the efficiency or effectiveness with which the operations of business are carried on. Profit margin varies with disproportionate variations in sales revenue in comparison to cost or the *vice versa*.

To judge profitability from the view point of financial management of selected South Indian private sector Sugar

Industry, the following ratios have been computed and analyzed.

Operating Profit-Margin Ratio

The first profitability ratio in relation to sales is the operating profit margin.[6] The operating profit margin reflects the efficiency with which the management produces each unit of product. This ratio indicates the average spread between the cost of goods sold and sales.[7] It is one of the most carefully watched measures of profitability. A high operating profit ratio is the sign of managerial effectiveness. Conversely, a low ratio should be carefully investigated and compared with the ratios of similar corporations to diagnoses as also to remedy problem.[8] There is no standard norm for operating profit ratio and it may vary from business to business but the operating profit should be adequate to provide for fixed charges, interest and dividend.

Table 4.1 and Fig. 4.1 show a fluctuating trend in the operating profit margin ratio of the selected South Indian private sector sugar industry during the 15-year study period. On an average the South Indian private sector sugar industry had the overall operating profit margin ratio of 18.70 per cent with a co-efficient of variation of 0.23. The average operating profit margin ratio varied from sector to sector, the highest average was 20.35 per cent in medium-sized sugar industry followed by large-sized (19.24%) and small-sized (16.11%) sugar industry. The mean operating profit margin was higher than the industry average in medium-sized and large-sized sugar industry. The CV value of these ratios shows high fluctuation in the operating profit margin ratio of the selected sector during the study period. Such fluctuation could be attributed to the differences in the growth rates of operating profit margin and sales because of the factors like high operating expenses, market condition, operational problems and change in demand of sugar. All the selected sectors and whole industry witnessed the positive compound annual growth rate of this ratio during the study period.

Table 4.1. Analysis of operating profit-margin ratio of selected South Indian private sector Sugar industry (1991-92 to 2005-06)

(Per cent)

Particulars	Initial phase [1992-96]	Growth phase [1997-2001]	Maturity phase [2002-2006]	Whole period [1992-2006]
Large-sized (n=7)				
Mean	20.38	20.0	17.35	**19.24**
CV	0.41	0.28	0.19	**0.24**
CAGR	0.74	5.53	5.31	**1.25**
Medium-sized (n=4)				
Mean	21.87	15.86	23.30	**20.35**
CV	0.31	0.76	0.42	**0.19**
CAGR	–4.55	–7.25	4.00	**–3.15**
Small-sized (n=4)				
Mean	16.61	14.67	17.05	**16.11**
CV	0.31	0.57	0.17	**0.29**
CAGR	16.78	2.41	–3.70	**1.66**
Whole Industry (n=15)				
Mean	19.77	17.48	18.86	18.70
CV	0.36	0.46	0.31	0.23
CAGR	0.81	0.21	0.75	0.68

CV - Co-efficient of variation
CAGR - Compound annual growth rate

In order to test the hypothesis, analysis of variance has been applied among the years and between the sectors. Since the calculated value of F (2.29) is more than the table value of F at 5 per cent level between the sectors, it is concluded that null hypothesis is rejected. The rejection of null hypothesis would indicate that there are significant differences in the operating profit margin ratio between the sectors.

By dividing the entire study period of 15 years after liberalization into three phases, initial phase, growth phase and maturity phase, it could find from Table 4.1 that the overall operating profit margin ratio of the selected South Indian private sector Sugar Industry showed a declining trend during the growth phase. It declined from 19.77 per cent during initial phase to 17.48 per cent during growth phase. Such a declining trend could be attributed to the poor performance of small and medium-sized sugar industry due to poor market condition, difficulty in getting raw material and all round rise in the input cost without corresponding increase in sales price. But during maturity phase all the selected sectors and whole industry registered an increasing trend in operating profit margin because of improved market conditions, upward revision of sales price and reduction in the cost of sales with the help of modernization and expansion.

The CV value of this ratio during the three phases showed high fluctuations. It is also inferred that the medium-sized sugar industry during the initial phase and growth phase and small-sized industry during maturity phase have registered a negative compound annual growth rate. In order to test the hypothesis, paired sample t-test has been applied among the different phases. It is evident from the table that there were no significant differences in operating profit margin of selected South Indian private sector sugar industry between phases.

Analysis of Variance

Sources of variation	F value	F critical value
Between the years	0.86	1.74
Between the sector	2.29**	1.74

Operating profit margin - Paired sample t-test

Industry	Initial phase and Growth Phase	Growth phase and Maturity phase	Initial phase and Maturity phase
Large-sized	0.35	1.65	1.41
Medium-sized	2.03	1.52	0.39
Small-sized	0.34	1.36	0.08
Whole industry	1.26	1.08	0.48

**Significant at 0.05 per cent level.

Source: Computed.

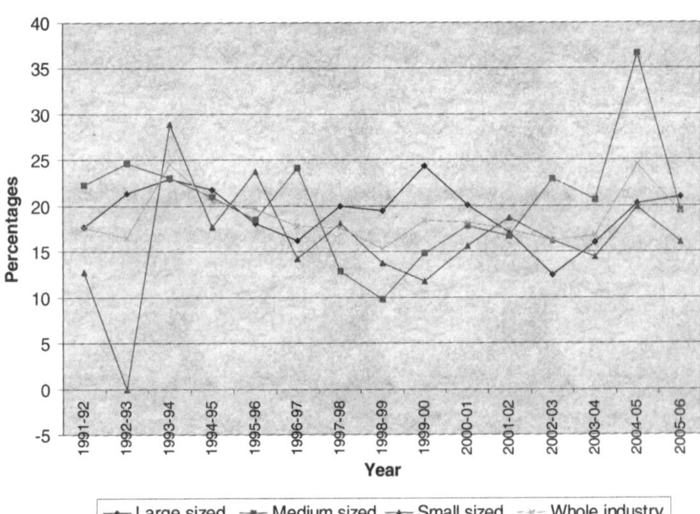

Fig. 4.1. Operating profit-margin ratio of selected South Indian Private Sector Sugar Industry.

The industry-wise operating profit margin ratio of different sectors of selected South Indian private sector sugar industry during three different phases and whole period is presented in Table 4.2. The performance of Bannari Amman Sugars Ltd, Jeypore Sugars and Chemicals Ltd, Rajshree Sugars and Chemicals Ltd, Sakthi Sugars Ltd, and Thiru Arooran Sugars Ltd was satisfactory because its average operating margin ratios were higher than the industry average. In medium-sized sugar industry the performance of Kothari Sugars and Chemicals Ltd, and Kakatiya Cements Sugar and Industries Ltd was satisfactory because its average operating profit margin ratios were higher than the industry average. Dharani Sugars and Chemicals Ltd under small-sized sugar industry showed better performance regarding operating profit margin ratio. Table 4.2 witnessed that all the selected South Indian private sector sugar industry have positive operating profit margin during the study period. The table also reveals a fluctuating trend of this ratio among the industry selected under different sectors of South Indian private sector sugar industry.

Table 4.3 refers that differences in the operating profit margin ratios were significant in between the industry under large-sized sector as calculated value of F was greater than the table value of F at five per cent level. However, they were insignificant in between the years and industry in all the remaining cases as the calculated value of F was lower than the table value of F at five per cent level of significance.

It can be viewed from the Table 4.3 that majority of the large-sized industry's operating profit margin ratios showed significant differences during initial phase and maturity phase as per the t-value. It is further noticed that such significant differences were observed in EID Parry Ltd and Rajshree Sugars and Chemicals Ltd under large-sized and Kothari Sugars Ltd under medium-sized sugar industry during initial phase and maturity phase. Such significant differences were also noticed in EID Parry Ltd, Rajshree Sugars and Chemicals Ltd, Sakthi Sugars Ltd and Thiru

Table 4.2. Analysis of industry-wise operating profit margin ratio of selected South Indian private sector Sugar Industry (1991-92 to 2005-06)

(Per cent)

Industry	Initial phase (1992-96)			Growth phase (1997-2001)			Maturity phase (2002-2006)			Whole period (1992-2006)		
	Mean	CV	CAGR	Mean	CV	CAGR	Mean	CV	CAGR	Mean	CV	CAGR
1	2	3	4	5	6	7	8	9	10	11	12	13
Large-sized												
Bannari Amman Sugars Ltd	21.56	0.14	-0.25	20.42	0.12	0.74	19.40	0.15	7.99	20.46	0.13	1.37
EID Parry Ltd	9.48	0.07	1.94	13.74	0.08	0.50	16.19	0.35	15.02	13.14	0.32	6.13
Jeypore Sugars and Chemicals Ltd	19.70	0.22	8.19	19.31	0.38	25.24	21.58	0.53	4.66	20.19	0.38	4.61
Rajshree Sugars and Chemicals Ltd	32.68	0.23	10.30	17.16	0.33	7.19	19.80	0.23	5.31	23.21	0.39	1.37
Sakthi Sugars Ltd	20.57	0.09	2.18	23.51	0.21	0.25	12.83	0.64	3.33	18.97	0.37	1.00
Thiru Arooran Sugars Ltd	27.87	0.24	-10.91	30.33	0.24	3.78	18.21	0.30	8.58	25.47	0.32	-2.82
Ugar Sugar Works Ltd	10.82	0.25	-10.91	15.53	0.20	9.92	13.44	0.32	-10.56	13.26	0.28	-2.42
Medium-sized												
Kothari Sugars and Chemicals Ltd	23.82	0.20	0.00	-1.87	-11.71	-22.01	37.46	0.98	14.52	19.80	1.42	-9.53
Sri Chamundeswari Sugars Ltd	15.41	0.51	-39.95	21.50	0.25	6.57	17.60	0.42	3.56	18.19	0.38	-2.60
Sri Sarvaraya Sugars Ltd	17.59	0.08	1.23	19.09	0.13	-4.84	16.01	0.21	5.95	17.56	0.16	4.56
Kakatiya Cements Sugar & Industries Ltd	30.66	0.11	5.53	24.67	0.22	-7.88	22.14	0.08	-2.60	25.83	0.20	-5.13

Small-sized												
Dharani Sugars and Chemicals Ltd	23.88	0.16	-6.33	25.02	0.37	25.11	16.88	0.45	-15.08	21.93	0.35	-4.56
Empee Sugars and Chemicals Ltd	15.55	2.66	1.64	18.03	0.27	13.34	20.07	0.70	-6.94	17.88	1.32	-9.80
India Sugars and Refineries Ltd	11.70	0.45	24.08	7.43	0.97	-52.71	17.98	0.57	5.74	12.37	0.69	7.41
Ponni Sugars Ltd	15.31	0.63	-36.75	8.22	1.26	0.0	13.27	0.25	3.78	12.27	0.68	-1.15

Source: Computed from the annual accounts of the respective industry.

Arooran Sugars Ltd under large-sized and Kakatiya Cements Sugar and Industries Ltd under medium-sized and Dharani Sugars and Chemicals Ltd under small-sized between initial phase and maturity phase. Similarly the significant differences in operating profit margin ratio of Sakthi Sugars Ltd and Thiru Arooran Sugars Ltd under large-sized and Sri Sarvaraya Sugars Ltd under medium-sized were noticed between growth phase and maturity phase. Thus, the overall analysis of profitability of the selected sectors of South Indian private sector Sugar Industry measured through operating profit margin ratio was satisfactory.

Table 4.3. Analysis of Variance - ANOVA

Particulars	Large-sized		Medium-sized		Small-sized	
	F value	F critical value	F value	F critical value	F value	F critical value
Between the years	1.71	1.81	0.64	1.96	0.79	1.94
Between the Industry	8.52**	2.21	0.89	2.83	1.65	2.83

Industry-wise operating profit margin ratio - Paired sample t-test

Industry	Paired sample t-test		
	Initial phase and growth phase	Initial phase and maturity phase	Growth phase and maturity phase
	1	2	3
Large-sized (n=7)			
Bannari Amman Sugars Ltd	0.85	0.91	0.55
EID Parry Ltd	12.59*	2.76***	0.98
Jeypore Sugars & Chemicals Ltd	0.14	0.36	0.38
Rajshree Sugars & Chemicals Ltd	3.05**	3.03**	1.55
Sakthi Sugars Ltd	1.86	2.15***	2.21***
Thiru Arooran Sugars Ltd	-0.64	3.15**	3.44**
Ugar Sugar Works Ltd	1.93	1.93	0.8

	1	2	3
Medium-sized (n=4)			
Kothari Sugars & Chemicals Ltd	2.49***	0.78	1.77
Sri Chamundeswari Sugars Ltd	1.29	0.42	0.71
Sri Sarvaraya Sugars Ltd	0.87	0.76	2.26***
Kakatiya Cements Sugar & Industries Ltd	1.66	4.86*	1.34
Small-sized (n=4)			
Dharani Sugars & Chemicals Ltd	0.26	2.31***	1.46
Empee Sugars & Chemicals Ltd	0.13	0.19	0.36
India Sugars and Refineries Ltd	0.82	2.10	1.65
Ponni Sugars Ltd	1.01	0.38	0.95

*-Significant at 0.01 level; **-Significant at 0.05 level; ***-Significant at 0.10 level

Source: Computed.

Gross Profit Margin

Generally excess of net sales over cost of goods sold is termed as gross profit margin. It reflects the efficiency with which management produces each unit of product. This ratio indicates the average spread between cost of goods sold and sales.[9] This ratio is of vital importance for gauging business results. It reflects pricing policies of a business. It also helps in ascertaining whether the average percentage of mark up on the goods is maintained. A low gross profit ratio will suggest a decline in business which may be due to insufficient sales, higher cost of production with the existing or reduced selling price or all round inefficient management. The Finance manager must be able to detect the causes of falling gross profit ratio and initiate action to improve the situation. A high gross profit margin is a sign of good and efficient management.

Table 4.4 and Fig. 4.2 show a fluctuating trend in the gross profit margin ratio of the selected South Indian private sector Sugar Industry during the fifteen-year study period. On an average the sample of South Indian private sector sugar industry had the overall gross profit margin ratio of 6.92 per cent with a co-efficient of variation of 0.84. The average gross profit margin ratio varies from sector to sector, the highest average was 9.32 per cent in large-sized sugar industry followed by medium-sized (8.65%) and small-sized (1.60%) sugar industry. The average ratio of gross profit margin was higher than the industry average in large-sized and medium-sized sugar industry. The CV value of these ratios shows very high fluctuation in the gross profit margin ratio of the selected sector during the study period. Such fluctuations could be attributed to the differences in the growth rates of gross profit margin and sales because of the factor such as higher financial charges, market condition and change in demand of sugar during the study period. All the selected sectors and whole industry witnessed the positive compound annual growth rate of this ratio during the study period. All the selected sectors and whole industry witnessed the positive compound annual growth rate of this ratio during the study period.

Table 4.4. Analysis of gross profit margin ratio of selected South Indian private sector Sugar Industry (1991-92 to 2005-06)

(Per cent)

Particulars	Initial phase [1992-96]	Growth phase [1997-2001]	Maturity phase [2002-2006]	Whole period [1992-2006]
1	2	3	4	5
Large-sized (n=7)				
Mean	10.37	7.96	9.63	**9.32**
CV	0.79	0.43	0.61	**0.46**
CAGR	10.28	16.74	17.58	**4.57**

1	2	3	4	5
Medium-sized (n=4)				
Mean	11.82	0.80	13.32	**8.65**
CV	0.89	24.39	0.63	**0.75**
CAGR	12.20	–29.53	54.62	**6.14**
Small-sized (n=4)				
Mean	2.60	–4.43	6.65	**1.60**
CV	3.89	–1.73	0.76	**2.05**
CAGR	38.33	—	24.85	**15.29**
Whole industry (n=15)				
Mean	**8.69**	**2.75**	**9.82**	**6.92**
CV	**1.09**	**4.14**	**0.66**	**0.84**
CAGR	**13.46**	**–1.13**	**25.67**	**6.28**

Analysis of Variance

Sources of variation	F value	F critical value
Between the years	2.70**	2.06
Between the sector	6.39**	3.34

Gross profit margin - Paired sample t-test

Industry	Initial phase and Growth phase	Growth phase and Maturity phase	Initial phase and Maturity phase
Large-sized	1.75	0.26	0.69
Medium-sized	2.43**	0.32	1.59
Small-sized	0.99	0.75	4.18**
Whole industry	**2.27****	**0.52**	**2.05**

**Significant at 0.05 level

Source: Computed.

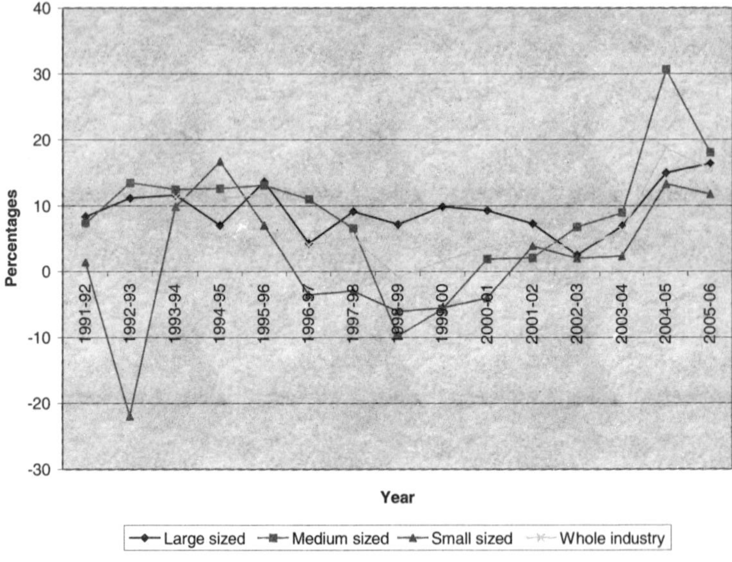

Fig. 4.2. Gross Profit margin ratio of selected South Indian Private Sector Sugar Industry.

In order to test the hypothesis, analysis of variance has been applied between the years and between the sectors. Since the calculated values of F (2.70 and 6.39) are more than the table values of F at five per cent level between the years and sectors respectively, it is concluded that null hypothesis is rejected. The rejection of the null hypothesis would indicate that there are significant differences in the gross profit margin ratio between the years and sectors.

By dividing the entire study period of 15 years after liberalisation into three phases, initial phase, growth phase and maturity phase, it could find from the Table 4.4 that the overall gross profit margin ratio of the selected South Indian private sector sugar industry showed a declining trend during the growth phase. It declined from 8.69 per cent during initial phase to 2.75 per cent during growth phase. Such a declining trend could be attributed to the poor performance of small and medium-sized sugar industry due to poor market condition, difficulty in getting raw materials and all round rise in the input cost without corresponding increase in sales.

But during maturity phase all the selected sector and whole industry registered an increasing trend in gross profit margin because of improved market conditions, upward revision of sales price and reduction in the cost of sales with the help of modernization and expansion.

The CV value of this ratio during the three phases showed very high fluctuations. It is also inferred that medium-sized, small-sized and the whole sugar industry registered a negative compound annual growth rate during the growth phase. In order to test the hypothesis, paired sample t-test has been applied among the different phases.

It is also evident from the table that there was a significant difference in gross profit margin between initial phase and growth phase in whole industry and medium-sized industry. Further such significant differences were also noticed in small-sized sugar industry during initial phase and maturity phase.

The industry-wise gross profit margin ratio of different sectors of selected South Indian private sector sugar industry during three different phases and whole period is presented in Table 4.5. The performance of Bannari Amman Sugars Ltd, EID Parry Ltd, Rajshree Sugars & Chemicals Ltd and Thiru Arooran Sugars Ltd was satisfactory because its average gross profit margin ratios were higher than the industry average. In medium-sized sugar industry the performance of Kakatiya Cements Sugar & Industries Ltd and Sri Sarvaraya Sugars Ltd. was satisfactory because its average gross profit margin ratio was higher than the industry average. Dharani Sugars & Chemicals Ltd, Empee Sugars & Chemicals Ltd and Ponni Sugars Ltd under small-sized sugar industry showed better performance regarding gross profit margin during the study period. Table 4.5 witnessed that the entire selected South Indian private sector Sugar Industry had positive gross profit margin during the study period except India Sugars and Refineries Ltd. The table also reveals a fluctuating trend of this ratio among the industry selected under different sectors of South Indian private sector Sugar Industry.

Table 4.5. Analysis of Industry-wise Gross profit margin ratio of selected South Indian private sector Sugar Industry (1991-92 to 2005-06)

(Per cent)

Industry	Initial phase (1992-96)			Growth phase (1997-2001)			Maturity phase (2002-2006)			Whole period (1992-2006)		
	Mean	CV	CAGR	Mean	CV	CAGR	Mean	CV	CAGR	Mean	CV	CAGR
1	2	3	4	5	6	7	8	9	10	11	12	13
Large-sized												
Bannari Amman Sugars Ltd	11.59	0.23	-4.13	13.03	0.14	0.40	16.17	0.25	12.10	13.59	0.25	3.05
EID Parry Ltd	6.47	0.18	-6.36	7.97	0.10	-1.02	13.75	0.50	21.34	9.40	0.53	5.83
Jeypore Sugars & Chemicals Ltd	5.19	0.96	-	2.64	3.03	-14.38	10.50	1.24	22.25	6.11	1.51	-
Rajshree Sugars & Chemicals Ltd	21.86	0.41	31.15	7.61	0.85	4.56	14.42	0.37	11.59	14.63	0.61	7.83
Sakthi Sugars Ltd	9.19	0.03	-0.61	5.74	0.22	-10.01	-0.43	-26.23	24.32	4.83	1.52	1.71
Thiru Arooran Sugars Ltd	19.66	1.07	13.70	11.43	0.41	20.30	5.78	1.50	96.71	12.29	1.12	-3.46
Ugar Sugar Works Ltd	-1.37	-2.24	-	7.29	0.66	-66.56	7.22	0.36	-4.61	4.38	1.23	-
Medium-sized												
Kothari Sugars & Chemicals Ltd	14.03	0.11	-1.44	-27.95	-1.05	-	24.87	1.72	-	3.65	9.98	0.0
Sri Chamundeswari Sugars Ltd	4.34	2.02	-	6.69	2.33	-	4.73	1.84	29.56	5.25	2.03	2.02
Sri Sarvaraya Sugars Ltd	3.17	4.56	-	8.64	0.23	-0.81	11.07	0.66	30.05	7.63	1.23	-
Kakatiya Cements Sugar & Industries Ltd	25.74	0.32	11.59	15.82	0.53	-16.74	12.60	0.15	5.39	18.06	0.47	-2.35

Small-sized												
Dharani Sugars & Chemicals Ltd	13.77	0.21	-6.89	-0.87	-11.58	-	0.29	30.85	12.72	4.40	2.29	-4.27
Empee Sugars & Chemicals Ltd	-9.36	-5.80	-	4.06	1.11	-	12.13	0.98	13.94	2.20	13.67	-
India Sugars and Refineries Ltd	-1.48	-8.34	-	-13.51	-0.86	-	5.55	2.80	73.30	-3.15	-4.68	-
Ponni Sugars Ltd	7.49	0.99	-	-7.41	-1.60		8.61	0.60	24.07	2.9	3.79	1.17

Source: Computed from the annual accounts of the respective industry.

Table 4.6 refers that differences in the gross profit margin ratio was significant in between the industry under large-sized sector as calculated value of F was greater than the table value of F at five per cent level. However, these were insignificant in between the years and industry in all the remaining cases as the calculated value of F was lower than the table value of F at five per cent level of significance.

It can be viewed from Table 4.6 that Bannari Amman Sugars Ltd, EID Parry Ltd, Rajshree Sugars & Chemicals Ltd, Sakthi Sugars Ltd and Ugar Sugar Works Ltd of the large-sized industry gross profit margin showed significant difference during initial phase and growth phase as per the t-value. It is further noticed that such significant differences were observed in Kothari Sugars & Chemicals Ltd under medium-sized sector and Dharani Sugars & Chemicals Ltd under small-sized sector during initial phase and growth phase. Such significant differences were also noticed in EID Parry Ltd, Ugar Sugar Works Ltd under large-sized and Dharani Sugars & Chemicals Ltd under small-sized between initial phase and maturity phase. Similarly, the significant differences in gross profit margin ratio of Rajshree Sugars & Chemicals Ltd under large-sized and Ponni Sugars Ltd under small-sized were noticed between growth phase and maturity phase.

Hence, the profitability of the selected sectors of South Indian private sector Sugar Industry except India Sugars & Refineries Ltd under small-sized measured through the gross profit margin ratio was satisfactory and should be adequate to cover the fixed charges during the study period.

Return on Capital Employed

The primary objective of making investment in any business is to obtain satisfactory return on the capital invested. Hence, the return on capital employed is used as a measure of success of a business in realizing this objective. It is the chief profitability ratio and the most important measure of

Table 4.6. Analysis of Variance - ANOVA

Particulars	Large-sized		Medium-sized		Small-sized	
	F value	F critical value	F value	F critical value	F value	F critical value
Between the years	1.62	1.81	0.90	1.94	1.09	1.94
Between the Industry	4.43**	2.21	1.54	2.83	0.47	2.83

Industry-wise gross profit margin ratio - Paired sample t-test

Industry	Paired sample t-test		
	Initial phase and growth phase	Initial phase and maturity phase	Growth phase and maturity phase
Large-sized (n=7)			
Bannari Amman Sugars Ltd	2.37***	1.73	1.46
EID Parry Ltd	2.60***	2.33***	1.91
Jeypore Sugars & Chemicals Ltd	0.89	0.76	1.23
Rajshree Sugars & Chemicals Ltd	2.70***	2.12	2.90**
Sakthi Sugars Ltd	6.45*	1.91	1.14
Thiru Arooran Sugars Ltd	0.79	1.32	1.37
Ugar Sugar Works Ltd	3.41**	3.45**	0.03
Medium-sized (n=4)			
Kothari Sugars & Chemicals Ltd	3.23**	0.55	1.85
Sri Chamundeswari Sugars Ltd	0.29	0.05	0.22
Sri Sarvaraya Sugars Ltd	0.80	1.25	0.82
Kakatiya Cements Sugar & Industries Ltd	1.57	4.58*	0.89
Small-sized (n=4)			
Dharani Sugars & Chemicals Ltd	3.18**	3.45**	0.27
Empee Sugars & Chemicals Ltd	0.54	0.74	1.81
India Sugars and Refineries Ltd	1.17	1.17	1.90
Ponni Sugars Ltd	1.95	0.22	2.59***

*-Significant at 0.01 level; **-Significant at 0.05 level; ***-Significant at 0.10 level

Source: Computed.

performance as it indicates the comparative efficiency with which the whole company runs properly. Therefore, return on capital employed is a valuable yardstick to measure the overall performance of an undertaking. The return on capital employed shows the earning power of the capital invested. It indicates how the management has used the funds supplied by creditors and owners. The higher the ratio, the more efficient can be considered the enterprise in using funds entrusted to it. The comparison of this ratio with the ratio of similar business organizations will reveal the relative operating efficiency of a business enterprise. Further, an investor can judge the future prospects of business enterprise by taking into consideration the earning capacity of capital employed. It shows the earning capacity of the capital.

Table 4.7 and Fig. 4.3 indicated that a fluctuating trend in the return on capital employed ratio in the selected South Indian private sector Sugar Industry during the study period. In the selected South Indian private sector sugar industry, the return on capital employed has been on an average of 19.63 per cent ranging from 15.72 per cent in 2001-02 to 28.92 per cent in 2005-06.

The average return on capital employed varied from sector to sector. The highest average was 23.10 per cent in large-sized sugar industry followed by small-sized (18.50%) and medium-sized (14.67%). The average ratio of return on capital employed was higher than the industry average only in large-sized sugar industry. The compound annual growth rate of this ratio was positive in all the three selected sectors. The CV value of this ratio shows vary high fluctuations during the study period. The fluctuation in this ratio can be attributed to the differences in growth rate of EBIT and the capital employed.

In order to test the hypothesis, the analysis of variance has been applied among all the selected sectors and between the

Table 4.7. Analysis of return on capital employed of selected South Indian private sector Sugar industry (1991-92 to 2005-06)

(Per cent)

Particulars	Initial phase [1992-96]	Growth phase [1997-2001]	Maturity phase [2002-2006]	Whole period [1992-2006]
Large-sized (n=7)				
Mean	26.77	21.22	21.32	**23.10**
CV	0.41	0.54	0.63	**0.42**
CAGR	-0.83	0.93	7.45	**0.89**
Medium-sized (n=4)				
Mean	15.09	14.96	10.38	**14.67**
CV	0.16	0.84	1.70	**0.73**
CAGR	-6.90	10.68	3.28	**0.91**
Small-sized (n=4)				
Mean	26.13	16.17	13.20	**18.50**
CV	0.82	0.34	0.52	**0.53**
CAGR	12.82	-2.83	63.68	**4.75**
Whole industry (n=15)				
Mean	**24.44**	**18.20**	**16.23**	**19.63**
CV	**0.52**	**0.56**	**0.83**	**0.51**
CAGR	**1.38**	**2.00**	**12.97**	**1.84**

Analysis of Variance

Sources of variation	F value	F critical value
Between the years	2.12**	2.06
Between the sector	2.50	3.34

Return on capital employed - Paired sample t-test

Industry	Initial phase and Growth phase	Growth phase and Maturity phase	Initial phase and Maturity phase
Large-sized	3.42**	0.03	1.27
Medium-sized	0.90	0.38	0.55
Small-sized	1.88	0.48	3.10**
Whole industry	**3.92****	**0.41**	**1.44**

**Significant at 0.05 level
Source: Computed

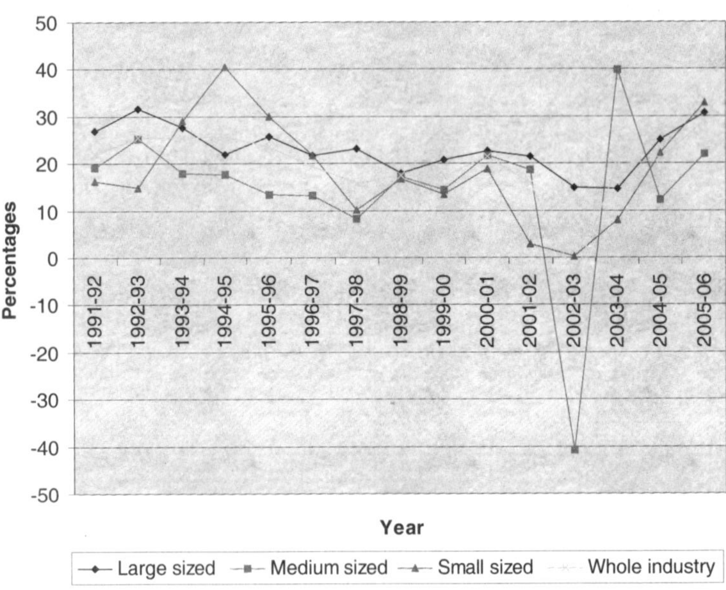

Fig. 4.3. Return on capital employed of selected South Indian

years. Table 4.7 showed that difference in the return on capital employed ratio was significant in between the years as the calculated value of F (2.12) was greater than the table value of F (2.06) at five per cent level of significance. However, these were insignificant in between the sectors as the calculated value of F (2.50) was lower than the table value of F at five per cent level of significance.

By dividing the entire study period of fifteen years after liberalization into three phases, it could find from the Table 4.7 that the overall average of return on capital employed ratio of the selected South Indian private sector sugar industry showed a declining trend during the study period. It declined from 24.44 per cent during initial phase to 18.20 per cent during growth phase. It was further declined to 16.23 per cent during maturity phase. The decline in this ratio was due to the fluctuations in the EBIT and increase in the capital employed of the selected South Indian private sector sugar industry during this period. The CV value of this ratio during three phases showed the very high fluctuation. It is also inferred that the selected South Indian private sector sugar industry registered positive compound annual growth rate during the period of three phases. Such growth was more during maturity phase when compared to initial phase and growth phase. It is evident from the Table 4.7 that return on capital employed was more in large-sized sugar industry followed by small-sized and medium-sized during the three phases. Similarly, all the three sectors registered very high fluctuations during the period of three phases. Further, large-sized and medium-sized sugar industry during the initial phase and small-sized sugar industry during growth phase period was registered a negative compound annual growth rate of these ratio. It is also evident from Table 4.7 that there was a significant difference in return on capital employed ratio between initial phase and growth phase in whole industry and large-sized sugar industry as per the t-value. Further such significant differences were also noticed in small-sized sugar industry during initial phase and maturity phase.

The industry wise return on capital employed ratio of different sectors of selected South Indian private sector sugar industry during the three different phases and the whole period is presented in Table 4.8. The performance of Bannari Amman Sugars Ltd, Jeypore Sugars & Chemicals Ltd,

Table 4.8. Analysis of Industry-wise return on capital employed of selected South Indian private sector Sugar Industry (1991-92 to 2005-06)

(Per cent)

Industry	Initial phase (1992-96)			Growth phase (1997-2001)			Maturity phase (2002-2006)			Whole period (1992-2006)		
	Mean	CV	CAGR	Mean	CV	CAGR	Mean	CV	CAGR	Mean	CV	CAGR
1	2	3	4	5	6	7	8	9	10	11	12	13
Large-sized												
Bannari Amman Sugars Ltd	18.47	0.29	6.19	20.74	0.06	-0.61	21.01	0.19	1.92	20.07	0.19	1.50
EID Parry Ltd	21.50	0.36	-18.48	14.11	0.12	6.50	16.09	0.33	4.56	17.25	0.35	-3.13
Jeypore Sugars & Chemicals Ltd	26.14	0.49	-35.69	26.45	0.30	19.73	48.10	0.54	17.19	33.56	0.57	6.87
Rajshree Sugars & Chemicals Ltd	34.59	0.36	16.76	16.28	0.46	5.39	24.16	0.23	10.40	25.01	0.45	2.73
Sakthi Sugars Ltd	19.65	0.15	-5.59	19.64	0.30	-2.09	9.66	1.11	-10.01	16.32	0.51	-4.97
Thiru Arooran Sugars Ltd	19.25	0.30	-8.54	7.83	0.33	-0.20	7.26	0.96	45.72	11.45	0.67	-0.70
Ugar Sugar Works Ltd	47.76	0.48	8.50	43.50	0.29	-8.54	22.94	0.47	-5.84	38.07	0.49	-3.39
Medium-sized												
Kothari Sugars & Chemicals Ltd	15.09	0.16	-0.71	-1.92	-4.74	-21.13	-14.19	-9.07	45.38	-0.34	-205.44	1.26
Sri Chamundeswari Sugars Ltd	18.47	0.62	-	24.84	0.76	300	12.66	0.98	-3.26	18.66	0.77	-1.75
Sri Sarvaraya Sugars Ltd	22.17	0.48	-7.28	24.45	0.36	8.21	27.84	0.26	1.13	24.82	0.35	2.63
Kakatiya Cements Sugar & Industries Ltd	18.94	0.31	19.52	12.48	0.20	-0.49	15.20	0.21	0.09	15.54	0.30	1.67

Small-sized												
Dharani Sugars & Chemicals Ltd	24.97	0.27	1.92	16.41	0.62	43.48	11.92	0.62	-5.59	17.77	0.53	-3.24
Empee Sugars & Chemicals Ltd	10.95	2.20	-	16.47	0.25	8.45	3.94	7.86	-	10.45	2.08	-
India Sugars and Refineries Ltd	56.72	0.48	33.31	22.53	1.12	-30.69	18.17	1.07	26.51	32.47	0.88	3.31
Ponni Sugars Ltd	11.90	0.74	-47.47	9.25	1.27	19.14	18.75	0.54	20.68	13.30	0.78	4.11

Source: Computed from the annual accounts of the respective industry.

Rajshree Sugars & Chemicals Ltd, and Ugar Sugar Works Ltd, under large-sized sector, Sri Sarvaraya Sugars Ltd., under medium-sized and India Sugar and Refineries Ltd., under small-sized sugar industry was satisfactory. Because its average return on capital employed ratio was higher than the industry average. The same position was also reflected during the three different phases. The table reveals that a fluctuating trend of this ratio among the industry selected under different sectors of South Indian private sector Sugar Industry.

Table 4.9 indicated that the differences in the return on capital employed ratio was significant in between the industry under large-sized and small-sized industry as calculated value of F was greater than the table value of F at five per cent level. However, these were insignificant in between the years and industry in all the remaining cases as the calculated value of F was lower than the table value of F at five per cent level of significance.

It can be viewed from the Table 4.9 that of the large-sized industries return on capital employed ratio showed significant differences during the different phases as per the t-value. During the Initial phase and maturity phase Rajshree Sugars & Chemicals Ltd, Sakthi Sugars Ltd and Thiru Arooran Sugars had significant differences in return on capital employed ratio. Among the medium-sized sugar industry, significant differences in this ratio were noticed only in Kothari Sugars & Cement Ltd during initial phase and growth phase. Among the small-sized sector such significant differences were noticed in Dharani Sugars and India Sugars Ltd & Refineries between initial phase and maturity phase.

The overall analysis of this ratio reveals that the ratio of return on capital employed decreased significantly between the three different phases. This was due to wide fluctuations in the growth rate of EBIT and capital employed in the selected South Indian private sector Sugar Industry during the study period.

Table 4.9. Analysis of Variance - ANOVA

Particulars	Large-sized		Medium-sized		Small-sized	
	F value	F critical value	F value	F critical value	F value	F critical value
Between the years	1.25	1.81	0.85	1.94	1.54	1.94
Between the Industry	9.89**	2.21	1.27	2.83	4.38**	2.83

Industry-wise return on capital employed - Paired sample t-test

Industry	Paired sample t-test		
	Initial phase and growth phase	Initial phase and maturity phase	Growth phase and maturity phase
Large-sized (n=7)			
Bannari Amman Sugars Ltd	0.95	1.38	0.13
EID Parry Ltd	1.77	1.09	0.85
Jeypore Sugars & Chemicals Ltd	0.04	1.35	2.26***
Rajshree Sugars & Chemicals Ltd	4.39**	2.58***	3.16**
Sakthi Sugars Ltd	0.00	2.23***	2.02
Thiru Arooran Sugars Ltd	5.27*	2.16***	0.16
Ugar Sugar Works Ltd	0.48	1.70	2.38***
Medium-sized (n=4)			
Kothari Sugars & Chemicals Ltd	3.65**	0.50	0.21
Sri Chamundeswari Sugars Ltd	0.55	0.75	0.96
Sri Sarvaraya Sugars Ltd	0.30	1.11	1.08
Kakatiya Cements Sugar & Industries Ltd	2.11	1.20	1.13
Small-sized (n=4)			
Dharani Sugars & Chemicals Ltd	1.76	3.62**	0.77
Empee Sugars & Chemicals Ltd	0.59	0.53	0.97
India Sugars and Refineries Ltd	1.63	4.46**	0.27
Ponni Sugars Ltd	0.37	0.84	1.91

*Significant at 0.01 level; **Significant at 0.05 level; ***Significant at 0.10 level

Source: Computed

Interest Coverage Ratio

It is relevant to analyze the interest burden in the sugar industry to have an idea of its impact on the net profit margins. Interest means a fixed burden that to a certain degree does not change with variation in volume of business operations. This ratio is very important from the lenders point of view, as this ratio reveals the fixed charges bearing funds such as debentures, long term borrowing as the extent covers the profit before interest and tax to fixed charges interest paid or payable. This ratio is an important factor which affects the capital structure and financial management at it measures debt-serving capacity of a firm. The ratio suggests that how many times the interest charges are covered by the earnings before interest and taxes. A high ratio is a sign of low burden of debt-servicing and lower utilization of borrowed funds but too high ratio suggests the firm is not taking the advantages of 'trading on equity' and is very conservative in using debt and credit facility. In contrast a very low ratio signifies the danger signal that the firm is highly dependent on borrowed funds and its earnings cannot meet the obligation fully.

Table 4.10 and Fig. 4.4 show a fluctuating trend in the interest coverage ratio of the selected South Indian private sector sugar industry during the 15-year study period. The sample South Indian private sector sugar industry on an average had overall interest coverage ratio of 1.92 times with a co-efficient of variation of 0.45. The average interest coverage ratio varied from sector to sector, the highest average was 2.35 times in medium-sized sugar industry followed by large-sized (2.04 times) and small-sized (1.28 times) sugar industry. The average ratio of interest coverage was higher than the industry average in medium-sized and large-sized sugar industry. The CV value of these ratios showed the high fluctuations in the interest payments during the study period. Such fluctuations could be attributed to the growth rates of

Table 4.10. Analysis of interest coverage ratio of selected South Indian private sector Sugar Industry (1991-92 to 2005-06)

(in times)

Particulars	**Initial phase [1992-96]**	**Growth phase [1997-2001]**	**Maturity phase [2002-2006]**	**Whole period [1992-2006]**
Large-sized (n=7)				
Mean	1.89	1.45	2.80	**2.04**
CV	0.42	0.32	0.69	**0.44**
CAGR	6.81	-0.40	27.35	**25.15**
Medium-sized (n=4)				
Mean	2.44	2.02	2.58	**2.35**
CV	0.75	0.53	0.59	**0.46**
CAGR	1.36	-12.94	24.74	**11.07**
Small-sized (n=4)				
Mean	1.09	0.69	2.07	**1.28**
CV	0.67	0.53	0.66	**0.33**
CAGR	1.55	2.41	66.67	**9.99**
Whole industry (n=15)				
Mean	**1.82**	**1.40**	**2.55**	**1.92**
CV	**0.64**	**0.56**	**0.63**	**0.45**
CAGR	**3.71**	**-5.59**	**31.35**	**6.66**

Analysis of Variance

Sources of variation	**F value**	**F critical value**
Between the years	7.40**	1.74
Between the sector	5.84**	1.74

Interest coverage ratio - Paired sample t-test

Industry	Initial phase and Growth phase	Growth phase and Maturity phase	Initial phase and Maturity phase
Large-sized	2.23***	4.73*	6.02*
Medium-sized	1.82	4.38**	23.24*
Small-sized	0.50	1.17	5.69*
Whole industry	**2.51*** **	**1.49**	**1.19**

*Significant at 0.01 level; **Significant at 0.05 level; ***Significant at 0.10 level

Source: Computed

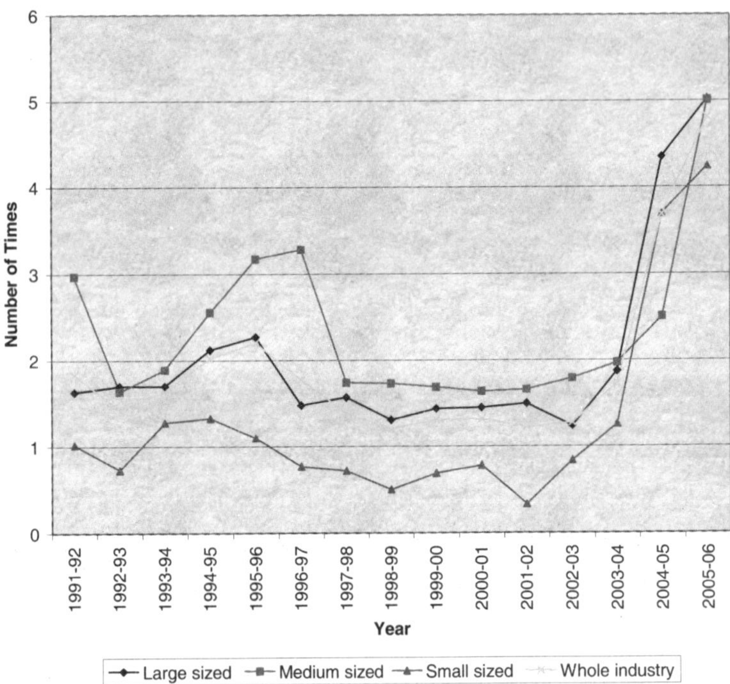

Fig. 4.4. Interest coverage ratio of selected South Indian Private Sector Sugar Industry

earnings before interest and tax, borrowings and fluctuation in the rates of financial charges arising out of financial market conditions and variation in the lending rates of banks and financial institutions. All the selected sectors and industry as whole witnessed a positive compound annual growth rate of this ratio during the study period.

In order to test the hypothesis, analysis of variance has been applied among years and between the sectors. Since the calculated value of F (7.40 and 5.84) are more than the table value of F at five per cent level between the years and sectors respectively, it is concluded that null hypothesis is rejected. The rejection of null hypothesis would indicate that there were significant differences in the interest coverage ratio between the years and sectors.

By dividing the entire study period of fifteen years after liberalization in to three phases, initial phase, growth phase and maturity phase, it could find from Table 4.10 that the overall interest coverage ratio of the selected South Indian private sector sugar industry showed a fluctuating trend during the growth phase. It declined from 1.82 times during initial phase to 1.40 times during growth phase. Such a declining trend could be attributed to the poor Earnings Before Interest and Tax, growth rates of borrowings and financial charges of all the three selected sectors. But during maturity phase all the selected sectors and the industry as a whole registered an upward trend in interest coverage ratio because of lower utilization of borrowed funds.

The CV values of this ratio during the three phases indicated very high fluctuations. It is also inferred that the large-sized and medium-sized sugar industries during the growth phase had registered a negative compound annual growth rate. All the selected sectors and whole industry had registered positive compound annual growth rate during initial phase and maturity phase. In order to test the hypothesis, paired sample t-test has been applied among the different phases.

It is observed from Table 4.10 that there was a significant difference in interest coverage ratio between initial phase and growth phase in whole industry. A significant difference in interest coverage ratio between growth phase and maturity phase and also between initial phase and maturity phase was also observed in large-sized industry. The small-sized industry had a significant difference in interest coverage ratio between initial phase and maturity phase.

The industry-wise interest coverage ratio of different sectors of selected South Indian private sector sugar industry during three different phases and whole period is presented in Table 4.11. A low burden of debt-servicing and lower utilisation of borrowed funds were observed in Bannari Amman Sugars Ltd., and Rajshree Sugars & Chemicals Ltd., among the large-sized and in Ponni Sugars Ltd among the small-sized selected sugar industry as its average interest coverage ratios are higher than the industry average. The table also disclosed the fact that EID Parry Ltd. among the large-sized and Kothari Sugars & Chemicals Ltd. and Kakatiya Cements Sugar & Industries Ltd. among medium-sized sugar industry are not taking the advantages of 'trading on equity' and are very conservative in using debt and credit facility as its average interest coverage ratios were too high. It was also noticed from the table that the Empee Sugars & Chemicals Ltd under small-sized among the selected South Indian private sector Sugar Industry signifies a danger signal as the firm was highly dependent on borrowed funds since the interest coverage ratio was very low. The Table 4.11 witnessed that a fluctuating trend of this ratio among industry selected under different sectors of South Indian private sector Sugar Industry.

Table 4.12 represents that the differences in the interest coverage ratio was significant in between the years under large-sized and small-sized sectors as calculated values of F were greater than the table value of F at five per cent level. Similarly, significant differences were noticed in between the industries under large-sized and medium-sized selected

South Indian private sector Sugar Industry at five per cent level. However, they were insignificant in between the years and industry in the remaining cases as the calculated values F were lower than the table value of F at five per cent level of significance.

It can be viewed from Table 4.12 that under large size sugar industry EID Parry Ltd and Thiru Arooran Sugars Ltd, under medium-sized Kothari Sugars & Chemicals Ltd and under small-sized Empee Sugars & Chemicals Ltd significant differences in interest coverage ratio were found during initial phase and growth phase. Significant differences were observed in the interest coverage ratio of Bannari Amman Sugars Ltd and Thiru Arooran Sugars Ltd among large-sized, Kothari Sugars & Chemicals Ltd and Kakatiya Cements Sugar & Industries Ltd among the medium-sized and Dharani Sugars & Chemicals Ltd among small-sized during the initial phase and maturity phase. Similarly, significant differences in the interest coverage of Rajshree Sugars & Chemicals Ltd under large-sized, Kothari Sugars & Chemicals Ltd under medium-sized and Ponni Sugars Ltd under small-sized selected South Indian private sector Sugar Industry were also identified between growth phase and maturity phase.

It is concluded from analysis of the interest coverage of the selected sectors of South Indian private sector Sugar Industry measured through the interest coverage ratio is satisfactory subject to variation in the coverage and the EBIT of all the sample industries is adequate to cover the financial charges of debt and credit facility.

PROFITABILITY FROM THE VIEW POINT OF SHAREHOLDERS

The owners - the shareholders - have permanent stake in the enterprise and as such they have to share prosperity marked by higher profitability and adversity marked by losses. The financial welfare of owners increases when net profit after tax has increased and also when they receive

Table 4.11. Analysis of Industry wise interest coverage ratio of selected South Indian private sector Sugar Industry (1991-92 to 2005-06)

(in times)

Industry	Initial phase (1992-96)			Growth phase (1997-2001)			Maturity phase (2002-2006)			Whole period (1992-2006)		
	Mean	CV	CAGR	Mean	CV	CAGR	Mean	CV	CAGR	Mean	CV	CAGR
1	2	3	4	5	6	7	8	9	10	11	12	13
Large-sized												
Bannari Amman Sugars Ltd	1.68	0.29	-3.66	2.22	0.11	-3.20	4.85	0.55	28.84	2.92	0.70	30.95
EID Parry Ltd	2.16	0.22	-2.75	1.80	0.08	-1.65	5.89	0.83	39.17	3.28	0.99	33.56
Jeypore Sugars & Chemicals Ltd	1.08	0.58	-54.27	0.98	0.44	41.49	1.92	0.84	27.05	1.32	0.79	30.60
Rajshree Sugars & Chemicals Ltd	3.42	0.69	45.32	1.47	0.49	-2.75	3.30	0.52	21.24	2.73	0.68	39.43
Sakthi Sugars Ltd	1.30	0.21	-5.59	1.12	0.09	-3.20	0.96	0.97	14.64	1.12	0.48	9.16
Thiru Arooran Sugars Ltd	2.13	0.24	14.64	0.99	0.60	-29.03	1.27	0.76	34.31	1.48	0.57	13.21
Ugar Sugar Works Ltd	1.43	0.21	-3.43	1.60	0.23	11.97	1.38	0.32	6.96	1.47	0.25	-5.34
Medium-sized												
Kothari Sugars & Chemicals Ltd	1.80	0.18	7.11	2.59	0.20	6.03	4.83	0.43	25.23	3.07	0.57	39.11
Sri Chamundeswari Sugars Ltd	1.10	0.65	-50.41	0.84	0.36	17.29	1.42	1.71	34.92	1.12	1.24	24.41
Sri Sarvaraya Sugars Ltd	1.71	0.09	0.40	1.43	0.16	3.37	2.16	0.58	23.99	1.77	0.42	18.23
Kakatiya Cements Sugar & Industries Ltd	5.17	0.57	5.22	3.21	1.11	-30.69	1.92	0.33	13.46	3.43	0.83	-15.53

Small-sized												
Dharani Sugars & Chemicals Ltd	1.99	0.13	0.20	0.77	0.52	25.11	1.00	0.74	16.54	1.25	0.58	0.45
Empee Sugars & Chemicals Ltd	0.26	2.92	-2.52	1.18	0.13	13.34	1.06	1.76	5.22	0.84	1.40	6.52
India Sugars and Refineries Ltd	0.84	0.64	32.54	0.46	1.07	-52.71	2.30	1.16	28.52	1.20	1.41	16.35
Ponni Sugars Ltd	1.26	0.53	-41.25	0.37	2.03	0.00	3.91	0.81	42.13	1.85	1.28	11.53

Source: Computed from the annual accounts of the respective industry.

Table 4.12. Analysis of Variance - ANOVA

Particulars	Large-sized		Medium-sized		Small-sized	
	F value	F critical value	F value	F critical value	F value	F critical value
Between the years	4.84**	1.81	1.04	1.94	2.92**	1.94
Between the Industry	12.01**	2.21	5.22**	2.83	1.50	2.83

Industry-wise interest coverage ratio - Paired sample t-test

Industry	Paired sample t-test		
	Initial phase and growth phase	Initial phase and maturity phase	Growth phase and maturity phase
Large-sized (n=7)			
Bannari Amman Sugars Ltd	1.82	2.63***	2.04
EID Parry Ltd	2.24***	1.82	1.90
Jeypore Sugars & Chemicals Ltd	0.29	0.85	1.35
Rajshree Sugars & Chemicals Ltd	1.91	0.34	2.59***
Sakthi Sugars Ltd	1.60	0.63	0.37
Thiru Arooran Sugars Ltd	2.59***	2.71***	0.41
Ugar Sugar Works Ltd	0.79	0.15	0.82
Medium-sized (n=4)			
Kothari Sugars & Chemicals Ltd	2.80***	3.82**	2.44***
Sri Chamundeswari Sugars Ltd	0.61	0.23	0.55
Sri Sarvaraya Sugars Ltd	2.08	0.79	1.51
Kakatiya Cements Sugar & Industries Ltd	1.13	2.86**	0.75
Small-sized (n=4)			
Dharani Sugars & Chemicals Ltd	6.94*	3.28**	0.80
Empee Sugars & Chemicals Ltd	2.34***	0.97	0.13
India Sugars and Refineries Ltd	1.08	1.47	1.59
Ponni Sugars Ltd	1.68	1.55	2.63***

*Significant at 0.01 level; **Significant at 0.05 level; *** Significant at 0.10 level

Source: Computed

larger share of dividend. Hence, in this part analysis has been made about profitability of selected South Indian private sector Sugar Industry from the viewpoint of shareholders. For this following ratios are computed and analyzed.

Net Profit Margin Ratio

Net profit margin enables one to measure the relationship between sales and net profit and it is an indicator of the efficiency of the management in manufacturing, selling and financing. Net profit margin refers from operating profit margin in as much as it is computed after adding the non operating surplus/deficit. A high net profit margin would ensure adequate return to the owners as well as enable a firm to withstand adverse economic conditions when the selling price is declining, cost of production is rising and demand for the product is falling.[10] In case the net profit margin is inadequate, the company will not be in a position to pay off its debts and give a satisfactory return to its shareholders.[11]

Table 4.13 and Fig. 4.5 showed a fluctuating trend in the net profit margin ratio of the selected South Indian private sector sugar industry during the fifteen-year study period. On an average the selected South Indian private sector sugar industry had the overall negative net profit margin ratio due to poor performance of medium-sized and small-sized sugar industry over the period of study. The average net profit margin ratio varied from sector to sector, the highest average was 3.14 per cent in large-sized sugar industry whereas the average of small-sized sugar industry was -6.06 per cent followed by -0.46 per cent in medium-sized industry over the period of study. The selected South Indian private sector sugar industry have registered an average net profit margin of 1.96 percent during initial phase, but it step down to a negative net profit margin of –3.25 per cent during growth phase and the industry recovered from loss zone to fetch a net profit margin of 0.48 per cent during maturity period. The average net profit margin of small-sized industry was continued to be negative at -9.72 per cent and -8.95 per cent during initial phase and growth phase respectively.

The industries slowly recovered and climb up to the profit zone of 0.49 per cent on an average during maturity phase. The medium-sized sugar industry had registered an average of 7.53 per cent of net profit margin during initial phase whereas the industry gone down to incur negative average net profit margin of -6.71 per cent and -2.19 per cent in growth phase and maturity phase respectively. Large-sized sugar industries were able to sustain its net profit margin during the study period but at declined rate. From the above it can be observed that no industry among the three sectors would really face of falling sales prices, rising costs of production or declining demand for the product.

Table 4.13. Analysis of Net profit margin of selected South Indian private sector Sugar Industry (1991-92 to 2005-06)

(Per cent)

Particulars	Initial phase [1992-96]	Growth phase [1997-2001]	Maturity phase [2002-2006]	Whole period [1992-2006]
Large-sized (n=7)				
Mean	5.45	1.97	2.00	**3.14**
CV	1.13	2.02	3.21	**0.56**
CAGR	0.45	-8.31	38.15	**6.46**
Medium-sized (n=4)				
Mean	7.53	-6.71	-2.19	**-0.46**
CV	1.12	-2.85	-3.99	**-22.88**
CAGR	-4.90	-	-	**1.77**
Small-sized (n=4)				
Mean	-9.72	-8.95	0.49	**-6.06**
CV	-2.65	-0.29	12.63	**-1.50**
CAGR	-30.05	-	-	**9.35**
Whole industry (n=15)				
Mean	**1.96**	**-3.25**	**0.48**	**-0.27**
CV	**7.70**	**-3.27**	**14.09**	**-29.08**
CAGR	**-4.78**	**-**	**-**	**4.93**

Analysis of Variance

Sources of variation	F value	F critical value
Between the years	1.24	2.06
Between the sector	3.75**	3.34

Net profit margin - Paired sample t-test

Industry	Initial phase and Growth phase	Growth phase and Maturity phase	Initial phase and Maturity phase
Large-sized	2.76***	0.01	1.36
Medium-sized	4.65**	1.05	2.52***
Small-sized	0.07	2.79**	0.98
Whole industry	**1.71**	**1.49**	**0.47**

**Significant at 0.05 level; ***Significant at 0.10 level.

Source: Computed

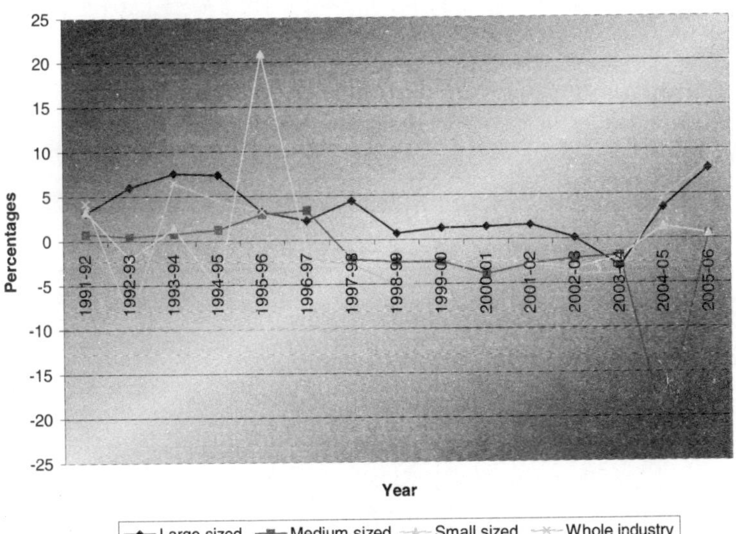

Fig. 4.5. Net Profit ratio of Selected South Indian Private Sector Sugar Industry.

Table 4.14. Analysis of Industry-wise Net profit margin of selected South Indian private sector Sugar industry (1991-92 to 2005-06)

(Per cent)

Industry	Initial phase (1992-96)			Growth phase (1997-2001)			Maturity phase (2002-2006)			Whole period (1992-2006)		
	Mean	CV	CAGR	Mean	CV	CAGR	Mean	CV	CAGR	Mean	CV	CAGR
1	2	3	4	5	6	7	8	9	10	11	12	13
Large-sized												
Bannari Amman Sugars Ltd	5.41	0.46	1.93	8.26	0.25	-6.10	8.57	0.29	11.84	7.41	0.35	3.52
EID Parry Ltd	2.86	0.39	12.60	3.69	0.12	-1.23	5.52	0.80	37.08	4.02	0.67	11.21
Jeypore Sugars & Chemicals Ltd	-0.36	-31.27	-	-1.09	-7.24	-	4.55	1.20	28.84	1.03	8.01	9.97
Rajshree Sugars & Chemicals Ltd	16.71	0.62	-	3.36	1.92	0.40	7.38	0.41	6.65	9.15	0.97	-
Sakthi Sugars Ltd	3.06	0.92	-39.66	1.73	0.72	24.83	-7.27	-1.56	-	-0.83	-9.53	1.19
Thiru Arooran Sugars Ltd	10.52	0.43	13.09	-4.47	-2.39	-	-6.30	-1.54	-	-0.08	139.09	-2.73
Ugar Sugar Works Ltd	-0.05	-18.44	-	2.32	0.56	31.62	1.53	2.90	-11.27	1.27	2.14	10.53
Medium-sized												
Kothari Sugars & Chemicals Ltd	8.07	0.13	3.71	-34.05	-0.80	-	-13.94	-1.77	-	-13.35	-2.00	2.02
Sri Chamundeswari Sugars Ltd	-0.17	-46.06	-	-4.91	-1.58	-	-3.02	-4.16	-	-2.70	-3.38	6.60
Sri Sarvaraya Sugars Ltd	3.05	0.94	-7.15	2.89	0.41	0.59	1.72	1.44	31.62	2.55	0.86	7.55
Kakatiya Cements Sugar & Industries Ltd	19.17	0.39	13.21	9.24	0.65	-17.17	6.48	0.26	11.07	11.63	0.66	-3.79

Small-sized												
Dharani Sugars & Chemicals Ltd	9.97	0.35	-1.87	-7.35	-1.52	-	-4.63	-1.88	-	-0.67	16.49	-9.33
Empee Sugars & Chemicals Ltd	-47.63	-1.86	-	-6.21	-2.91	-45.07	-5.01	-4.64	-	-19.62	-2.75	-
India Sugars and Refineries Ltd	-1.86	-2.69	-	-11.83	-0.68	-	6.71	2.73	10.67	-2.33	-5.81	-
Ponni Sugars Ltd	0.65	8.02	-	10.41	-1.09	-	4.89	0.49	20.97	-1.62	-5.87	3.92

Source: Computed from the annual accounts of the respective industry.

It would be possible to interpret the firm's profitability more meaningfully if both gross profit margin and net profit margin jointly. By comparing Table 4.4 with Table 4.13, it may be observed that the average gross profit margin of whole industry has increased to 9.82 per cent in maturity phase from 8.69 per cent in initial phase, whereas there was a sharp decrease in the average net profit margin to 0.48 per cent during maturity phase from 1.96 per cent during initial phase. It implies that the operating expenses relating to sales have been increasing. The increasing expenses should be identified and controlled.

Table 4.13 showed that the CV value of these ratios is at higher side that indicates high fluctuation in the net profit margin ratios of selected sectors during the study period. Such fluctuation could be attributed to the differences in the growth rates of net profit margin and sales because of the adverse economic conditions such as falling in sales prices, rising cost of production or declining demand for the product. All the selected sectors and whole industry witnessed positive compound annual growth rate of this ratio over the period of study.

In order to test the hypothesis, analysis of variance has been applied between the years and between the sectors. It is concluded that the null hypothesis is rejected, since the calculated value of F is greater than the table value of F at five per cent level between the sectors. The rejection of null hypothesis would indicate that there were significant differences in net profit margin ratios between the sectors.

The post-liberalization period of fifteen years was divided into three different phases as initial phase, growth phase and maturity phase. Table 4.13 showed that the overall net profit margin of the selected South Indian private sector sugar industry has been declined from 1.96 per cent in the initial phase to 0.48 per cent during maturity phase. The declining trend could be attributed to the poor performance of small-sized and medium-sized sugar industry due to increasing operating expenses, decreases in selling prices and demand. But during maturity phase all the selected sectors and whole industry registered an increasing trend in net profit margin ratio because of upward revision of sales price and reduction of cost of sales. The CV values of this ratio during the three phases showed high fluctuations. It is also clear from the table that the large-sized industry during growth phase and medium-sized and small-sized during initial phase have registered a negative compound annual growth rate of net profit margin ratio.

Paired sample t-test has been applied among the different phases in order to test the hypothesis. It is observed from Table 4.13 that there were significant differences in net profit margin ratio between the initial phase and growth phase under large-sized selected sugary industry and in between initial phase and maturity phase under medium-sized industry at ten per cent level of significance. Similarly the significant differences were also identified between initial phase and growth phase under medium-sized industry and growth phase and maturity phase under small-sized sugar industry at five per cent level. It is also evident from table that there were no significant differences in net profit margin of whole South Indian private sector Sugar Industry in between the phases.

Industry-wise and whole industry's net profit margin ratios of different sectors of selected South Indian private sector sugar industry during the post liberalization period in different phases are presented in Table 4.14. The performance of Bannari Amman Sugars Ltd, EID Parry Ltd, Rajshree Sugars & Chemicals Ltd, Ugar Sugar Works Ltd and Jeypore Sugar Ltd under large-sized and Sri Sarvaraya Sugars Ltd and Kakatiya Cements Sugar & Industries Ltd under medium-sized sugar industry was satisfactory because its average net profit margin ratios were better than the industry average. No industry under small-sized sector has performed well during the whole period of study, as its average net profit margin ratios were higher negative than the industry negative average. Moreover, only these industries made the industry average down to negative. In these circumstances, the industries under small-sized sector failed to achieve satisfactory return on shareholder funds and these can not withstand adverse economic conditions such as falling sales price, rising costs of production or declining demand for the product. High average net profit margin ratios were observed in Rajshree Sugars & Chemicals Ltd and Bannari Amman Sugars Ltd under large-sized and Kakatiya Cements Sugar & Industries Ltd under medium-sized sector. These industries would be in advantageous position to survive in the face of falling in sales prices, rising costs of production or declining demand for the product. These industries can make better use of favourable conditions such as rising sales prices, falling in costs of production or increasing demand for the product. These industries will be able to accelerate its profit at a faster rate than the industries with a low net profit margin.

Table 4.15 gives an idea about the differences in net profit margin ratios between the years and industry. It is clear from table that there was a significant difference in this ratio between the industries in large-sized sector and medium-sized sector at five percent level of significance. However there were no such significant differences between the industries in small-sized sector. Similarly there were no significant differences in net profit margins of all industries in between the years.

It can be viewed from Table 4.15 that the net profit ratios of Rajshree Sugars & Chemicals Ltd, Thiru Arooran Sugars Ltd and Ugar Sugar Works Ltd showed significant differences during initial phase and growth phase at 10 per cent level of significance. Bannari Amman Sugars Ltd signified that its net profit margin was differed during initial phase and maturity phase at ten percent level of significance. Thiru Arooran Sugars Ltd under large-sized registered a significant difference in net profit ratio at five per cent level of significance during initial phase and maturity phase.

Table 4.15. Analysis of Variance - ANOVA

Particulars	Large-sized		Medium-sized		Small-sized	
	F value	F critical value	F value	F critical value	F value	F critical value
Between the years	1.39	1.81	1.50	1.94	0.95	1.94
Between the Industry	4.62**	2.21	8.60**	2.83	1.47	2.83

Industry-wise Net profit Margin - Paired sample t-test

Industry	Paired sample t-test		
	Initial phase and growth phase	Initial phase and maturity phase	Growth phase and maturity phase
Large-sized (n=7)			
Bannari Amman Sugars Ltd	2.05	2.41***	0.16
EID Parry Ltd	1.38	1.75	0.90
Jeypore Sugars & Chemicals Ltd	0.11	0.70	1.42
Rajshree Sugars & Chemicals Ltd	2.29***	2.08	1.85
Sakthi Sugars Ltd	1.13	1.98	1.86
Thiru Arooran Sugars Ltd	2.74***	3.05**	0.23
Ugar Sugar Works Ltd	2.44***	0.74	0.39
Medium-sized (n=4)			
Kothari Sugars & Chemicals Ltd	3.47**	2.03	1.12
Sri Chamundeswari Sugars Ltd	0.75	0.34	0.29
Sri Sarvaraya Sugars Ltd	0.11	0.59	0.85
Kakatiya Cements Sugar & Industries Ltd	1.99	4.46**	0.95
Small-sized (n=4)			
Dharani Sugars & Chemicals Ltd	3.80**	4.41**	0.62
Empee Sugars & Chemicals Ltd	0.96	0.97	0.38
India Sugars and Refineries Ltd	1.81	1.21	1.80
Ponni Sugars Ltd	1.78	1.28	2.88**

*Significant at 0.01 level; **Significant at 0.05 level; ***Significant at 0.10 level

Source: Computed.

Some other significant differences in net profit margin ratios were also recorded during initial phase and growth phase and at initial phase and maturity phases at five per cent level of significance. They were Kothari Sugars & Chemicals Ltd under large-sized sector, Dharani Sugars & Chemicals Ltd under small-sized sector during initial phase and growth phase, Kakatiya Cements Sugar & Industries Ltd under medium-sized and Dharani Sugars & Chemicals Ltd under small-sized during initial phase and maturity phase and Ponni Sugars Ltd under small-sized during growth phase and maturity phase at five per cent level of significance.

To sum up the above inferences it may be concluded that the industries under large-sized sector are performing well and they indicate the efficiency in manufacturing, and selling the products was proved to be satisfactory. Industries under medium-sized sector also performing but at the industry average level. In case of industries under small-sized sector have failed to achieve satisfactory return. In contrast they incurred net losses over the period of study. But positive sign was occurred during the maturity phase giving good hope for the industries in the years to come from the view point of shareholders.

Return on Total Assets

Profitability of business enterprises is measured in relation to investment. It is the prime measure of the overall profitability of an enterprise. Return on investment measures the overall effectiveness of management in generating profit with its available assets.[12] This ratio reveals how profitability of the firm's assets has been utilized. The rate of return on investment is the end product of the two-fold sequence of the profit margin path and can be ascertained by the multiplication of the investment turnover with the percentage of profit margin on sales.[13]

The return on assets of a company determines its ability

to utilize the assets employed in the enterprises efficiently and effectively to earn good return. This ratio measures the percentage of profit earned per rupee of assets and thus is a measure of efficiency of the company in generating profits on its asset. The ratio can be very well used for inter-firm and inter-industry comparison. Notably, neither the operating profit margin nor the turnover ratio by itself provides an adequate measure of operating efficiency. Further, while the net profit margin ignores the utilization of assets, the turnover ratio ignores profitability on sales, the return an assets ratio or earning power reveals these short comings.[14] An improvement in the earning power of the firm will result if there is an increase in turnover on existing assets and an increase in the net profit margin.

Most industries acquire assets to produce sales revenues and ultimately, profits. Asset utilization ratios indicate how effectively or efficiently an industry uses its assets. The asset efficiencies and the returns on assets for various sectors of selected South Indian private sector Sugar Industry were shown in Table 4.16 and Fig. 4.6. The selected South Indian private sector sugar industry has registered 1.28 per cent average rate of return on total assets over the period of study. The average return on total asset ratio varied from sector to sector, the highest average was 3.25 per cent in large-sized sugar industry followed by medium-sized (1.65%) sugar industry. The CV value of these ratios shows very high fluctuations in the return on total assets ratio of the selected sectors during the study period. Such fluctuations could be attributed to the differences in the growth rates of profit after tax and total assets because of the over investment in assets, under utilization of assets due to seasonal factors in getting raw materials. All the selected sectors of South Indian private sector sugar industry and whole industry have recorded a positive compound annual growth rate of this ratio during the study period.

Table 4.16. Analysis of Return on total assets of selected South Indian private sector Sugar Industry (1991-92 to 2005-06)

(Per cent)

Particulars	Initial phase [1992-96]	Growth phase [1997-2001]	Maturity phase [2002-2006]	Whole period [1992-2006]
Large-sized (n=7)				
Mean	4.68	2.23	2.84	**3.25**
CV	1.01	1.11	1.31	**0.87**
CAGR	6.29	-7.98	27.31	**5.84**
Medium-sized (n=4)				
Mean	5.74	-0.89	0.11	**1.65**
CV	0.71	-6.75	40.69	**2.65**
CAGR	2.61	-	-	**4.54**
Small-sized (n=4)				
Mean	-0.38	-5.81	-1.38	**-2.52**
CV	-18.04	-0.74	-3.24	**-1.09**
CAGR	-	-	-	**9.69**
Whole industry (n=15)				
Mean	**3.61**	**-0.75**	**0.98**	**1.28**
CV	**1.51**	**-6.84**	**4.35**	**3.05**
CAGR	**-5.02**	**-**	**-**	**6.40**

Analysis of Variance

Sources of variation	F value	F critical value
Between the years	2.39**	2.06
Between the sector	3.44**	3.34

Return on total assets - Paired sample t-test

Industry	Initial phase and Growth phase	Growth phase and Maturity phase	Initial phase and Maturity phase
Large-sized	0.80	0.41	0.71
Medium-sized	3.74**	0.75	2.13***
Small-sized	2.79**	1.15	0.21
Whole industry	**0.64**	**0.89**	**0.01**

**Significant at 0.05 level; ***Significant at 0.10 level

Source: Computed

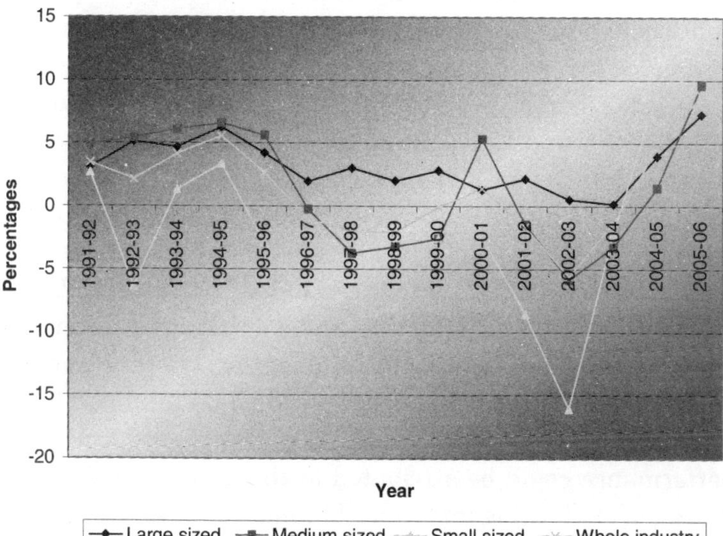

Fig. 4.6. Return on total assets ratio of Selected South Indian Private Sector Sugar Industry

The hypothesis framed was tested by applying analysis of variance between the years and between the sectors. The calculated values of F (2.39 and 3.44) are greater than the table values of F at 5 per cent level of significance, hence it is concluded that the null hypothesis is rejected. The rejection of null hypothesis would reveal that there are significant differences in return on total assets ratios between the years and sectors. The table also revealed that there were significant differences in return on total assets ratios of medium-sized and small-sized sugar industry during initial phase and growth phase at five per cent level of significance. Similarly the return on total assets ratios of medium-sized sector differed significantly during initial phase and maturity phase at 10 per cent level of significance.

The industry wise return on total assets ratio of sample industries under different sectors of selected South Indian private sector Sugar Industry during three different phases and whole period is presented in Table 4.17. The efficiency in generating profits on its asset was better in Rajshree Sugars & Chemicals Ltd (7.70%), Bannari Amman Sugars Ltd (6.02%), and EID Parry Ltd (4.40%) under large-sized sugar industry and Kakatiya Cements Sugar & Industries Ltd (6.86%) and Sri Sarvaraya Sugars Ltd (3.57%) under medium-sized sugar industry because its average return an total assets was for better than the industry average (1.28%). It is observed that no industries under small-sized sector was operated efficiently in utilizing its assets for generating profits on its assets. Because its average return on total assets for the study period incurred only negative signs. This poor performance could be attributed to the under utilization of assets, over stocking and capital intensive. Of great interest to shareholders looking at the industry's financial performance is how rapidly various items are growing, in particular revenues and profits. Indeed, these growth rates have their own names: top line growth for revenues, and bottom-line growth for profits. The South Indian private sector Sugar Industry's compound annual growth rate was 6.40 per cent during the study period which was exceeded by few industries such as Jeypore Sugar Company Ltd. (10.87%).

and Ugar Sugar Works Ltd. (10.36%) under large-sized, Kothari Sugars & Chemicals Ltd. (19.04%) and Sri Sarvaraya Sugars Ltd. (30.67%) under medium-sized and Ponni Sugars Ltd. (23.13%) under small-sized. The Sri Sarvaraya Sugars Ltd. under medium-sized sugar industry tops the list and placed as fast growing industry with compound annual growth rate of 30.67 per cent during the post-liberalization period. Few industries have registered a negative compound annual growth rate during the study period such as Sakthi Sugars Ltd. and Thiru Arooran Sugars Ltd. under large-sized and Dharani Sugars & Chemicals Ltd. under small-sized sugar industry. Dharani Sugars & Chemicals Ltd. under small-sized sugar industry was the worst among the selected industries in the list of poorly performing industries, as its compound annual growth rate was -21.40 per cent during the post-liberalization period.

Growth by acquisition or expansion can make natural growth that comes as a result of growing sales alone. It seems to be the natural growth in the return on total assets of Sri Sarvaraya Sugars Ltd under medium-sized as its average return on assets over the phases constantly increased. From the table, it is clear that the Sakthi Sugars Ltd was more volatile industry in utilizing its assets efficiently as its CV was the highest among the sample industries. To sum up the above, Jeypore Sugar and Chemicals Ltd among large-sized, Sri Sarvaraya Sugars Ltd among the medium-sized and Ponni Sugars Ltd among the small-sized are the fast growing industries and Sri Sarvaraya Sugars Ltd is the fast growing among the selected South Indian private sector Sugar Industry during the post-liberalisation period in relation to asset utilization.

Table 4.18 reveals that the difference in the return on total asset ratio was significant in between the industry under large-sized sector, in between the industry and the years under medium-sized industry and in between the years under

Table 4.17. Analysis of Industry-wise Return on total assets of selected South Indian private sector Sugar Industry (1991-92 to 2005-06)

(Per cent)

Industry	Initial phase (1992-96)			Growth phase (1997-2001)			Maturity phase (2002-2006)			Whole period (1992-2006)		
	Mean	CV	CAGR	Mean	CV	CAGR	Mean	CV	CAGR	Mean	CV	CAGR
1	2	3	4	5	6	7	8	9	10	11	12	13
Large-sized												
Bannari Amman Sugars Ltd	4.45	0.67	1.55	6.40	0.26	-7.42	7.22	0.40	13.82	6.02	0.51	3.35
EID Parry Ltd	4.32	0.20	-1.65	3.79	0.09	2.11	5.11	0.84	32.80	4.40	0.68	5.83
Jeypore Sugars & Chemicals Ltd	0.45	12.79	-	-0.63	-7.19	-	3.50	1.32	41.24	1.11	4.46	10.87
Rajshree Sugars & Chemicals Ltd	14.21	0.73	-	2.72	1.72	-1.02	6.16	0.36	10.40	7.70	1.09	-
Sakthi Sugars Ltd	2.64	0.90	-43.03	0.07	38.65	-	-2.32	-1.85	-	0.13	27.53	-1.48
Thiru Arooran Sugars Ltd	6.31	0.40	11.59	0.42	10.07	-	-1.47	-2.09	-	1.75	2.53	-2.44
Ugar Sugar Works Ltd	0.37	5.95	-	2.82	0.57	17.40	1.65	2.63	-6.10	1.61	1.80	10.36
Medium-sized												
Kothari Sugars & Chemicals Ltd	5.30	0.05	-0.26	-7.66	-1.81	22.60	-5.72	-2.76	-	-2.70	-4.71	19.04
Sri Chamundeswari Sugars Ltd	2.07	1.13	-	-4.19	-1.77	-	-1.29	-5.26	-	-1.13	-5.39	16.11
Sri Sarvaraya Sugars Ltd	4.07	0.71	-	3.19	0.48	24.90	2.78	1.22	14.41	3.59	0.74	30.67
Kakatiya Cements Sugar & Industries Ltd	11.50	0.41	17.92	4.39	0.72	-17.59	4.68	0.46	25.39	6.86	0.68	0.40

Small-sized												
Dharani Sugars & Chemicals Ltd	7.82	0.34	-12.26	-2.52	-1.62	-	-1.87	2.83	-	1.14	5.47	-21.40
Empee Sugars & Chemicals Ltd	-8.80	-1.61	-11.92	-5.33	-1.58	-45.07	-2.55	-5.62	-	-5.56	-2.15	-
India Sugars and Refineries Ltd	-1.63	-2.70	-	-12.03	-0.62	-	4.81	2.75	31.82	-2.95	-3.76	-
Ponni Sugars Ltd	1.08	3.09	-	-3.33	-1.87	-	-5.92	-3.25	-	-2.72	-4.17	23.13

Source: Computed from the annual accounts of the respective industry.

small-sized sugar industry as the calculated values of F were greater than the table values at five per cent level of significance. However, they were insignificant in between the years under large-sized and in between industry under small-sized sectors of the selected South Indian private sector sugar industry.

Significant differences in return on total asset in between the phases were tested by applying paired t-test (Table 4.18). The differences in return on total assets of Kakatiya Cements Sugar & Industries Ltd under medium-sized, India Sugars and Refineries Ltd under small-sized and Dharani Sugars & Chemicals Ltd small-sized at were significant at different level of significance. During the initial phase and maturity phase differences in the ratio of Bannari Amman Sugars Ltd under large-sized, Kakatiya Cements Sugar & Industries Ltd under medium-sized and Dharani Sugars & Chemicals Ltd under small-sized were significant. Similarly the return on total asset ratios of Rajshree Sugars & Chemicals Ltd under large-sized were differed significantly at 10 per cent level and India Sugars and Refineries Ltd ratios varied significantly at five per cent level between growth phase and maturity phase.

Return on Shareholders Fund

Return on shareholders fund is of utmost importance to shareholders. Since it reflects the earning power of the funds belonging to them after all debts and charges of every description have been paid. The profitability of a company from the owner's point of view should, therefore be assessed in terms of the return on the owner's equity. The ratio measures the ability of the management of enterprise to generate adequate returns for the capital invested by the owners of the company. The ratio is meaningful in the sense that it measures the residue of income, which really belongs to the owners.

Table 4.18. Analysis of Variance - ANOVA

Particulars	Large-sized		Medium-sized		Small-sized	
	F value	F critical value	F value	F critical value	F value	F critical value
Between the years	1.49	1.81	2.08**	1.94	2.67**	1.94
Between the Industry	6.22**	2.21	6.42**	2.83	1.49	2.83

Industry-wise Return on total assets - Paired sample t-test

Industry	Paired sample t-test		
	Initial phase and growth phase	Initial phase and maturity phase	Growth phase and maturity phase
Large-sized (n=7)			
Bannari Amman Sugars Ltd	1.17	2.31***	0.43
EID Parry Ltd	1.23	0.45	0.69
Jeypore Sugars & Chemicals Ltd	0.30	0.68	1.63
Rajshree Sugars & Chemicals Ltd	0.63	1.40	2.17***
Sakthi Sugars Ltd	0.61	0.08	0.88
Thiru Arooran Sugars Ltd	0.88	0.40	0.64
Ugar Sugar Works Ltd	1.00	0.81	0.54
Medium-sized (n=4)			
Kothari Sugars & Chemicals Ltd	2.10	1.58	0.27
Sri Chamundeswari Sugars Ltd	1.49	0.98	0.65
Sri Sarvaraya Sugars Ltd	0.09	0.47	0.77
Kakatiya Cements Sugar & Industries Ltd	2.26***	4.72*	0.15
Small-sized (n=4)			
Dharani Sugars & Chemicals Ltd	3.79**	3.58**	0.34
Empee Sugars & Chemicals Ltd	0.50	0.74	0.94
India Sugars and Refineries Ltd	2.61***	1.45	2.89**
Ponni Sugars Ltd	1.21	0.71	0.29

*Significant at 0.01 level; **Significant at 0.05 level; ***Significant at 0.10 level

Source: Computed

This residue is measured in relation to the capital base, which takes into account not only the share capital paid by the owners, but also accumulated surplus or deficit. The earning of a satisfactory return is the most desirable objective of business. Thus, this ratio is of great interest to present as well as prospective shareholders and also of great concern to management.[15] As is the case for return on assets, the estimate of market value will have a large impact on this ratio. The return on owners' equity of the company should be compared with the ratios for other similar companies. This will reveal the relative performance and also the relative strength of the enterprise in attracting future investments.

A look on Table 4.19 and Fig. 4.7 would make us to observe how well the selected sectors of South Indian private sector sugar industry have used the resources of owners during the three phases and whole period. The average return on shareholders fund was varied from sector to sector. The highest average return was 9.98 per cent in large-sized sugar industry followed by medium-sized 8.35 per cent. In the small-sized sugar industry negative return of -8.85 was registered during the period of study. The table indicates that the average return on shareholders fund was fluctuating during the post liberalization period under the study. The average return on shareholders' fund 9.83 per cent during initial phase was declined to negative average return during growth phase and reached a positive average return 13.63 per cent in the maturity phase. The wide fluctuation was caused by the differences in the rates of small-sized (-29.95%) and medium-sized (-16.25%) during growth phase. The compound annual growth rate of this ratio was positive in all the selected sectors. The CV value of this ratio shows very high fluctuations during the study period. The fluctuations in this ratio could be attributed to the differences in growth rates of profit after tax and shareholders fund.

Table 4.19. Analysis of Return on shareholders funds of selected South Indian private sector Sugar Industry (1991-92 to 2005-06)

(Per cent)

Particulars	Initial phase [1992-96]	Growth phase [1997-2001]	Maturity phase [2002-2006]	Whole period [1992-2006]
Large-sized (n=7)				
Mean	13.06	5.19	11.69	**9.98**
CV	0.96	2.16	1.16	**0.69**
CAGR	-	-	24.63	**4.42**
Medium-sized (n=4)				
Mean	16.36	-16.25	24.93	**8.35**
CV	0.35	-2.39	1.93	**1.59**
CAGR	-12.40	-	34.16	**4.72**
Small-sized (n=4)				
Mean	-2.34	-29.95	5.74	**-8.85**
CV	-14.53	-1.22	2.75	**-2.38**
CAGR	29.27	-	-	**26.99**
Whole industry (n=15)				
Mean	**9.83**	**-9.90**	**13.63**	**4.52**
CV	**1.99**	**-3.04**	**1.92**	**3.31**
CAGR	**-29.47**	**-**	**48.74**	**8.74**

Analysis of Variance

Sources of variation	F value	F critical value
Between the years	2.69**	2.06
Between the sector	2.28	3.34

Return on shareholders funds - Paired sample t-test

Industry	Initial phase and Growth phase	Growth phase and Maturity phase	Initial phase and Maturity phase
Large-sized	1.67	1.02	0.14
Medium-sized	1.57	3.64**	0.47
Small-sized	1.04	1.18	0.40
Whole industry	**1.53**	**2.61*** **	**0.37**

**Significant at 0.05 level; ***Significant at 0.10 level
Source: Computed

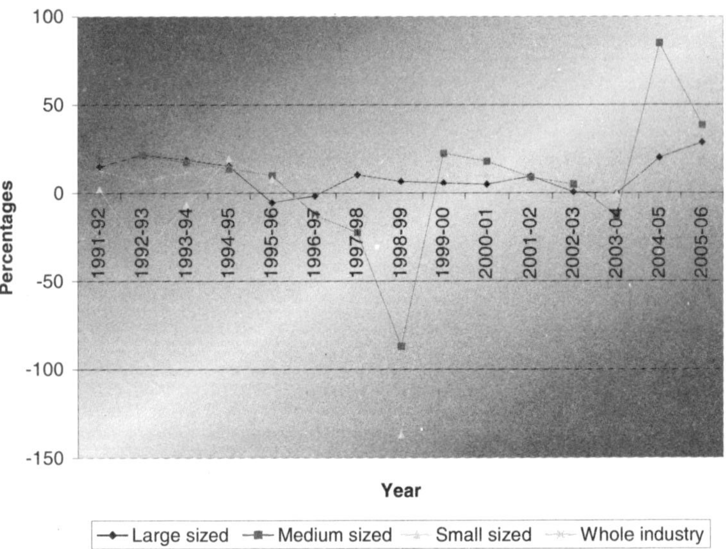

Fig. 4.7. Return on Shareholders fund of Selected South Indian Private Sector Sugar Industry

In order to test the hypothesis, the analysis of variance has been applied among the selected sectors and between the years. Differences in the average return on shareholders fund was significant in between the years as the calculated value of F (2.69) is greater that the table value of F (2.06) at five per cent level of significance. However, this was insignificant in between the sectors as the calculated value of F (2.28) is lower than the table value of F (3.34) at five per cent level of significance.

The study period of fifteen years was divided into three phases as initial phase (1992-96), growth phase (1997-2001) and maturity phase (2002-06). Table 4.19 indicates that there were significant differences in return on shareholders fund between growth phase and maturity phase in whole industry and medium-sized sugar industry as per the t-value. In the remaining cases no such differences were observed.

The industry-wise return on shareholders fund ratio of different sectors of selected South Indian private sector sugar industry during the three different phases and the whole period is presented in Table 4.20. Among the selected South Indian private sector Sugar Industry Rajshree Sugars & Chemicals Ltd, Bannari Amman Sugars Ltd, EID Parry Ltd and Ugar Sugar Works Ltd under large-sized sector have performed well in generating adequate return for the capital invested by the owners and the industries have used the resources of owners well. These industries have accomplished the most desirable objective of the industries. This achievement attracted the present shareholders and will attract the prospective shareholders. In the medium-sized sector Sri Sarvaraya Sugars Ltd is the best performed industry as the highest average return on shareholders fund of 15.52 per cent was recorded. It was followed by Kakatiya Cements Sugar & Industries Ltd 15.33 per cent and Kothari Sugars & Chemicals Ltd 14.05 per cent during the study period. These industries have maximized its owner's welfare and accomplished the most desirable objective of the industry. No industry under small-sized sector fetched the industry average of 4.52 per cent and the average return of the small-sized sectors were far below the industry average during the study period. It may be inferred from the table that the small-sized sector failed to attain the most desirable objective of the industry and failed to attract the future investments.

Table 4.20. Analysis of Industry-wise Return on shareholders funds of selected South Indian private sector Sugar industry (1991-92 to 2005-06)

(Per cent)

Industry	Initial phase (1992-96)			Growth phase (1997-2001)			Maturity phase (2002-2006)			Whole period (1992-2006)		
	Mean	CV	CAGR	Mean	CV	CAGR	Mean	CV	CAGR	Mean	CV	CAGR
1	2	3	4	5	6	7	8	9	10	11	12	13
Large-sized												
Bannari Amman Sugars Ltd	14.07	0.57	-1.23	15.28	0.19	-4.36	23.09	0.27	9.30	17.48	0.40	2.22
EID Parry Ltd	14.63	0.26	-13.30	9.58	0.11	5.22	1142	0.69	22.07	11.88	0.44	0.39
Jeypore Sugars & Chemicals Ltd	-1.46	-37.01	-	-7.83	-5.11	-	28.56	1.26	39.96	6.42	6.85	10.96
Rajshree Sugars & Chemicals Ltd	32.43	0.65	76.19	6.57	1.79	5.06	20.68	0.45	16.76	19.89	0.89	18.69
Sakthi Sugars Ltd	12.10	0.87	-45.07	-1.05	-15.55	-	-7.34	-1.99	-	1.24	12.53	-4.14
Thiru Arooran Sugars Ltd	22.72	0.46	6.19	-7.55	-2.00	-	-4.06	-2.47	-	3.70	4.84	-2.73
Ugar Sugar Works Ltd	-3.07	-6.34	-	21.34	0.49	19.33	9.47	2.58	-9.71	9.24	2.21	3.96
Medium-sized												
Kothari Sugars & Chemicals Ltd	18.53	0.35	-11.27	-68.94	-2.59	16.54	92.55	1.72	15.55	14.05	10.32	2.59
Sri Chamundeswari Sugars Ltd	8.04	1.11	-	-21.56	-1.91	-	-21.03	-2.32	-	-11.51	-3.24	7.83
Sri Sarvaraya Sugars Ltd	17.64	0.73	-	16.36	0.47	18.02	12.55	1.33	19.53	15.52	0.79	9.61
Kakatiya Cements Sugar & Industries Ltd	21.22	0.15	2.83	9.14	042	-3.89	15.62	0.29	13.09	15.33	0.41	-0.77

Small-sized												
Dharani Sugars & Chemicals Ltd	36.33	0.37	-2.75	-14.83	-1.67	-	-15.16	-2.29	-19.41	2.11	16.38	-694
Empee Sugars & Chemicals Ltd	2.02	-3.82	-	4.18	0.96	-	8.24	1.21	31.42	3.46	2.40	11.01
India Sugars and Refineries Ltd	-46.53	-1.82	-	-81.21	-2.26	-	6.69	21.86	-	-40.35	-3.43	-
Ponni Sugars Ltd	2.85	4.03	-	-27.94	-2.47	-	23.21	0.40	13.21	-0.63	-69.63	7.72

Source: Computed from the annual accounts of the respective industry.

Table 4.21 showed that the differences in the ratio of return on shareholders fund were insignificant in between the years and industry selected as the calculated values of F were lower than the table values of F at five per cent level of significance.

It is clear from Table 4.21 that in the majority of the large-sized sugar industries among the sample showed a significant differences in the return on shareholders fund ratios during initial phase and growth phase. Such significant differences were occurred in EID Parry Ltd, Rajshree Sugars & Chemicals Ltd, Sakthi Sugars Ltd and Thiru Arooran Sugars Ltd under large-sized sector at varied level of significance ranging from five per cent to ten per cent. Among the medium-sized industry return on shareholders fund ratio varied significantly in Kakatiya Cements Sugar & Industries Ltd during initial phase and growth phase and also during growth phase and maturity phase. The rest of the industries under medium-sized were remain stable during the three phases. In the small-sized sector, the differences in the ratio of return on shareholders fund were significant in Dharani Sugars & Chemicals Ltd and Empee Sugars & Chemicals Ltd during initial phase and growth phase at five per cent and ten per cent level of significance respectively. During initial phase and maturity phase the differences were observed significant in Dharani Sugars & Chemicals Ltd and Ponni Sugars Ltd under the small-sized sector of selected South Indian private sector sugar industry.

Table 4.21. Analysis of Variance - ANOVA

Particulars	Large-sized		Medium-sized		Small-sized	
	F value	F critical value	F value	F critical value	F value	F critical value
Between the years	1.51	1.81	0.91	1.94	1.61	1.94
Between the Industry	1.64	2.21	0.46	2.83	1.37	2.83

Industry-wise Return on shareholders funds - Paired sample t-test

Industry	Paired sample t-test		
	Initial phase and growth phase	Initial phase and maturity phase	Growth phase and maturity phase
Large-sized (n=7)			
Bannari Amman Sugars Ltd	0.38	2.05	1.97
EID Parry Ltd	2.43***	0.67	0.53
Jeypore Sugars & Chemicals Ltd	0.19	0.80	1.76
Rajshree Sugars & Chemicals Ltd	2.63***	1.39	3.54**
Sakthi Sugars Ltd	2.31***	2.20***	0.53
Thiru Arooran Sugars Ltd	4.55**	3.55**	0.33
Ugar Sugar Works Ltd	2.01	0.80	0.95
Medium-sized (n=4)			
Kothari Sugars & Chemicals Ltd	1.11	1.85	2.05
Sri Chamundeswari Sugars Ltd	1.36	1.28	0.02
Sri Sarvaraya Sugars Ltd	0.15	0.41	0.54
Kakatiya Cements Sugar & Industries Ltd	4.83*	1.87	2.34***
Small-sized (n=4)			
Dharani Sugars & Chemicals Ltd	3.95**	3.89**	0.03
Empee Sugars & Chemicals Ltd	2.16***	1.32	0.78
India Sugars and Refineries Ltd	0.39	0.72	0.85
Ponni Sugars Ltd	0.92	2.24***	1.74

*Significant at 0.01 level; **Significant at 0.05 level; ***Significant at 0.10 level

Source: Computed

For manufacturing enterprises the usual standard of return on owners fund is 10-15 per cent.[16] In the selected sugar industry majority of the industries have to make struggle for achieving this standard, as sugar pricing depends on the forces of demand and supply and it is also statutorily and administratively controlled. Further, the prices of the inputs are also not favourable. To sum up the above, the fluctuating returns among the three sectors over the period denote unstable return in the whole industry, wide fluctuation trend in small-sized sector, upward trend in the medium-sized sector and low deviation in large-sized sector were observed. Industry wise analysis indicates majority of the large-sized and medium-sized sugar industry had performed well in relation to the return on shareholders fund, whereas small-sized industry failed to attain the most desirable objective of earning adequate return on shareholders fund.

Earnings Per Share

Apart from the rates of return, the profitability of a company from the point of view of the equity shareholders is the Earnings Per Share (EPS). It measures the profit available to the equity shareholders on a per share basis. Many enterprises fix their growth targets in terms of growth in earnings per share.[17] Shareholders and financial analyst place considerable emphasis on reported earnings per share and anticipated growth in earnings per share. The earnings per share calculations made over years indicate whether or not the firms' earning power on per share basis has changed over that period.

The earnings per share simply show the profitability of the firm on a per share basis it does not reflect how much is paid as dividend and how much it retained in the business. But as a profitability index, it is valuable and widely used ratio.[18] Further, earning per share is a good measure of profitability and when compared with earnings per share of similar other companies, it gives a view of the comparative earnings or earning power of the firm.

Average earnings per share, co-efficient of variations, compound annual growth rates, analysis of variance and paired sample t-test analysis are presented in the Table 4.22 and Fig. 4.8. A look on the table gives us an idea about the profitability of the common shareholders' investment in the South Indian private sector sugar industry during the post liberalization period of fifteen years and phased manner as well. The industry average earnings per share was Rs. 19.94 per share ranging from Rs.4.03 per share in 2002-03 to Rs.152 per share in 2000-01. This indicates a wide fluctuation in the earnings per share in the selected South Indian private sector sugar industry during the period of study.

The average earnings per share varied from sector to sector also. The highest average was Rs.38.71 per share in small-sized sugar industry followed by Rs.14.27 per share in medium-sized sector and Rs.12.45 per share in large-sized sector. The average earnings per share was higher than the industry average only in small-sized industry. The compound annual growth rate of this was positive in all the selected sectors. The CV values of this ratio showed very high fluctuations in the earnings per share during the study period. The fluctuation in this ratio could be attributed to the differences in the growth rates of earnings available to equity shareholders, utilization of borrowed and owners fund by the selected South Indian private sector sugar industry during the study period.

In order to test the hypothesis, the analysis of variance has been applied among all the selected sectors and between the years. Table 4.22 shows that there was no significant difference in the earnings per share in between the sectors and years as the calculated values of F were lower than the table values F at five per cent level of significance. Analysis of paired samples t-test makes it clear from the table

Table 4.22. Analysis of Earnings per share of selected South Indian private sector Sugar Industry (1991-92 to 2005-06)

(in Rupees)

Particulars	**Initial phase [1992-96]**	**Growth phase [1997-2001]**	**Maturity phase [2002-2006]**	**Whole period [1992-2006]**
Large-sized (n=7)				
Mean	12.69	9.31	15.36	**12.45**
CV	0.73	0.79	0.90	**0.62**
CAGR	-1.04	11.05	30.09	**6.47**
Medium-sized (n=4)				
Mean	12.72	10.08	19.82	**14.27**
CV	0.69	1.35	1.29	**1.12**
CAGR	-14.11	11.52	18.50	**5.62**
Small-sized (n=4)				
Mean	4.06	107.29	4.28	**38.71**
CV	0.75	1.99	1.08	**1.84**
CAGR	26.09	428.30	37.87	**11.33**
Whole industry (n=15)				
Mean	**10.40**	**35.64**	**13.73**	**19.94**
CV	**0.81**	**3.06**	**1.18**	**1.81**
CAGR	**-1.27**	**94.29**	**26.85**	**6.64**

Analysis of Variance

Sources of variation	**F value**	**F critical value**
Between the years	1.01	2.06
Between the sector	0.51	3.34

Earnings per share - Paired sample t-test

Industry	Initial phase and Growth phase	Growth phase and Maturity phase	Initial phase and Maturity phase
Large-sized	3.42**	0.03	1.27
Large-sized	1.68	1.45	0.57
Medium-sized	0.73	1.41	0.90
Small-sized	0.97	0.97	0.65
Whole industry	0.86	0.82	0.77

Source: Computed.

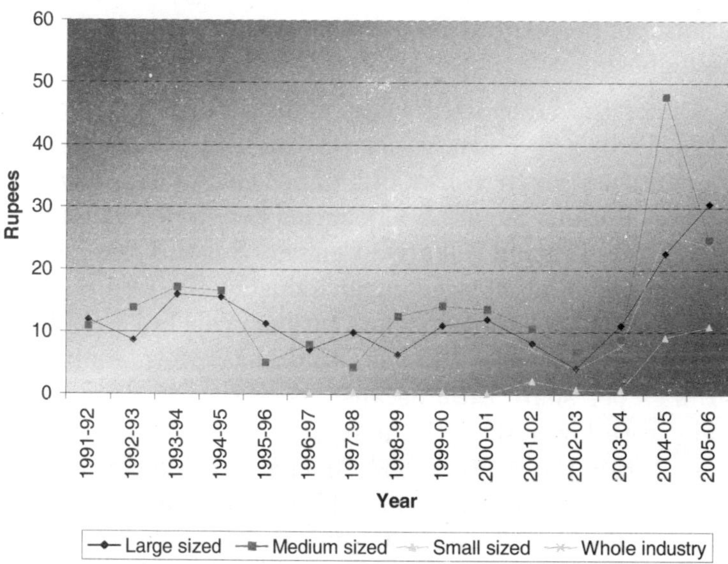

Fig. 4.8. Earnings per share of Selected South Indian Private Sector Sugar Industry

that the differences in the earnings per share of all the selected sectors and whole industry were insignificant during initial phase and growth phase, growth phase and maturity phase and initial phase and maturity phase.

The post-liberalization period was divided equally into three phases as initial phase, growth phase and maturity phase for this study. Industry-wise earnings per share in each phase and for the whole period are given in Table 4.23. The profitability performance of Bannari Amman Sugars Ltd and Jeypore Sugars & Chemicals Ltd under large-sized sugar industry, Sri Sarvaraya Sugars Ltd under medium-sized sugar industry and Ponni Sugars Ltd under small-sized sugar industry was satisfactory on a per share basis as its average earnings per share was higher than the industry average earnings per share of Rs.19.94 per share. Among the above top performers in relation to earnings per share Ponni Sugars Ltd under small-sized sugar industry was the best performing industry as its average earnings per share was the highest.

Under the large-sized sugar industry Rajshree Sugars & Chemicals Ltd, Thiru Arooran Sugars Ltd, Sakthi Sugars Ltd and Ugar Sugar Works Ltd, under medium-sized sugar industry Kothari Sugars & Chemicals Ltd, Sri Chamundeswari Sugars Ltd and Kakatiya Cements Sugar & Industries Ltd and under small-sized sugar industry, Dharani Sugars & Chemicals Ltd, Empee Sugars & Chemicals Ltd and India Sugars and Refineries Ltd were the poor performers in the earnings per share ratio because its average earnings per share were lower than the industry average Rs.19.94 per share during the study period. Among the poor performers Rajshree Sugars & Chemicals Ltd under large-sized sugar industry, Kothari Sugars & Chemicals Ltd under medium-sized sugar industry and Empee Sugars & Chemicals Ltd under small-sized sugar industry were the worst performers in the respective sector because its average earnings per share were least among the sector average.

The Bannari Amman Sugars Ltd and EID Parry Ltd under large-sized sugar industry, Sri Sarvaraya Sugars Ltd under medium-sized sugar industry and Empee Sugars &

Chemicals Ltd under small-sized sugar industry were the steady performers in relation to earnings per share as its average earnings per share during initial phase, growth phase and maturity phase showed steadily upward trend. Few of industries in the selected South Indian private sector Sugar Industry were mixed performers during the study period viz., Jeypore Sugars & Chemicals Ltd, Rajshree Sugars & Chemicals Ltd, Sakthi Sugars Ltd and Ugar Sugar Works Ltd under large-sized sugar industry and Kothari Sugars & Chemicals Ltd, Sri Chamundeswari Sugars Ltd and Kakatiya Cements Sugar & Industries Ltd under medium-sized sugar industry. Thiru Arooran Sugars Ltd under large-sized and Dharani Sugars & Chemicals Ltd under medium-sized were dipping performers as the numbers in relation to the earnings per share have been on the slide during the phases.

Table 4.24 indicated that the differences in the earnings per share in between the years and industry were significant in the large-sized sector. Similarly in the medium-sized sector the differences between industry were significant, as the calculated value was higher than the table values of F at five per cent level. However, these were insignificant between the years and industry in the small-sized sugar industry. Further it can be observed from the Table 4.24 that the differences in earnings per share of majority of the large-sized sugar industry were significant in between the industry as per the t-value. Such significant differences were obtained in Bannari Amman Sugars Ltd, EID Parry Ltd, Sakthi Sugars Ltd and Thiru Arooran Sugars Ltd under large-sized, Kothari Sugars & Chemicals Ltd and Kakatiya Cements Sugar & Industries Ltd under medium-sized sugar industry and Dharani Sugars & Chemicals Ltd under small-sized during initial phase and growth phase. Similarly significant differences in average earnings per share of Bannari Amman Sugars Ltd and Thiru Arooran Sugars Ltd under large-sized and Dharani Sugars & Chemicals Ltd under small-sized during initial phase and maturity phase were observed.

Table 4.23. Analysis of Industry-wise Earnings per share of selected South Indian private sector Sugar industry (1991-92 to 2005-06)

(in Rupees)

Industry	Initial phase (1992-96)			Growth phase (1997-2001)			Maturity phase (2002-2006)			Whole period (1992-2006)		
	Mean	CV	CAGR	Mean	CV	CAGR	Mean	CV	CAGR	Mean	CV	CAGR
1	2	3	4	5	6	7	8	9	10	11	12	13
Large-sized												
Bannari Amman Sugars Ltd	7.32	0.64	10.40	15.84	0.15	5.71	38.91	0.66	55.56	20.69	0.95	13.31
EID Parry Ltd	13.61	0.13	6.03	20.45	0.27	9.58	25.17	0.72	2.01	19.74	0.57	4.15
Jeypore Sugars & Chemicals Ltd	32.60	0.88	-	7.28	0.62	-6.36	23.17	1.27	29.84	21.02	1.17	0.99
Rajshree Sugars & Chemicals Ltd	4.16	0.89	-	1.98	0.93	3.19	5.85	0.73	-	4.00	0.89	5.07
Sakthi Sugars Ltd	9.57	0.29	7.42	2.59	1.11	-41.25	7.57	1.58	24.07	6.57	1.13	1.92
Thiru Arooran Sugars Ltd	9.40	0.45	34.37	3.28	0.68	-15.53	3.14	1.67	30.88	5.27	0.92	-5.93
Ugar Sugar Works Ltd	12.19	1.02	-15.53	13.75	0.66	27.50	3.73	1.79	-50.41	9.89	1.01	-1.39
Medium-sized												
Kothari Sugars & Chemicals Ltd	6.08	0.17	2.66	1.08	2.24	-	3.68	1.81	-	3.61	1.21	-4.52
Sri Chamundeswari Sugars Ltd	8.44	0.64	-11.50	2.85	1.70	-	7.11	1.43	10.13	6.37	1.13	-10.63
Sri Sarvaraya Sugars Ltd	25.55	0.72	26.51	30.30	0.54	16.54	58.02	1.05	20.97	37.96	1.00	4.15
Kakatiya Cements Sugar & Industries Ltd	10.83	0.28	5.55	6.09	0.44	-2.75	10.46	0.38	20.11	9.13	0.41	2.69

Small-sized												
Dharani Sugars & Chemicals Ltd	5.00	0.49	13.82	0.47	0.99	-	0.73	1.62	47.58	2.07	1.26	-2.54
Empee Sugars & Chemicals Ltd	0.50	1.93	-	0.59	1.11	-	1.13	1.02	2.47	0.74	1.24	15.32
India Sugars and Refineries Ltd	7.68	1.16	-	0.10	2.24	-	11.85	1.15	32.08	6.55	1.54	13.16
Ponni Sugars Ltd	3.07	0.65	-11.92	428.0	2.24	-	5.42	0.95	43.81	145.50	3.79	0.51

Source: Computed from the annual accounts of the respective industry.

Table 4.24. Analysis of Variance - ANOVA

Particulars	Large-sized		Medium-sized		Small-sized	
	F value	F critical value	F value	F critical value	F value	F critical value
Between the years	1.91**	1.81	1.29	1.94	0.99	1.94
Between the Industry	5.40**	2.21	10.71**	2.83	1.00	2.83

Industry-wise Earnings per share - Paired sample t-test

Industry	Paired sample t-test		
	Initial phase and growth phase	Initial phase and maturity phase	Growth phase and maturity phase
Large-sized (n=7)			
Bannari Amman Sugars Ltd	5.04*	3.07**	2.05
EID Parry Ltd	3.24**	1.47	0.68
Jeypore Sugars & Chemicals Ltd	2.03	0.43	1.23
Rajshree Sugars & Chemicals Ltd	1.47	1.87	2.66**
Sakthi Sugars Ltd	2.97**	0.46	0.81
Thiru Arooran Sugars Ltd	2.36***	3.57**	0.05
Ugar Sugar Works Ltd	0.23	1.17	1.72
Medium-sized (n=4)			
Kothari Sugars & Chemicals Ltd	4.26**	0.80	0.75
Sri Chamundeswari Sugars Ltd	1.02	0.22	1.55
Sri Sarvaraya Sugars Ltd	0.51	1.28	1.29
Kakatiya Cements Sugar & Industries Ltd	2.54***	0.20	2.01
Small-sized (n=4)			
Dharani Sugars & Chemicals Ltd	4.16**	5.59*	0.49
Empee Sugars & Chemicals Ltd	0.14	1.47	1.07
India Sugars and Refineries Ltd	1.88	1.53	1.91
Ponni Sugars Ltd	0.99	0.74	0.99

*Significant at 0.01 level; **Significant at 0.05 level; ***Significant at 0.10 level

Source: Computed

Significant differences in the average of earnings per share of Rajshree Sugars & Chemicals Ltd under large-sized were also observed during growth phase and maturity phase.

The above overall analysis shows that the performance of the three sectors during the study period was varied between the sectors, between the phases and in between the industry. The multiple results indicate that the industry selected for the study consists of mixed performers with relation to its earnings per share.

Dividend Pay Out Ratio

This ratio indicates what percentage of firms' earnings after tax less preference dividend is being paid to equity shareholders in the form of dividend. Dividend pay out ratio is a major aspect of the dividend policy of a company. It measures the relationship between the earnings belonging to the equity shareholders and the dividend paid to them. A ratio lower than 100 per cent denotes the retention of distributable earnings whereas a ratio higher than 100 per cent indicates the distribution of a part of resources by way of dividends. The investors have a marked performer for higher dividend pay out ratio. The ratio is a list of managerial ability and reputation of company.

Table 4.25 and Fig. 4.9 showed a fluctuating trend in the dividend pay out ratio of the selected South Indian private sector sugar industry during the 15 year study period. On an average the sample South Indian sugar industry had the overall dividend pay out ratio of 68.19 per cent with a co-efficient variation of 1.43. The average dividend pay out ratio varied from sector to sector, the highest average was 33.97 in large-sized sugar industry followed by medium-sized sector (14.36%) and small-sized (8.77%) sugar industry. The CV value of these ratios show a very high fluctuation in the dividend pay out ratio of the selected sectors during the study period. Such fluctuations could be attributed to the industries' efforts to maintain stable dividend policy, irrespective of their

Table 4.25. Analysis of Dividend pay out ratio of selected South Indian private sector Sugar Industry (1991-92 to 2005-06)

(Per cent)

Particulars	**Initial phase [1992-96]**	**Growth phase [1997-2001]**	**Maturity phase [2002-2006]**	**Whole period [1992-2006]**
Large-sized (n=7)				
Mean	94.07	95.53	14.96	**68.19**
CV	1.89	1.25	1.67	**1.02**
CAGR	65.78	45.32	-6.89	**-1.52**
Medium-sized (n=4)				
Mean	19.01	16.85	7.22	**14.36**
CV	0.68	1.13	1.39	**0.67**
CAGR	-9.09	12.08	-7.36	**-8.66**
Small-sized (n=4)				
Mean	19.40	5.56	1.35	**8.77**
CV	1.07	2.00	2.00	**0.71**
CAGR	-1.35	-	-	**-7.65**
Whole industry (n=15)				
Mean	**54.14**	**50.56**	**9.27**	**37.99**
CV	**2.28**	**1.79**	**1.95**	**1.43**
CAGR	**51.06**	**27.94**	**-5.62**	**-3.47**

Analysis of Variance

Sources of variation	**F value**	**F critical value**
Between the years	0.97	2.06
Between the sector	4.69**	3.34

actual earnings. These fluctuations could also be resulted from the industry policy in the light of economic conditions and industry practices.

Dividend pay out ratio - Paired sample t-test

Industry	Initial phase and Growth phase	Growth phase and Maturity phase	Initial phase and Maturity phase
Large-sized	0.03	1.77	1.25
Medium-sized	1.41	6.08*	7.01*
Small-sized	1.65	0.71	4.12**
Whole industry	**0.15**	**2.04**	**1.57**

*Significant at 0.01 level; **Significant at 0.05 level

Source: Computed.

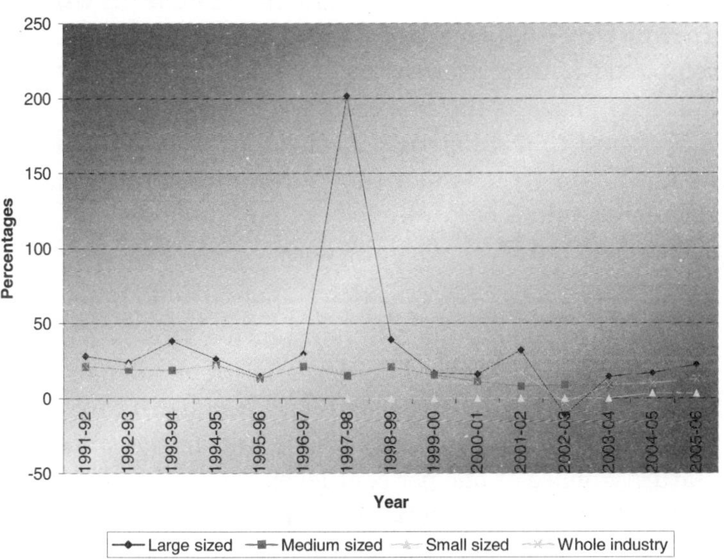

Fig. 4.9. Dividend pay out ratio of Selected South Indian Private Sector Sugar Industry

Higher pay out ratio in the whole industry was registered during initial phase and growth phase because of the highest average pay out ratio in the large-sized sugar industry during the phases. The average dividend pay out ratio of large-sized sugar industry was very high during growth phase and the ratio deeply declined to 14.96 per cent in maturity phase. This sudden decrease or lower pay out ratio could be attributed to the retention of slightly over 85 per cent of its net income to reinvest for the shareholders' future benefit. Similarly the pay out ratio of medium-sized and small-sized sugar industry had the comparatively higher ratio during initial phase and growth phase than maturity phase.

The CV value of this ratio during the three phases showed very high fluctuations. It is also inferred that the large-sized sugar industry, medium-sized and small-sized sugar industry have registered negative compound annual growth rate during three phases and whole period. Similarly the compound annual growth rate was not able obtain during maturity phase as the average pay out ratio was zero. Table 4.25 shows that differences in dividend pay out ratio was insignificant in between the years and industry as the calculated values of F were lower than the table values of F at five per cent level of significance.

In order to test the hypothesis, paired sample t-test has been applied among the different phases. It is also evident from the table that the differences in the dividend pay out ratio of medium-sized sugar industry was significant during growth phase and maturity phase and initial phase and maturity phase at one per cent level. Similarly such significant differences were noticed in small-sized sugar industry during initial phase and maturity phase. However, the differences were insignificant in rest of the cases. A notable inference could be observed from this analysis that there were no significant differences among the ratios of large-sized sugar industry during three phases because it maintained sustained policy over divided payment.

The analysis of industry wise dividend pay out ratio during three different phases has been given in Table 4.26. Higher dividend pay out ratios were found in Rajshree Sugars & Chemicals Ltd, Ugar Sugar Works Ltd, Thiru Arooran Sugars Ltd, EID Parry Ltd and Bannari Amman Sugars Ltd under large-sized sugar industry. These industries were slower growing companies as they have higher pay out ratios. Perhaps these industries retain two third of its net income for the future benefit of the shareholders. Only Kakatiya Cements Sugar & Industries Ltd under medium-sized sugar industry had paid on an average of 27.70 per cent dividend, which is higher than the industry average of 22.02 per cent. The rest of the industries under medium-sized sugar industry have paid minimum of 8.65 per cent and maximum of 15.06 per cent over the study period. It is inferred from the table that no industry under small-sized sugar industry had paid dividend more than the industry average. The Empee Sugars & Chemicals Ltd under small-sized sugar industry had not paid dividend during the whole period of post liberalization as it incurred loss during the period.

In brief majority of the large-sized sugar industry has been making higher rates of dividend payment annually. This higher pay out ratio indicates that the industries are slower growing as the retention ratio is less.

Table 4.27 reveals that differences in the dividend pay out ratio was significant in between the industry under medium-sized sector as the calculated value of F was greater than the table value of F at five per cent level of significance. However they were insignificant in between the years in medium-sized sugar industry. Similarly the differences in this ratio were insignificant in between the years and the sectors in the remaining cases, as the calculated values of F were lower than the table values of F at five per cent level of significance.

Table 4.26. Analysis of Industry-wise Dividend pay out ratio of selected South Indian private sector Sugar industry (1991-92 to 2005-06)

(Per cent)

Industry	Initial phase (1992-96)			Growth phase (1997-2001)			Maturity phase (2002-2006)			Whole period (1992-2006)		
	Mean	CV	CAGR	Mean	CV	CAGR	Mean	CV	CAGR	Mean	CV	CAGR
1	2	3	4	5	6	7	8	9	10	11	12	13
Large-sized												
Bannari Amman Sugars Ltd	48.56	0.98	-9.71	16.51	0.11	-3.89	13.36	0.43	-10.01	26.14	1.17	-6.41
EID Parry Ltd	495.87	2.14	-	29.06	0.21	2.11	33.83	0.22	0	186.25	3.28	3.48
Jeypore Sugars & Chemicals Ltd	7.66	1.06	-	25.83	0.66	-	-28.31	-3.94	0.40	1.73	37.54	9.38
Rajshree Sugars & Chemicals Ltd	9.96	1.39	-	272.55	2.03	-10.63	44.79	0.29	2.29	109.10	2.93	-
Sakthi Sugars Ltd	22.22	0.20	-6.62	10.89	1.54	-	1.07	2.24	-	11.40	1.14	-8.59
Thiru Arooran Sugars Ltd	32.50	0.54	-21.93	46.01	1.24	-	6.34	1.38	-	28.28	1.29	-9.33
Ugar Sugar Works Ltd	41.76	0.47	-23.04	267.88	2.02	-7.70	33.67	1.29	-26.81	114.44	2.72	-6.08
Medium-sized												
Kothari Sugars & Chemicals Ltd	36.99	0.11	-1.65	8.18	2.24	-	0	-	-	15.06	1.28	-
Sri Chamundeswari Sugars Ltd	15.72	0.70	-	2.37	2.24	-	0	-	-	6.03	1.61	-
Sri Sarvaraya Sugars Ltd	6.11	0.89	-	12.21	0.54	-14.02	7.64	0.69	52.98	8.65	0.69	-2.83
Kakatiya Cements Sugar & Industries Ltd	17.21	0.15	1.36	44.65	0.48	1.65	21.24	0.35	-16.74	27.70	0.63	-2.26

Small-sized												
Dharani Sugars & Chemicals Ltd	41.56	0.76	-	0	-	-	0	-	-	13.85	1.91	-
Empee Sugars & Chemicals Ltd	0	-	-	0	-	-	0	-	-	0	-	-
India Sugars and Refineries Ltd	3.50	1.45	-	22.22	2.24	-	0	-	-	8.57	3.33	-
Ponni Sugars Ltd	32.54	0.56	-	0	-	-	5.41	1.37	-	12.65	1.43	-7.71

Source: Computed from the annual accounts of the respective industry.

It can also be viewed from the table that Rajshree Sugars Chemicals Ltd, Sakthi Sugars Ltd and Thiru Arooran Sugars Ltd of large-sized sugar industry dividend pay out ratios showed significant differences during initial phase and maturity phase as per the t-values. It was further noticed that such significant differences were noticed in Kothari Sugars & Chemicals Ltd and Sri Chamundeswari Sugars Ltd under medium-sized sugar industry during initial phase and maturity phase, Kothari Sugars & Chemicals Ltd and Kakatiya Cements Sugar & Industries Ltd under medium-sized sugar industry during initial phase and growth phase. The difference in this ratio was significant in Kakatiya Cements Sugar & Industries Ltd during growth phase and maturity phase at ten per cent level of significance.

PROFITABILITY FROM THE VIEW POINT OF UTILIZATION OF ASSETS

The overall profitability of any business largely depends on two factors viz, the rate of return on capital employed and turnover. The turnover refers the number of times an asset flows through a business firms' operations and into sales. The triangular relationship among the sales, profits and assets greatly affect the profitability of a business. The relationship between the sales and profits is known as profit margin and relationship between the sales and assets is known as asset turnover. Any change in assts turnover would effect the profitability of the business. Profitability is the end product of profit margin and assets turnover[19].

Table 4.27. Analysis of Variance - ANOVA

Particulars	Large-sized		Medium-sized		Small-sized	
	F value	F critical value	F value	F critical value	F value	F critical value
Between the years	0.83	1.81	0.70	1.94	1.21	1.94
Between the Industry	0.85	2.21	6.47**	2.83	1.35	2.83

Industry-wise Dividend pay out ratio - Paired sample t-test

Industry	Paired sample t-test		
	Initial phase and growth phase	Initial phase and maturity phase	Growth phase and maturity phase
Large-sized (n=7)			
Bannari Amman Sugars Ltd	1.54	1.60	1.10
EID Parry Ltd	0.98	0.97	1.08
Jeypore Sugars & Chemicals Ltd	2.06	0.71	1.05
Rajshree Sugars & Chemicals Ltd	1.05	3.67**	0.94
Sakthi Sugars Ltd	1.46	7.03*	1.24
Thiru Arooran Sugars Ltd	0.52	2.63***	1.45
Ugar Sugar Works Ltd	0.91	0.47	0.96
Medium-sized (n=4)			
Kothari Sugars & Chemicals Ltd	3.71**	20.75*	1.00
Sri Chamundeswari Sugars Ltd	1.88	3.19**	1.00
Sri Sarvaraya Sugars Ltd	2.11	0.36	1.32
Kakatiya Cements Sugar & Industries Ltd	2.65***	1.15	2.34***
Small-sized (n=4)			
Dharani Sugars & Chemicals Ltd	2.94**	2.94**	-
Empee Sugars & Chemicals Ltd	-	-	-
India Sugars and Refineries Ltd	0.81	1.55	1.00
Ponni Sugars Ltd	-	-	-

*Significant at 0.01 level; **Significant at 0.05 level; ***Significant at 0.10 level
Source: Computed

Assets are the economic resources owned by the business which can be conveniently expressed in monetary term.[20] The assets are usually significant for the owners, investors, management, bankers, creditors, government and public. The assets communicate the financial fact about an enterprise or economic entity to those who have an interest in interpreting and using those facts. These serve as means for analyzing and controlling the operation of the enterprise and planning future action.[21] Turnover ratios are concerned with how efficiently the assets of the firm are managed or utilised. These ratios indicate the rate at which different assets are turned over in the process of doing business. The greater the rate of turnover, the more efficient the utilization, other things being equal, resulting in higher profitability. Thus, the assets turnover helps us to know the efficiency of use of assets in generating the profits. Hence, a detailed analysis of assets turnover has been made for better study and tracing out the factors responsible for changes in the profitability.

Total Assets Turnover

The total assets turnover ratio is an indication of financial soundness of the business in terms of the sales revenue generated against total funds employed in the business. This ratio indicates the overall efficiency with which total assets are used. The total assets taken here are after deducting the depreciation provision, intangible assets and miscellaneous non-current assets. Using the total asset turnover ratio alone does not lead to any firm conclusions about a company's efficiency. However, when the information about asset efficiency is joined with information about the nature of the business, the industry and economic conditions, it is possible to gain real insight.

The total assets turnover ratio of the selected South private sector Indian Sugar Industry during the period of study has been given in Table 4.28 and Fig. 4.10. The table implies that the sector average ratio of asset turnover was very close to the industry average. The overall ratio of the selected South Indian private sector sugar industry was 0.87 times with co-efficient variation of 0.29. The highest average total assets turnover ratio 0.94 times was recorded in small-sized sugar industry followed by 0.87 times in large-sized sugar industry and 0.80 times in medium-sized sugar industry. The CV value of these ratios shows the low fluctuation in total assets turnover ratio of selected South Indian private sector sugar industry during the study period. Such low fluctuation could be attributed to the stable investment in fixed assets and current assets and steady sales revenue over the period of study. The whole industry witnessed a bottom side positive compound annual growth rate in this ratio whereas large-sized sugar industry registered a negative compound annual rate on the one hand and medium-sized sugar industry have posted slightly over the industry average growth rate. It could be observed that the small-sized sugar industry have utilized its assets more efficiently to generate sales than the large-sized and medium-sized sugar industry as its average total assets turnover ratio was higher than the other sectors.

Analysis of variance has been applied among the years and between the sectors to test the hypothesis. Since the calculated values of F (1.11 and 2.48) are lower than the table values of F (2.06 and 3.34) at five per cent level between the years and sectors, it is concluded the null hypothesis is accepted. The acceptance of the null hypothesis would indicate that there is no significant difference in the mean percentage of asset turnover ratio between the years and sectors.

It could find from Table 4.28 by dividing the entire study period of fifteen years after liberalization into three phases initial phase, growth phase and maturity phase, that the overall total assets turnover ratio of selected South Indian private sector Sugar Industry showed declining trend during growth phase. It declined from 0.96 times during initial phase to 0.82 times during growth phase. Such a declining trend could be characterized by the increase in sales was not in tune with that of total assets, due to market conditions, revaluation of assets, development of plans etc. But during maturity phase the small-sized sugar industry has posted an increasing trend in the ratio, because of increased sales resulted from improved market conditions.

The CV value of this ratio during three phases showed low fluctuations. It is also inferred that the large-sized sugar industry during initial phase and growth phase, medium-sized sugar industry and small-sized sugar industry during initial phase have registered a negative compound annual growth rate. It is also evident from the table that there were no significant differences in total assets turnover ratio of selected South Indian private sector sugar industry in between years and sectors as the calculated values of F were lower than the table values of F at five per cent level of significance.

Table 4.28. Analysis of Total assets turnover ratio of selected South Indian private sector Sugar Industry (1991-92 to 2005-06)

(in times)

Particulars	Initial phase [1992-96]	Growth phase [1997-2001]	Maturity phase [2002-2006]	Whole period [1992-2006]
Large-sized (n=7)				
Mean	1.04	0.82	0.74	**0.87**
CV	0.37	0.34	0.30	**0.32**
CAGR	-3.09	-0.25	3.99	**-1.73**
Medium-sized (n=4)				
Mean	0.91	0.76	0.72	**0.80**
CV	0.37	0.56	0.35	**0.39**
CAGR	-3.88	0.89	7.01	**1.25**
Small-sized (n=4)				
Mean	0.85	0.86	1.10	**0.94**
CV	0.18	0.42	0.26	**0.20**
CAGR	-4.47	6.17	9.01	**2.99**
Whole industry (n=15)				
Mean	**0.96**	**0.82**	**0.83**	**0.87**
CV	**0.33**	**0.39**	**0.34**	**0.29**
CAGR	**-3.70**	**1.95**	**6.27**	**0.26**

Analysis of Variance

Sources of variation	F value	F critical value
Between the years	1.11	2.06
Between the sector	2.48	3.34

Total assets turnover ratio - Paired sample t-test

Industry	Initial phase and Growth phase	Growth phase and Maturity phase	Initial phase and Maturity phase
Large-sized	4.38**	1.30	4.60**
Medium-sized	2.13***	0.44	1.30
Small-sized	0.14	3.10**	2.04
Whole industry	**2.74*** **	**0.33**	**1.46**

**Significant at 0.05 level; ***Significant at 0.10 level

Source: Computed

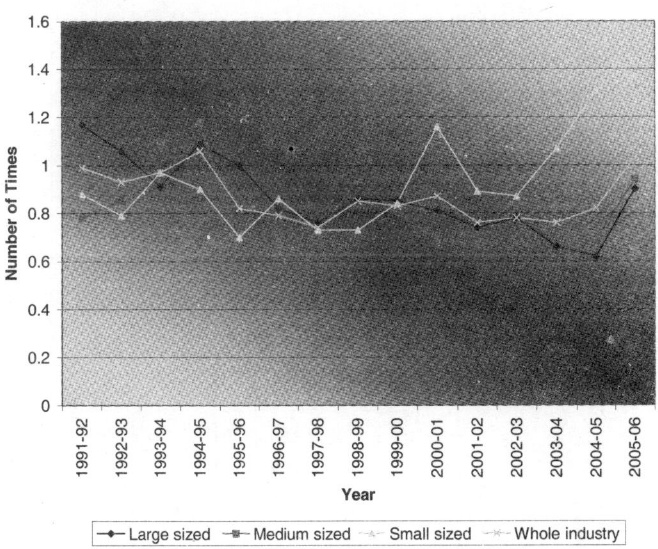

Fig. 4.10. Total Assets Turnover ratio of selected South Indian Private Sector Sugar Industry.

Table 4.29. Analysis of Industry wise Total assets turnover ratio of selected South Indian private sector Sugar industry (1991-92 to 2005-06)

(in times)

Industry	Initial phase (1992-96)			Growth phase (1997-2001)			Maturity phase (2002-2006)			Whole period (1992-2006)		
	Mean	CV	CAGR	Mean	CV	CAGR	Mean	CV	CAGR	Mean	CV	CAGR
1	2	3	4	5	6	7	8	9	10	11	12	13
Large-sized												
Bannari Amman Sugars Ltd	0.84	0.21	-1.65	0.86	0.10	-0.20	0.83	0.09	1.36	0.84	0.13	-0.55
EID Parry Ltd	1.66	0.27	-13.65	1.06	0.09	4.73	0.91	0.26	-4.61	1.21	0.36	-5.77
Jeypore Sugars & Chemicals Ltd	0.76	0.17	-7.70	0.63	0.09	5.06	0.70	0.16	5.39	0.69	0.16	-0.63
Rajshree Sugars & Chemicals Ltd	0.97	0.25	4.40	0.75	0.07	-2.09	0.89	0.24	7.42	0.87	0.23	0.13
Sakthi Sugars Ltd	0.88	0.05	-0.20	0.71	0.18	-4.85	0.49	0.33	4.06	0.69	0.29	-1.73
Thiru Arooran Sugars Ltd	0.67	0.15	-6.89	0.45	0.24	5.71	0.38	0.56	21.61	0.50	0.38	0.26
Ugar Sugar Works Ltd	1.53	0.20	4.40	1.29	0.11	-4.61	0.96	0.17	2.66	1.26	0.25	-1.39
Medium-sized												
Kothari Sugars & Chemicals Ltd	0.69	0.16	-3.89	0.38	0.41	-1.87	0.72	0.42	22.07	0.60	0.39	4.00
Sri Chamundeswari Sugars Ltd	0.99	0.17	-3.43	0.77	0.42	-6.89	0.42	0.31	-1.87	0.74	0.41	-3.35
Sri Sarvaraya Sugars Ltd	1.34	0.51	-9.41	1.35	0.31	9.58	1.06	0.13	4.06	1.25	0.36	1.39
Kakatiya Cements Sugar & Industries Ltd	0.61	0.18	4.40	0.53	0.04	1.17	0.62	0.16	5.71	0.59	0.15	3.01

Small-sized												
Dharani Sugars & Chemicals Ltd	0.90	0.33	-11.59	0.55	0.34	8.73	0.70	0.50	13.34	0.72	0.42	-4.36
Empee Sugars & Chemicals Ltd	0.73	1.06	23.42	0.55	0.15	-5.34	1.23	0.63	44.82	0.84	0.79	14.77
India Sugars and Refineries Ltd	1.05	0.16	0.98	1.15	0.37	-17.17	1.12	0.23	-1.65	1.11	0.26	1.11
Ponni Sugars Ltd	0.71	0.45	-17.59	1.20	0.79	34.06	1.36	0.17	1.92	1.09	0.57	1.51

Source: Computed from the annual accounts of the respective industry.

In order to test the hypothesis paired sample t-test has been applied among the different phases. The analysis showed that there were significant differences in total assets turnover ratios in large-sized sugar industry, medium-sized sugar industry and whole industry during initial phase and growth phase. Such significant differences were also found in small-sized sugar industry during growth phase and maturity phase and in large-sized sugar industry during initial phase and maturity phase.

The industry-wise total assets turnover ratios at different phases and for the whole period are presented in Table 4.29. The efficiency of EID Parry Ltd and Ugar Sugar Works Ltd under large-sized sugar industry was satisfactory because its average total assets turnover ratios were higher than the industry average. In medium-sized sugar industry the efficiency of Sri Sarvaraya Sugars Ltd was satisfactory. In small-sized sugar industry the efficiency of India Sugars and Refineries Ltd and Ponni Sugars Ltd was satisfactory because its average ratios were higher than the industry average. The assets utilization efficiency of Thiru Arooran Sugars Ltd was the worst among the selected South Indian private sector Sugar Industry during the study period because its average ratio (0.50 times) was the least among the industry and below the industry average. The table also reveals that the low fluctuating trend of this ratio among the industry selected under different sectors of South Indian private sector Sugar Industry.

Table 4.30 shows that differences in the total assets turnover ratio were significant in between the years and the industry under large-sized sugar industry as calculated values of F were higher than the table values of F at five per cent level of significance. Similarly the difference was significant in between the industry under medium-sized sugar industry. However, they were insignificant in between the years and industry in all the remaining cases as the calculated values of F were lower than the table values of F at five per cent level of significance.

Table 4.30. Analysis of Variance - ANOVA

Particulars	Large-sized		Medium-sized		Small-sized	
	F value	F critical value	F value	F critical value	F value	F critical value
Between the years	4.07**	1.81	1.43	1.94	0.62	1.94
Between the Industry	27.63**	2.21	17.96**	2.83	2.01	2.83

Industry-wise Total assets turnover ratio - Paired sample t-test

Industry	Paired sample t-test		
	Initial phase and growth phase	Initial phase and maturity phase	Growth phase and maturity phase
Large-sized (n=7)			
Bannari Amman Sugars Ltd	0.18	0.07	0.71
EID Parry Ltd	2.46***	4.06**	1.19
Jeypore Sugars & Chemicals Ltd	1.74	0.70	1.49
Rajshree Sugars & Chemicals Ltd	1.95	0.50	1.25
Sakthi Sugars Ltd	4.12**	4.74*	1.79
Thiru Arooran Sugars Ltd	2.76***	2.09	0.96
Ugar Sugar Works Ltd	1.42	3.54	3.09**
Medium-sized (n=4)			
Kothari Sugars & Chemicals Ltd	5.17*	0.18	2.49***
Sri Chamundeswari Sugars Ltd	1.09	4.00**	2.11
Sri Sarvaraya Sugars Ltd	0.04	0.78	1.30
Kakatiya Cements Sugar & Industries Ltd	1.55	0.23	2.15***
Small-sized (n=4)			
Dharani Sugars & Chemicals Ltd	1.78	0.88	1.38
Empee Sugars & Chemicals Ltd	0.53	1.78	1.88
India Sugars and Refineries Ltd	0.46	0.79	0.15
Ponni Sugars Ltd	0.94	3.65**	0.39

*Significant at 0.01 level; **Significant at 0.05 level; ***Significant at 0.10 level

Source: Computed

Table 4.30 also depicts from the paired samples t-test analysis that there were significant differences in the total assets turnover ratios of few large-sized sugar industry during initial phase and growth phase as per the t-value. Such significant differences were noticed in EID Parry Ltd, Sakthi Sugars Ltd and Thiru Arooran Sugars Ltd under large-sized sugar industry and Kothari Sugars & Chemicals Ltd under medium-sized sugar industry. Similarly the differences were also noticed in EID Parry Ltd, Sakthi Sugars Ltd and Ugar Sugar Works Ltd under large-sized sugar industry, Sri Chamundeswari Sugars Ltd under medium-sized sugar industry and Ponni Sugars Ltd under small-sized sugar industry during initial phase and maturity phase. During growth phase and maturity phase the differences were significant in Ugar Sugar Works Ltd, Kothari Sugars & Chemicals Ltd and Kakatiya Cements Sugar & Industries Ltd.

In brief most of the selected South Indian private sector Sugar industry have maintained stable total assets turnover ratio over the period of study. The overall assets utilization efficiency of the selected South Indian private sector sugar industry was satisfactory. Among the selected sectors small-sized sector was found more efficient than others in respect of asset utilisation. These ratios indicated that the industries have utilized its assets effectively to generate sales revenue.

Fixed Assets Turnover Ratio

The fixed assets turnover ratio represents the extent of utilization of fixed assets in terms of the sales achieved. The ratio indicated whether the investment in fixed asset was judicious or not if compared with a previous period. It has been calculated to determine whether investment decision has been good or bad in the sense of their efficient utilization. A high ratio will show that the concern is over trading on its assets, while a low ratio will indicate that excessive investment have been made in the fixed assets. It is also essential that the assets should be effectively utilized to generate sufficient earning. The fixed assets turnover ratio of selected South Indian private sector Sugar Industry has been catalogued in Table 4.31 and Appendix Fig. 4.11.

Table 4.31 shows a fluctuating trend in the fixed asset turnover ratio of the selected South Indian private sector sugar industry during fifteen year study period. On an average the sample South Indian private sector sugar industry had the overall fixed asset turnover ratio of 1.40 times with a co-efficient of variation of 0.35. The average fixed assets turnover ratio was varied from sector to sector, the highest average was 1.63 times in large-sized sugar industry followed by small-sized (1.32 times) and medium-sized (1.22 times) sugar industry. The average ratio of fixed assets turnover was higher than the industry average in large-sized sugar industry. The CV value of these ratios shows high fluctuation in the fixed asset turnover ratio of selected sectors of South Indian private sector sugar industry during the study period. Such fluctuation could be attributed to the differences in the growth rates of sales and fixed assets because of the external factors such as government policy and market conditions. All the selected sectors and whole industry witnessed negative compound annual growth rate of this ratio during the study period.

By dividing the entire study period of fifteen years after liberalization into three phases, initial phase, growth phase and maturity phase, it could find from Table 4.31 that the overall fixed asset turnover ratio of the selected South Indian private sector Sugar Industry showed a declining trend during the growth phase. It declined from 1.80 times during initial phase to 1.29 times during growth phase. Such a declining trend could be attributed to all the selected sectors in general and large-sized sector to a large extent in particular due to downward market and economic conditions. Further it declined from 1.29 times during growth phase to 1.23 times during maturity phase. The decline caused due to decrease in the ratio of large-sized and medium-sized sugar industry.

Table 4.31. Analysis of Fixed assets turnover ratio of selected South Indian private sector Sugar Industry (1991-92 to 2005-06)

(in times)

Particulars	Initial phase [1992-96]	Growth phase [1997-2001]	Maturity phase [2002-2006]	Whole period [1992-2006]
Large-sized (n=7)				
Mean	2.21	1.46	1.23	**1.63**
CV	0.50	0.35	0.21	**0.36**
CAGR	-2.32	-3.60	0	**-3.91**
Medium-sized (n=4)				
Mean	1.48	1.16	1.02	**1.22**
CV	0.44	0.51	0.31	**0.40**
CAGR	-3.64	-1.67	0	**-1.28**
Small-sized (n=4)				
Mean	1.40	1.13	1.43	**1.32**
CV	0.31	0.26	0.33	**0.19**
CAGR	1.40	-7.79	11.46	**2.32**
Whole industry (n=15)				
Mean	**1.80**	**1.29**	**1.23**	**1.40**
CV	**0.50**	**0.38**	**0.29**	**0.35**
CAGR	**-1.71**	**-4.01**	**3.38**	**-1.70**

Analysis of Variance

Sources of variation	F value	F critical value
Between the years	2.73**	2.06
Between the sector	8.75**	3.34

Fixed assets turnover ratio - Paired sample t-test

Industry	Initial phase and Growth phase	Growth phase and Maturity phase	Initial phase and Maturity phase
Large-sized	14.75*	3.22**	13.96*
Medium-sized	2.04	1.22	2.60***
Small-sized	1.68	1.32	0.25
Whole Industry	**4.89***	**0.22**	**3.49***

*Significant at 0.01 level; **Significant at 0.05 level; *** Significant at 0.10 level
Source: Computed

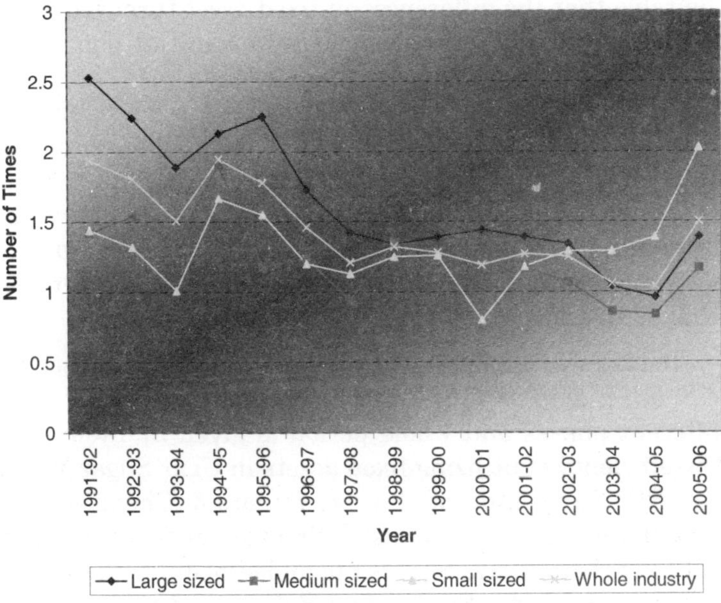

Fig. 4.11. Fixed Assets Turnover ratio of Selected South Indian Private Sector Sugar Industry

In order to test the hypothesis, analysis of variance has been applied among the years and between the sectors. It is concluded that null hypothesis is rejected since the calculated values of F (2.73 and 8.75) were greater than the table values of F (2.06 and 3.34) at five per cent level of significance. The rejection of null hypothesis indicated that there were significant differences in the fixed asset turnover ratio between the years and sectors.

• The CV value of this ratio during three phases showed low fluctuations. It is also inferred that the large-sized and medium-sized sugar industry have registered a negative compound annual growth rate in all the three phases, while in the small-sized sugar industry such negative compound annual growth rate was only during growth phase.

In order to test the hypothesis, paired samples t-test has been applied among the different phases. It is evident from the table that the differences in fixed asset turnover ratios of large-sized sugar industry between initial phase and growth phase, growth phase and maturity phase and initial phase and maturity phase were significant. Such significant differences in the industry under medium-sized sector during initial phase and maturity phase were noticed at ten per cent level of significance. In the whole industry the differences were found in between initial phase and growth phase and initial phase and maturity phase at one per cent level of significance.

Industry wise fixed asset turnover ratio of different sectors of South Indian private sector Sugar Industry during three different phases and whole period is given in Table 4.32. The efficiency of utilizing fixed assets in Ugar Sugar Works Ltd, EID Parry Ltd and Jeypore Sugars & Chemicals Ltd under large-sized sugar industry, Sri Chamundeswari Sugars Ltd and Sri Sarvaraya Sugars Ltd under medium-sized sugar industry and India Sugars and Refineries Ltd and Ponni Sugars Ltd under small-sized sugar industry was satisfactory during the period of study because its average ratios of fixed asset turnover was higher than the industry average of 1.44 times. Among the sample industries Ugar Sugar Works Ltd was the most efficient in generating sales revenue from its investment in fixed assets because it generated the highest average sale of Rs.2.48 for one rupee investment in fixed asset during the study period. Kakatiya Cements Sugar & Industries Ltd was the worst performer in generating sales revenue utilizing its fixed asset because the least average sale of Re. 0.78 for one rupee investment in fixed asset. Table 4.32 witnessed that majority of the selected industry under large-sized industry and medium-sized sugar industry had negative compound annual growth rate in fixed asset turnover ratio during the study period. The table also reveals that a fluctuating trend of this ratio among industries selected under different sectors of South Indian private sector Sugar Industry.

Table 4.33 exhibits that differences in the fixed asset turnover ratio was significant in between the years and industry in large-sized sugar industry as the calculated values of F were greater than the table values of F at five per cent level of significance. Similarly such differences in between the industry were insignificant. However, they were insignificant in between the years and industry under medium-sized sector and insignificant in between years under small-sized sugar industry.

It can be viewed from Table 4.33 that majority of the large-sized sugar industry's fixed asset turnover ratio showed significant differences during initial phase and growth phase and initial phase and maturity phase as per the t-values. It is further noticed that such significant difference in Kothari Sugars & Chemicals Ltd under medium-sized sugar industry and Dharani Sugars & Chemicals Ltd under small-sized sugar industry during initial phase and growth phase. It was also observed that the differences in the ratios of Kothari Sugars & Chemicals Ltd and Sri Chamundeswari Sugars Ltd under medium-sized and Dharani Sugars & Chemicals Ltd and Empee Sugars & Chemicals Ltd under small-sized sugar industry were significant during initial phase and maturity phase. Such significant differences were found in EID Parry Ltd and Ugar Sugar Works Ltd among the selected sectors of South Indian private sector Sugar Industry.

Table 4.32. Analysis of Industry wise Fixed assets turnover ratio of selected South Indian private sector Sugar industry (1991-92 to 2005-06)

(in times)

Industry	Initial phase (1992-96)			Growth phase (1997-2001)			Maturity phase (2002-2006)			Whole period (1992-2006)		
	Mean	CV	CAGR	Mean	CV	CAGR	Mean	CV	CAGR	Mean	CV	CAGR
1	2	3	4	5	6	7	8	9	10	11	12	13
Large-sized												
Bannari Amman Sugars Ltd	1.36	0.28	-3.43	1.33	0.11	0.59	1.30	0.13	-4.13	1.33	0.18	-2.63
EID Parry Ltd	4.00	0.27	-13.30	1.82	0.10	-0.40	1.39	0.29	-4.61	2.40	0.56	-23.62
Jeypore Sugars & Chemicals Ltd	1.94	0.37	-12.60	1.38	0.10	5.22	1.39	0.08	-1.87	1.55	0.31	-13.30
Rajshree Sugars & Chemicals Ltd	1.59	0.36	13.94	1.32	0.17	-8.83	1.25	0.21	4.90	1.39	0.28	1.92
Sakthi Sugars Ltd	1.86	0.13	0.40	1.25	0.15	-3.66	1.01	0.42	-0.40	1.37	0.34	-4.36
Thiru Arooran Sugars Ltd	1.18	0.18	6.19	0.77	0.31	-3.89	0.74	0.48	19.73	0.90	0.37	5.39
Ugar Sugar Works Ltd	3.53	0.16	6.03	2.42	0.22	-9.71	1.50	0.18	-2.75	2.48	0.39	-13.65
Medium-sized												
Kothari Sugars & Chemicals Ltd	1.23	0.19	-6.36	0.56	0.43	-15.14	0.64	0.48	21.24	0.81	0.48	-1.23
Sri Chamundeswari Sugars Ltd	2.19	0.23	-1.65	1.79	0.39	-1.65	1.19	0.42	-7.70	1.72	0.39	-2.54
Sri Sarvaraya Sugars Ltd	1.79	0.28	-9.12	1.51	0.13	5.06	1.36	0.09	-1.02	1.55	0.23	-1.90
Kakatiya Cements Sugar & Industries Ltd	0.70	0.23	10.53	0.77	0.05	-1.02	0.88	0.19	-0.81	0.78	0.19	3.39

Small-sized												
Dharani Sugars & Chemicals Ltd	1.68	0.34	5.06	0.98	0.30	3.37	1.16	0.55	17.50	1.27	0.45	1.61
Empee Sugars & Chemicals Ltd	0.83	0.31	6.81	0.93	0.14	-5.34	1.19	0.47	32.41	0.98	0.38	6.41
India Sugars and Refineries Ltd	1.80	0.25	6.50	1.56	0.19	-8.25	1.25	0.12	5.55	1.54	0.25	-0.70
Ponni Sugars Ltd	1.27	0.30	-15.14	1.03	0.47	-30.69	2.14	0.19	4.06	1.48	0.43	3.14

Source: Computed from the annual accounts of the respective industry.

Table 4.33. Analysis of Variance - ANOVA

Particulars	Large-sized		Medium-sized		Small-sized	
	F value	F critical value	F value	F critical value	F value	F critical value
Between the years	4.83**	1.81	1.97	1.94	1.30	1.94
Between the Industry	16.12**	2.21	23.37	2.83	4.43**	2.83

Industry-wise Fixed assets turnover ratio - Paired sample t-test

Industry	Paired sample t-test		
	Initial phase and growth phase	Initial phase and maturity phase	Growth phase and maturity phase
Large-sized (n=7)			
Bannari Amman Sugars Ltd	0.13	0.35	0.43
EID Parry Ltd	4.66**	6.40*	3.42**
Jeypore Sugars & Chemicals Ltd	1.71	1.97	0.68
Rajshree Sugars & Chemicals Ltd	0.85	1.26	C.43
Sakthi Sugars Ltd	3.29**	3.10**	1.46
Thiru Arooran Sugars Ltd	3.34**	3.46**	0.16
Ugar Sugar Works Ltd	2.69**	7.97*	5.35*
Medium-sized (n=4)			
Kothari Sugars & Chemicals Ltd	7.87*	2.77**	0.39
Sri Chamundeswari Sugars Ltd	0.84	2.50***	1.59
Sri Sarvaraya Sugars Ltd	1.22	167	1.26
Kakatiya Cements Sugar & Industries Ltd	0.79	1.62	1.46
Small-sized (n=4)			
Dharani Sugars & Chemicals Ltd	3.09**	2.77**	0.74
Empee Sugars & Chemicals Ltd	1.00	4.50**	0.92
India Sugars and Refineries Ltd	0.73	2.66	1.87
Ponni Sugars Ltd	1.45	3.17	2.90

*Significant at 0.01 level; **Significant at 0.05 level; ***Significant at 0.10 level
Source: Computed

Hence, the overall analysis of fixed assets turnover ratio indicates that there were mixed performers in utilizing the fixed assets to generate sales revenue ranging from Re.1.22 by the medium-sized sector to Rs.1.63 by the large-sized sugar industry for one rupee investment in fixed asset. Among the sectors selected large-sized sector has comparatively been the best performer in this respect.

Current Asset Turnover Ratio

This ratio is applied to measure the turnover and profitability of total current assets applied to conduct the operations of the firm. The idea behind the current assets turnover ratio is to give an overall impression of how rapidly the total investment in current assets is being turned and is thought of by some as an index of "efficiency" or profitability. The lower the turnover of current assets, the worse is the utilization of current assets and vice-versa. Table 4.34 and Fig. 4.12 reveal the current assets turnover ratio in selected South Indian private sector Sugar Industry under study.

It is clear from Table 4.34 that on an average the sample South Indian private sector Sugar Industry had the overall current asset turnover ratio of 1.58 times with a co-efficient of variation of 0.18. The average current asset turnover ratio slightly varied from sector to sector. The highest average was 1.61 times in the large-sized sugar industry followed by 1.59 times in medium-sized sugar industry and 1.49 times in small-sized sugar industry. The average ratio of current asset turnover was higher than the industry average in large-sized and medium-sized sugar industry. The CV value of these ratios shows less fluctuation in the current asset turnover ratio of the selected sectors during the study period. Such low fluctuation could be attributed to the marginal differences in the growth rates of sales and current assets. Medium-sized sector, small-sized sector and whole industry have witnessed positive compound annual growth

Table 4.34. Analysis of Current assets turnover ratio of selected South Indian private sector Sugar Industry (1991-92 to 2005-06)

(in times)

Particulars	Initial phase [1992-96]	Growth phase [1997-2001]	Maturity phase [2002-2006]	Whole period [1992-2006]
Large-sized (n=7)				
Mean	1.80	1.59	1.45	**1.61**
CV	0.22	0.26	0.27	**0.21**
CAGR	-3.90	0.26	5.27	**-0.86**
Medium-sized (n=4)				
Mean	1.66	1.51	1.60	**1.59**
CV	0.21	0.29	0.47	**0.21**
CAGR	-5.28	3.36	7.02	**1.06**
Small-sized (n=4)				
Mean	1.48	1.26	1.73	**1.49**
CV	0.28	0.11	0.39	**0.11**
CAGR	-2.56	-0.70	25.45	**4.20**
Whole industry (n=15)				
Mean	**1.68**	**1.48**	**1.56**	**1.58**
CV	**0.23**	**0.25**	**0.35**	**0.18**
CAGR	**-3.85**	**0.99**	**11.24**	**1.10**

Analysis of Variance ANOVA

Sources of variation	F value	F critical value
Between the years	2.83**	2.06
Between the sector	0.99	3.34

Current assets turnover ratio - Paired sample t-test

Industry	Initial phase and Growth phase	Growth phase and Maturity phase	Initial phase and Maturity phase
Large-sized	2.07	1.15	2.67***
Medium-sized	0.98	-0.65	0.32
Small-sized	2.11	-1.37	-0.70
Whole industry	**1.93**	**-0.48**	**0.55**

**Significant at 0.05 level; ***Significant at 0.10 level
Source: Computed

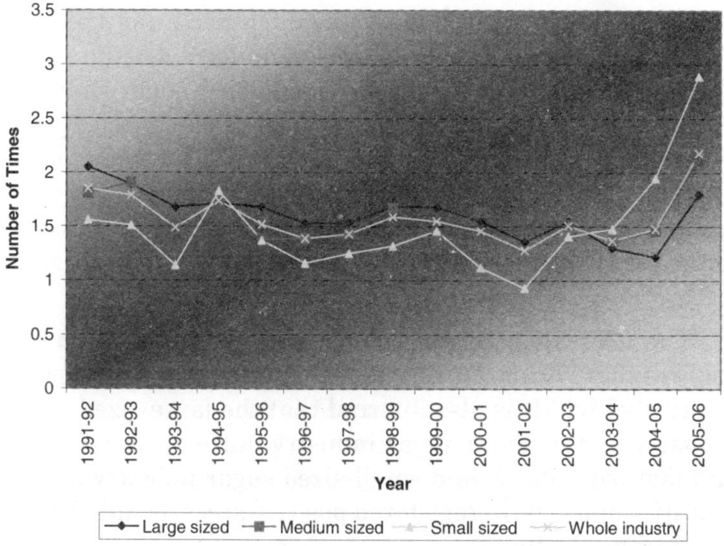

Fig. 4.12. Current Assets Turnover ratio of Selected South Indian Private Sector Sugar Industry

rate of this ratio during the study period, while large-sized sugar industry had registered a negative compound annual growth rate in this ratio during the study period.

Analysis of variance has been applied among the years and between the sectors for testing the hypothesis framed.

The hypothesis was rejected since the calculated value of F was greater than the table value of F at five per cent level of significance between the years. The rejection of hypothesis would indicate that there are significant differences in the current asset turnover ratio between the years. However, such differences between the sectors were insignificant as the calculated value of F was lower than the table value of F at five per cent level of significance.

Analysis of current asset turnover ratio between the three phases of post liberalization reveals that the overall current asset turnover ratio of the selected South Indian private sector sugar industry showed declining trend during growth phase. It declined from 1.68 times during initial phase to 1.48 times during growth phase. Such declining trend in the average ratio was resulted from uniform decline in the large-sized, medium-sized and small-sized sugar industry during the growth phase due to poor sales caused by the market and economic conditions. But during maturity phase medium-sized sugar industry, small-sized sugar industry and whole industry have posted a hike in the ratio because of improved market conditions and upward revision in sales price.

The CV values of all the sectors during three phases confirm that variations in this ratio during the phases were relatively high. It is also inferred that the large-sized sugar industry and medium sugar industry during growth phase and maturity phase, and small-sized sugar industry during maturity phase have registered positive and growing growth rates dramatically.

In order to test the hypothesis, paired sample t-test has been applied among the different phases. It is evident from the analysis that there was a significant difference in this ratio of large-sized sugar industry in between the initial phase and maturity phase at ten per cent level of significance. However, such differences in the rest of the cases were insignificant.

Industry-wise current asset turnover ratio of different sectors of selected South Indian private sector Sugar Industry during three phases has been presented in Table 4.35. The performance in utilizing current assets of EID Parry Ltd (2.13 times), Rajshree Sugars & Chemicals Ltd (1.92 times), Bannari Amman Sugars Ltd (1.72 times) and Ugar Sugar Works Ltd (1.65 times) under large-sized sector and Ponni Sugars Ltd (1.72 times) under small-sized sugar industry was better during the study period because its average current asset turnover ratios were higher than the industry average. Among the better performers EID Parry Ltd under large-sized sugar industry was the most efficient industry as its average ratio was the highest among the better performers. The best performance indicates that the industry needs one rupee investment in current asset to generate a sales revenue of Rs.2.13. Among sample industries Jeypore Sugars & Chemicals Ltd was the poor performing industry as its average during the period was the least (1.13 times). That is one rupee investment in current asset can generate slightly over one rupee by way of sales revenue i.e Re.1.13. This was the least average among the sample industries. Table 4.35 witnessed that majority of the industries under large-sized industry recorded positive compound annual growth rate ranging from 0.98 per cent to 3.71 per cent during the study period. Half of the industries under medium-sized sugar industry have registered negative compound annual growth rate viz., Sri Chamundeswari Sugars Ltd and Kakatiya Cements Sugar & Industries Ltd during the study period. Majority of the small-sized industry has posted positive and high compound annual growth rate during the period of study.

Table 4.36 depicts that differences in the current assets turnover ratio was significant in between years and industry under large-sized sector since the calculated values F were greater than the table values of F at five per cent level. The difference in the current asset turnover ratio was also

Table 4.35. Analysis of Industry-wise Current assets turnover ratio of selected South Indian private sector Sugar industry (1991-92 to 2005-06)

(in times)

Industry	Initial phase (1992-96)			Growth phase (1997-2001)			Maturity phase (2002-2006)			Whole period (1992-2006)		
	Mean	CV	CAGR	Mean	CV	CAGR	Mean	CV	CAGR	Mean	CV	CAGR
1	2	3	4	5	6	7	8	9	10	11	12	13
Large-sized												
Bannari Amman Sugars Ltd	1.87	0.18	-3.43	1.72	0.10	-2.30	1.59	0.11	3.01	1.72	0.15	-3.89
EID Parry Ltd	2.44	0.19	-9.41	2.26	0.09	3.89	1.68	0.29	-7.42	2.13	0.24	-13.30
Jeypore Sugars & Chemicals Ltd	1.27	0.11	-534	0.98	0.09	1.74	1.15	0.20	8.59	1.13	0.17	0.98
Rajshree Sugars & Chemicals Ltd	2.17	0.20	-7.15	1.48	0.09	-0.20	2.10	0.29	7.86	1.92	0.27	-3.89
Sakthi Sugars Ltd	1.75	0.12	3.19	1.48	0.20	-6.62	1.09	0.37	13.82	1.44	0.28	3.71
Thiru Arooran Sugars Ltd	1.60	0.13	-5.09	1.31	0.21	5.22	1.04	0.50	22.87	1.32	0.31	2.29
Ugar Sugar Works Ltd	1.53	0.17	3.71	1.93	0.21	-0.20	1.48	0.60	2.66	1.65	0.22	1.36
Medium-sized												
Kothari Sugars & Chemicals Ltd	1.73	0.15	-4.61	1.67	0.13	3.71	1.76	0.10	4.06	1.72	0.12	0.99
Sri Chamundeswari Sugars Ltd	1.54	0.11	2.47	1.16	0.42	-9.71	0.81	0.35	7.57	1.17	0.38	-1.08
Sri Sarvaraya Sugars Ltd	1.29	0.17	-1.65	2.08	0.25	13.70	2.55	0.29	10.80	1.97	0.37	6.74
Kakatiya Cements Sugar & Industries Ltd	2.10	0.33	-15.14	1.15	0.05	-0.20	1.27	0.17	2.47	1.51	0.39	-4.27

Small-sized												
Dharani Sugars & Chemicals Ltd	2.08	0.30	-9.12	1.25	0.25	-0.40	1.08	0.38	11.71	1.47	0.47	-3.35
Empee Sugars & Chemicals Ltd	1.17	0.72	5.33	1.08	0.18	-6.36	2.54	0.72	53.46	1.59	0.80	10.50
India Sugars and Refineries Ltd	1.24	0.17	1.17	1.29	0.24	-1.44	1.28	0.55	26.89	1.27	0.34	4.83
Ponni Sugars Ltd	1.44	0.27	-12.60	1.41	0.23	3.37	2.03	0.31	13.70	1.63	0.32	1.60

Source: Computed from the annual accounts of respective industry.

significant in between the years and industry under the small-sized sector. Similarly no significant differences in this ratio was found in between the years under medium-sized sugar industry.

It can be observed from Table 4.36 that current assets turnover ratio of some of the industries under large-sized sector, medium-sized sector and small-sized sector showed significant differences during different phases as per t-value. It is further observed that such significant differences were noticed in Jeypore Sugars & Chemicals Ltd and Rajshree Sugars & Chemicals Ltd under large-sized sugar industry, Sri Sarvaraya Sugars Ltd and Kakatiya Cements Sugar & Industries Ltd under medium-sized and Dharani Sugars & Chemicals Ltd under small-sized during initial phase and growth phase. Similarly the significant differences were also found in EID Parry Ltd and Sakthi Sugars Ltd under large-sized, Sri Chamundeswari Sugars Ltd, Sri Sarvaraya Sugars Ltd and Kakatiya Cements Sugar & Industries Ltd under medium-sized and Dharani Sugars & Chemicals Ltd and Empee Sugars & Chemicals Ltd under small sugar industry during initial phase and maturity phase. However, no such significant differences were observed between the growth phase and maturity phase in all the selected industry.

To sum up the above, the selected South Indian private sector Sugar Industry was capable of generating a minimum sales revenue of Re.1.13 and a maximum of Rs.2.13 from one rupee investment in current asset with a wider fluctuation between the sectors and within the sector as well.

Table 4.36. Analysis of Variance - ANOVA

Particulars	Large-sized		Medium-sized		Small-sized	
	F value	F critical value	F value	F critical value	F value	F critical value
Between the years	2.71**	1.81	0.61	1.94	1.66	1.94
Between the Industry	14.45**	2.21	5.53**	2.83	0.74	2.83

Industry-wise Current assets turnover ratio - Paired sample t-test

Industry	Paired sample t-test		
	Initial phase and growth phase	Initial phase and maturity phase	Growth phase and maturity phase
Large-sized (n=7)			
Bannari Amman Sugars Ltd	0.62	1.53	1.26
EID Parry Ltd	0.66	3.76**	2.02
Jeypore Sugars & Chemicals Ltd	4.00**	0.79	1.34
Rajshree Sugars & Chemicals Ltd	3.08**	0.20	2.12
Sakthi Sugars Ltd	1.40	3.03**	1.41
Thiru Arooran Sugars Ltd	1.49	1.78	1.87
Ugar Sugar Works Ltd	1.50	0.60	1.77
Medium-sized (n=4)			
Kothari Sugars & Chemicals Ltd	0.36	0.18	0.69
Sri Chamundeswari Sugars Ltd	1.27	5.22*	1.40
Sri Sarvaraya Sugars Ltd	2.84**	3.98**	1.67
Kakatiya Cements Sugar & Industries Ltd	3.03**	2.76***	1.41
Small-sized (n=4)			
Dharani Sugars & Chemicals Ltd	2.33***	2.81**	0.66
Empee Sugars & Chemicals Ltd	0.22	2.36***	1.65
India Sugars and Refineries Ltd	0.05	0.03	0.01
Ponni Sugars Ltd	0.03	0.59	0.62

*Significant at 0.01 level; **Significant at 0.05 level; ***Significant at 0.10 level
Source: Computed

Inventory Turnover Ratio

Inventory turnover indicates the efficiency of the firm's inventory management. It shows rapidity turning inventories into sales. Generally, a high turnover is good indicative of inventory management. Simultaneously, a low inventory turnover implies excessive inventory level that warranted by production and sales activities, or a slow moving or obsolete inventory. A high level of sluggish inventory amounts to unnecessary tie-up of funds, impairment of profit and increased cost. On the other hand a very high inventory turnover may be the result in frequent stock outs. The inventory will also be high if the firm replenishes its inventory in too many small lot sizes. The situation of frequent stock outs and too many small inventory replacements are costly for the firm. Thus, too high and too low inventory turnover rates are not preferred.

The inventory turnover ratio has been calculated for the selected South Indian private sector sugar industry during the study period and represented in Table 4.37 and Fig. 4.13. A fluctuating trend in the industry turnover ratio could be drawn from Table 4.37. On an average the sample South Indian private sector sugar industry had the overall inventor turnover ratio of 2.97 times with a co-efficient of variation of 0.47. The average inventory turnover ratio varied from sector to sector, the highest average was 4.07 times in medium-sized sugar industry followed by 2.89 times in large-sized sugar industry and 2.11 times in small-sized sugar industry. The CV value of this ratio shows very high fluctuation in inventory turnover ratio of the selected sector during the study period. Such fluctuation could be attributed to the differences in the growth rates of inventory and sales because of the factors such as market conditions, rise in raw material price and upward revision of selling price. All the selected sectors and whole industry witnessed positive compound annual growth rate of this ratio during the study period.

In order to test the hypothesis, analysis of variance has been applied between the years and between the sectors. Since the calculated values of F (8.02 and 21.94) are greater

Table 4.37. Analysis of Inventory turnover ratio of selected South Indian private sector Sugar Industry (1991-92 to 2005-06)

(in times)

Particulars	Initial phase [1992-96]	Growth phase [1997-2001]	Maturity phase [2002-2006]	Whole period [1992-2006]
Large-sized (n=7)				
Mean	2.74	2.62	3.32	**2.89**
C.V	0.67	0.88	0.73	**0.63**
CAGR	-3.40	-6.95	23.58	**3.86**
Medium-sized (n=4)				
Mean	3.68	3.12	5.42	**4.07**
C.V	0.73	0.28	0.35	**0.13**
CAGR	3.83	-8.78	32.72	**8.61**
Small-sized (n=4)				
Mean	1.85	1.65	2.83	**2.11**
C.V	0.35	0.29	0.52	**0.18**
CAGR	-3.56	8.05	25.43	**7.05**
Whole industry (n=15)				
Mean	**2.75**	**2.49**	**3.75**	**2.97**
C.V	**0.66**	**0.65**	**0.57**	**0.47**
CAGR	**-1.09**	**-5.06**	**27.35**	**6.10**

Analysis of Variance-ANOVA

Sources of variation	F value	F critical value
Between the years	8.02**	2.06
Between the sector	21.94**	3.34

Inventory turnover ratio - Paired sample t-test

Industry	Initial phase and Growth phase	Growth phase and Maturity phase	Initial phase and Maturity phase
Large-sized	0.41	0.76	0.77
Medium-sized	1.29	1.26	1.18
Small-sized	0.88	2.04	1.31
Whole industry	**1.40**	**1.18**	**1.07**

**Significant at 0.05 level
Source: Computed

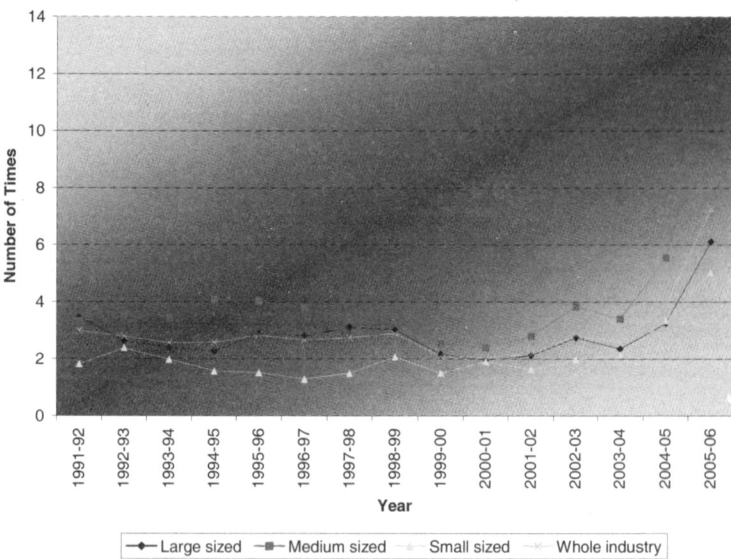

Fig. 4.13. Inventory Turnover ratio of Selected South Indian Private Sector Sugar Industry.

than the table values of F (2.06 and 3.34) at five per cent level between the years and sector, it is concluded that null hypothesis is rejected. The rejection of null hypothesis would indicate that there are significant differences in the inventory turnover ratio between the years and sectors.

The entire study period of 15 years of post-liberalization divided into three phases namely initial phase, growth phase and maturity phase. It could find from the Table 4.37 that the overall inventory turnover ratio of selected South Indian private sector sugar industry showed a declining trend during the growth phase. It declined from 2.75 times during initial phase to 2.49 times during growth phase. Such a declining trend could be attributed mainly to the poor performance of medium-sized sugar industry and small-sized sugar industry due to decreased production, difficulty in getting raw materials and an over abundance of obsolete inventory. But during maturity phase the entire selected sector and whole industry registered a dramatically increasing trend in inventory turnover ratio because of upward revision of sales price and low inventory.

The CV value of this ratio during three phases showed very high fluctuations. It is inferred that the large-sized sugar industry, small-sized sugar industry and whole industry have posted negative compound annual growth rate during initial phase, large-sized, medium-sized and whole industry have registered negative compound annual growth rate during growth phase and the entire selected sectors have recorded positive compound annual growth rate during maturity phase.

Paired sample t-test has been applied among the different phases for testing the hypothesis framed. Since the calculated t-values are lower than the table values, it is concluded that the null hypothesis is rejected. The rejection of the null hypothesis would indicate that the differences in this ratio of selected sectors of South Indian private sector Sugar Industry between the phases were insignificant.

Industry-wise inventory turnover ratio of selected sectors of South Indian private sector sugar industry during three phases and whole period is presented in Table 4.38. High inventory turnover ratios maintained in EID Parry Ltd (6.48 times) and Sakthi Sugars Ltd (4.03 times) under large-sized

Table 4.38. Analysis of Industry-wise Inventory turnover ratio of selected South Indian private sector Sugar Industry (1991-92 to 2005-06)

(in times)

Industry	Initial phase (1992-96)			Growth phase (1997-2001)			Maturity phase (2002-2006)			Whole period (1992-2006)		
	Mean	CV	CAGR	Mean	CV	CAGR	Mean	CV	CAGR	Mean	CV	CAGR
1	2	3	4	5	6	7	8	9	10	11	12	13
Large-sized												
Bannari Amman Sugars Ltd	2.41	0.41	-8.83	1.71	0.24	-4.85	2.07	0.17	5.22	2.07	0.33	-2.75
EID Parry Ltd	6.83	0.12	-1.23	7.68	0.30	-11.59	4.94	0.56	14.41	6.48	0.35	1.28
Jeypore Sugars & Chemicals Ltd	1.41	0.16	-5.34	1.08	0.20	-1.87	1.41	0.26	16.00	1.30	0.24	1.17
Rajshree Sugars & Chemicals Ltd	2.13	0.48	-12.94	1.83	0.13	-4.36	2.74	0.36	6.03	2.23	0.39	-1.56
Sakthi Sugars Ltd	2.39	0.17	-4.13	1.62	0.15	-7.42	8.07	0.86	76.30	4.03	1.18	13.95
Thiru Arooran Sugars Ltd	1.87	0.13	-2.09	1.50	0.08	-1.87	1.37	0.41	11.20	1.58	0.31	-0.55
Ugar Sugar Works Ltd	2.17	0.27	8.73	2.88	0.37	-2.30	2.60	0.52	20.59	2.55	0.40	5.95
Medium-sized												
Kothari Sugars & Chemicals Ltd	3.24	0.16	4.40	3.37	0.27	-5.84	6.64	0.36	12.10	4.41	0.48	7.08
Sri Chamundeswari Sugars Ltd	1.68	0.14	7.11	1.81	0.45	-14.76	6.70	1.22	66.64	3.40	1.48	20.20
Sri Sarvaraya Sugars Ltd	2.21	0.34	16.65	3.76	0.38	19.63	5.73	0.72	32.86	3.90	0.72	16.43
Kakatiya Cements Sugar & Industries Ltd	7.57	0.05	0	3.53	0.67	-23.04	2.61	0.42	19.63	4.57	0.58	-3.79

Small-sized												
Dharani Sugars & Chemicals Ltd	2.64	0.35	-10.01	1.34	0.19	-10.01	1.60	0.54	22.82	1.86	0.49	-0.85
Empee Sugars & Chemicals Ltd	1.43	0.62	-11.27	1.15	0.25	-5.34	4.90	0.68	38.57	2.49	1.03	10.21
India Sugars and Refineries Ltd	1.21	0.15	-0.40	1.99	0.59	1.55	1.96	0.59	24.32	1.72	0.56	8.59
Ponni Sugars Ltd	2.12	0.21	-8.83	2.11	0.63	31.42	2.84	0.20	10.40	2.36	0.37	2.32

Source: Computed from the annual accounts of the respective industry.

sugar industry and Kakatiya Cements Sugar & Industries Ltd (4.57 times), Kothari Sugars & Chemicals Ltd (4.41 times), Sri Sarvaraya Sugars Ltd (3.90 times) and Sri Chamundeswari Sugars Ltd (3.40 times) under medium-sized sugar industry indicated that these industries had utilized its financial resources efficiently by maintaining low inventories. Among the above better performing industries EID Parry Ltd was fastest inventory turning industry as it had the fastest rate during the reporting period. No industry under small-sized sugar industry had performed well regarding inventory turnover ratio because its average ratios were lower than the industry average. Overstocking, poor sales and economic conditions could characterize this poor performance. The table also indicated that there was a fluctuating trend of this ratio among the industry selected under different sectors of South Indian private sector Sugar Industry.

Table 4.39 depicts that differences in the inventory turnover ratio was significant in between industry under large-sized sugar industry and in between the years under medium-sized sugar industry and small-sized sugar industry as calculated values of F are greater than the table values of F at five per cent level. However, they were insignificant in between years under large-sized sugar industry and in between industry under medium-sized and small-sized sugar industry as calculated values F are lower than the table values of F at five per cent level of significance.

It can be viewed from the Table 4.39 that inventory turnover ratios of few industries selected under different sectors showed significant differences during initial phase and growth phase as per the t-values. In detail Jeypore Sugars & Chemicals Ltd and Sakthi Sugars Ltd under large-sized sugar industry, Sri Sarvaraya Sugars Ltd and Kakatiya Cements Sugar & Industries Ltd under medium-sized sugar industry and Dharani Sugars & Chemicals Ltd under small-sized sugar industry the differences in this ratio were significant during initial phase and growth phase. Such

Table 4.39. Analysis of Variance - ANOVA

Particulars	Large-sized		Medium-sized		Small-sized	
	F value	F critical value	F value	F critical value	F value	F critical value
Between the years	1.77	1.81	2.26**	1.94	1.98**	1.94
Between the Industry	12.57**	2.21	0.50	2.83	1.15	2.83

Industry-wise Inventory turnover ratio - Paired sample t-test

Industry	Paired sample t-test		
	Initial phase and growth phase	Initial phase and maturity phase	Growth phase and maturity phase
Large-sized (n=7)			
Bannari Amman Sugars Ltd	1.75	0.82	1.42
EID Parry Ltd	0.70	1.62	1.39
Jeypore Sugars & Chemicals Ltd	2.91**	0.02	1.60
Rajshree Sugars & Chemicals Ltd	0.71	1.15	2.32***
Sakthi Sugars Ltd	4.90*	1.76	2.02
Thiru Arooran Sugars Ltd	1.29	2.28***	0.43
Ugar Sugar Works Ltd	1.08	1.17	0.30
Medium-sized (n=4)			
Kothari Sugars & Chemicals Ltd	0.21	3.23**	3.11**
Sri Chamundeswari Sugars Ltd	0.32	1.38	1.26
Sri Sarvaraya Sugars Ltd4	3.46**	2.15***	1.09
Kakatiya Cements Sugar & Industries Ltd	3.92**	11.06*	0.65
Small-sized (n=4)			
Dharani Sugars & Chemicals Ltd	3.96**	1.61	0.54
Empee Sugars & Chemicals Ltd	0.76	2.31***	2.34***
India Sugars and Refineries Ltd	1.77	1.35	0.04
Ponni Sugars Ltd	0.02	1.87	1.86

*Significant at 0.01 level; **Significant at 0.05 level; ***Significant at 0.10 level

Source: Computed

significant differences were also noticed in Thiru Arooran Sugars Ltd under large-sized, Kothari Sugars & Chemicals Ltd, Sri Sarvaraya Sugars Ltd and Kakatiya Cements Sugar & Industries Ltd under medium-sized and Empee Sugars & Chemicals Ltd under small-sized sugar industry during initial phase and maturity phase. Similarly, the differences in this ratio of Rajshree Sugars & Chemicals Ltd under large-sized sugar industry, Kothari Sugars & Chemicals Ltd under medium-sized sugar industry and Empee Sugars & Chemicals Ltd under small-sized sugar industry were also observed significant during growth phase and maturity phase.

To conclude the selected South Indian private sector sugar industry having higher average inventory turnover ratio consists of mixed performers within the industry and widely varied performance within the sectors as well. A notable point in this analysis was that the small-sized sugar industry failed or struggling to maintain its inventory turnover on par with the industry average.

ANALYSIS OF PROFITABILITY TREND

Profitability of various industries would hardly diverge in a world of perfection, because, future can easily be predicted. However, real world is far from perfection. A number of dynamic forces (e.g., changes in income, technology, population, etc.) operate simultaneously in a real imperfect and uncertain world. Consequently, profitability of different concerns and industries etc. greatly affected.

Rate of profit, which is one of the most used and popular financial measure of performance of a concern and an industry, plays a pivotal role in the growth process of the concern, the industry and the whole economy. It reflects the financial stability and also enhances the earning capacity of the concern. It plays dual role in the investment process of the economy by attracting fresh investment on one hand, and generating internal source of finance on the other hand.

However, low rate of profit or loss reports any fresh inflow of investment and induces existing capital to quit towards the fields of higher rates of profit. It thus reflects investors' and lenders' need of knowing financial indicator of performance and is a key factor in determining the commercial viability of the concern and the industry.

The current rate of profit is an indicator and source of and a need for the expansions of business through re-investment and through attracting and observing new capital in the industry. Hence, investors and lenders are interested in knowing the profitability of concern and industry over time or at a point of time. The celebrated tendency of rates of profit to fall over long period of time had been theoretically developed by classical economists like Adam Smith, David Ricardo, etc., their critic Karl Marx and also by neoclassical writers such as Alfred Marshall. The study therefore indents to empirically examine whether the rate of profit is selected South Indian private sector sugar industry has a tendency to rise or fall over a period of 1991-92 to 2005-06. The objective is not to test the validity of classical hypothesis, as the economic conditions as assumed by classical writers do not prevail in the country. However, knowledge about whether profitability is raising or falling over the period 1991-92 to 2005-06 would throw interesting results for formulation of future policies.

An attempt has been made in the study to examine the trends in rates of profit of selected South Indian private sector sugar industry over the period 1991-92 to 2005-06. Further, an attempt has also been made to capture the industry wise variations in the series of profit rates, which reveals the dispersion of the series for each industry over the study period. In this study a ratio of profits to capital employed and expressed in percentage terms has been used for this purpose. The rate of profit on capital indicates the earning power of capital of long term nature and thus examines long-term profitability better. The linear regression model fitted is as follows:

$$P = \alpha + \beta t + e$$

Where P is rate of profit, t is the time and α and β are the parameters (intercept and co-efficient respectively) and e is the error term. The results of the application of above-stated model to the profitability of selected South Indian private sector sugar industry are presented in Table 4.40.

Table 4.40 reveals that the linear model of time trend of profitability has proved to be a "good fit" in case eight out of 15 industries, i.e., 53.33 per cent of the industries examined. This is revealed from the value of R^2, the co-efficient of determination. Among these industries, Sakthi Sugars Ltd, Thiru Arooran Sugars Ltd, Ugar Sugar Works Ltd (large-sized), Kothari Sugars & Chemicals Ltd and Sri Chamundeswari Sugars Ltd (medium-sized) and India Sugars and Refineries Ltd (small-sized) experienced a strong tendency in profitability to decline over the study period. The negative values of β, the time trend co-efficient, confirms this trend as these are observed to be statistical significant. Statistically significant negative value of β indicates steep negative relationship between profitability and time over the study period. Only in case of Jeypore Sugars & Chemicals Ltd (large-sized) and Ponni Sugars Ltd (small-sized), the sign for β, the time trend co-efficient is positive, implying the tendency of profit rate to rise over time.

Table 4.40 further reveals that β assumes different values (negative) for different industries and ranging from –0.23 for Kakatiya Cements Sugar & Industries Ltd to –2.89 for India Sugars and Refineries Ltd during the study period. This implies that profitability of different industries declined at different rates over this period. Bannari Amman Sugars Ltd and Empee Sugars Ltd, the sign for β the time trend co-efficient is positive, implying a tendency a profit rate to rise over time. However, β is being statistically non-significant the results are not discussed. In case of seven industries, no definite trend could be observed, as the results are statistically not significant. The value of co-efficient of

Table 4.40. Results of regression rates of Profit on time for South Indian private sector Sugar Industries (1991-92 to 2005-06)

Sl. No.	Industry	P = α + βt + e α	ß	R^2	F value
1.	Bannari Amman Sugars Ltd	17.65	0.30 (1.37)	0.13	1.87
2.	EID Parry Ltd	21.69	-0.55 (1.61)	0.17	2.60
3.	Jeypore Sugars & Chemicals Ltd	14.32	2.42** (2.46)	0.32	6.04**
4.	Rajshree Sugars & Chemicals Ltd	29.23	-0.53 (0.77)	0.04	0.59
5.	Sakthi Sugars Ltd	25.03	-1.09** (2.62)	0.35	6.89**
6.	Thiru Arooran Sugars Ltd	19.90	-1.06** (2.84)	0.38	8.08**
7.	Ugar Sugar Works Ltd	57.97	-2.49** (2.64)	0.35	6.97**
	Large-sized Industry	**26.53**	**-0.43** (2.92)**	**0.32**	**8.19****
8.	Kothari Sugars & Chemicals Ltd	13.28	-1.70** (2.430	0.30	6.72**
9.	Sri Chamundeswari Sugars Ltd	23.32	-0.58** (2.66)	0.33	6.98**
10.	Sri Sarvaraya Sugars Ltd	21.10	-0.47 (-0.47)	0.06	0.80
11.	Kakatiya Cements Sugar & Industries Ltd	17.38	-0.23 (0.81)	0.05	0.65
	Medium-sized Industry	**18.78**	**-0.51** (2.49)**	**0.22**	**6.24****
12.	Dharani Sugars & Chemicals Ltd	25.07	-0.91 (1.73)	0.19	2.99
13.	Empee Sugars & Chemicals Ltd	6.98	0.44 (0.32)	0.01	0.01
14.	India Sugars and Refineries Ltd	55.59	-2.89** (1.83)	0.20	4.16**
15.	Ponni Sugars Ltd	8.18	0.64** (2.52)	0.28	4.28**
	Small-sized Industry	**23.96**	**-0.68 (1.62)**	**0.07**	**1.04**
	Whole Industry	**23.77**	**-0.52** (2.85)**	**0.39**	**4.32**

Figures in parentheses are t values. **Significant at 0.05 level.
Source: Computed.

determination R^2 varied in case of industry having strong declining tendency of profit rate over time, from 0.20 for India Sugars and Refineries Ltd to 0.38 for Thiru Arooran Sugars Ltd. Such variations in the value of R^2 implies that time explain the profitability variation of different industry in different degree over the time. This means that time explain variation in profitability of the above two industries to the extent of 20 per cent and 38 per cent respectively over the study period.

Sector-wise trend regression results are also presented in Table 4.40. It may be noted from the table that all the three sectors and as well as whole industry, all had a strong tendency for profit rate to fall over the study period as the results for R^2 and ß, are statistically significant, while results are non-significant for small-sized industry. The value of R^2 varied between 0.07 (small-sized) to 0.32 (large-sized) indicating that time explaining profitability variation of the sector to the tune of three per cent and 51 per cent respectively. For whole industry the time explains the variations in profitability to the extent of 39 per cent over the study period. The time trend co-efficient also varies in value from –0.43 (large-sized) to –0.68 (small-sized), indicating that as time increases, profit rates of sector fall between this range.

Dispersion in Rate of Profit

The industry-wise dispersion in rates of selected South Indian private sector sugar industry over the study period is achieved through estimation mean, standard deviation and co-efficient of variations. The estimates are presented in Table 4.41. It is observed from the table that on an average, Ugar Sugar Works Ltd experienced highest profit rate (38.07 per cent), while Kothari Sugars & Chemicals Ltd experienced lowest rate of profit (-0.34%) over the study period. The whole selected South Indian private sector Sugar Industry on an average, enjoy 19.63 per cent rate of profit. Amongst the sector, large-sized sugar industry (23.10%) on an average, had a profit rate above the whole industry, while medium-sized and small-sized industries (14.67% and 18.50%) had below it.

Table 4.41. Industry-wise variation in profitability of South Indian private sector Sugar Industry (1991-92 to 2005-06)

Sl. No.	Industry	Mean	SD	CV
1.	Bannari Amman Sugars Ltd	20.07	3.82	0.19
2.	EID Parry Ltd	17.25	6.07	0.35
3.	Jeypore Sugars & Chemicals Ltd	33.56	19.20	0.57
4.	Rajshree Sugars & Chemicals Ltd	25.01	11.37	0.45
5.	Sakthi Sugars Ltd	16.32	8.29	0.51
6.	Thiru Arooran Sugars Ltd	11.45	7.63	0.67
7.	Ugar Sugar Works Ltd	38.07	18.83	0.49
	Large-sized industry	**23.10**	**10.75**	**0.42**
8.	Kothari Sugars & Chemicals Ltd	10.34	3.65	10.74
9.	Sri Chamundeswari Sugars Ltd	18.66	14.41	0.77
10.	Sri Sarvaraya Sugars Ltd	24.82	8.63	0.35
11.	Kakatiya Cements Sugar & Industries Ltd	15.54	4.69	0.30
	Medium-sized industry	**14.67**	**24.46**	**0.73**
12.	Dharani Sugars & Chemicals Ltd	17.77	9.44	0.53
13.	Empee Sugars & Chemicals Ltd	10.45	21.72	2.08
14.	India Sugars and Refineries Ltd	32.47	28.60	0.88
15.	Ponni Sugars Ltd	13.30	10.41	0.78
	Small-sized industry	**18.50**	**17.55**	**0.53**
	Whole industry	**19.63**	**9.94**	**0.51**

Sources: Computed from the annual reports of the respective industry.

Out of total of 15 industries, six industries (40% industries) viz., Bannari Amman Sugars Ltd, Jeypore Sugars & Chemicals Ltd, Rajshree Sugars & Chemicals Ltd, and Ugar Sugar Works Ltd (large-sized), Sri Sarvaraya Sugars Ltd (medium-sized) and India Sugars and Refineries Ltd (small-sized) enjoyed, on an average, a higher rate of profit than whole industry. Another important observation from the Table 4.41 is that mean rates of profit vary greatly in case all the industries, irrespective of sector of which they belong.

In order to study year to year variation in the profit rates the estimates of standard deviation and co-efficient variation for profit rate series of selected South Indian private sector sugar industry are worked out and presented in Table 4.41. These measures reveal the extent of variation of actual values of profit rate of each industry from its mean value of the series. The higher vales of co-efficient of variation indicate larger dispersion among the profit rate series of respective industry and vice versa. Bannari Amman Sugars Ltd with co-efficient of variation of being 0.19 experienced the lowest variation in profit rate over the study period while Kothari Sugars & Chemicals Ltd with lowest profit rates suffered from the largest dispersion, co-efficient of variation is equal to 10.74. Among the sectors large-sized industry has the lowest variation in profit rates (CV = 0.42) while medium-sized industry suffered from the largest variation (CV = 0.73) during the study period.

The selected South Indian private sector sugar industries are divided arbitrarily into relatively stable (CV with value up to 0.25), moderately fluctuating (CV lying between 0.251 and 0.500), highly fluctuating (CV lying between 0.501 and 0.750) and erratically fluctuating (CV above 0.75). It is observed from the Table 4.41 that five out of 15 industries (33.33%) experienced erratically fluctuating in profit rate series. These industries are Kothari Sugars & Chemicals Ltd,

Sri Chamundeswari Sugars Ltd (medium-sized) and Empee Sugars Ltd, India Sugars and Refineries Ltd and Ponni Sugars Ltd (small-sized) industry. Four out of 15 industries (26.67%) experienced highly fluctuating variations in profit rate series. These industries are Jeypore Sugars & Chemicals Ltd, Sakthi Sugars Ltd and Thiru Arooran Sugars Ltd (large-sized) and Dharani Sugars & Chemicals Ltd (small-sized industry). Five out of 15 industries (33.33%) experienced moderately fluctuating variation in profit rate series. These industries are EID Parry Ltd, Rajshree Sugars & Chemicals Ltd and Ugar Sugar Works Ltd (large-sized) and Sri Sarvaraya Sugars Ltd and Kakatiya Cements Sugar & Industries Ltd (medium-sized). Only one industry Bannari Amman Sugars Ltd (large-sized) experienced relatively stable variation in profit rate series. As far as the whole South Indian private sector Sugar Industry variations are concerned, it experienced highly fluctuating profit rate series over the period.

NOTES

1. Bradley, J.P. (1968). *Administrative Financial Management* (NewYork: Holt Rinechart and Winston, Inc.), p. 173.
2. Duck, R.E.V. and Jervis, F.R.J. (1964), *Management Accounting*, George G. Harrap & Company p. 98.
3. Kulshrestha, R.S., Profitability in India's Steel Industry - During the decade 1960-70 (A thesis submitted for the degree of Ph.D., Department of E.A.F.M. University of Rajasthan, (1973), p. 83.
4. James, C.Van Horne (1978), *Fundamentals of Financial Management*, (New Delhi: Prentice Hall), p. 40.
5. *Ibid.,* p. 43.
6. Waston, J.F and Brigham E.F (1978). *Managerial Finance* (6th Edn. The Dryden Press, Hinsdale. Illinois), p. 148.
7. Anthony, R.N. and Reece, J.S. (1975), *Management Accounting-Principles* (Horne Wood, Illinois, Richard D. Irwin, Inc.,) , p. 245.
8. Ralph, D. Kennedy and Stewart, M. (1968), *Financial Statement* (Home Wood Ill; Richard D Irwin, Inc.), p. 404.

9. Kulkarni, P.V., *Financial Management*, Bombay; Himalaya Publishing House, 1987, p. 192.

10. Khan, M.Y., and Jain, P.K., (1996), *Financial Management* (New Delhi: Tata McGraw-Hill Publishing Co.Ltd), p. 139.

11. Pandey I.M., (1980), Concept of Earning Power, *Accounting Journal*, Vol.W, (Rajastan Accounting Association), p. 46.

12. Lawrence, J.Gitman(1982). *Principles of Management Finance* (New York; Herper & Row Publishers), p. 204.

13. *Ibid.,* p. 204.

14. James, C. Van Horne (1981). *Fundamentals of Financial Management* (New Delhi, Prentice-Hall), p. 155.

15. Pandey, I.M., (1996), *Financial Management* (New Delhi; Vikas Publishing House Private Ltd) p. 449.

16. Weston, J.F. and E.F. *Brigham, Managerial Finance*, (New York: Holt, Rinchart, Winston, 1969), p. 88.

17. Sizer, John (1979). *An insight into the Management Accounting* (London; Pitman), p. 170.

18. Pandey, I.M.*, op.cit.,* p. 552.

19. Gupta, M.C (1989), *Profitability Analysis*, Jaipur: Pointer Publisher, p. 36.

20. Basant, A.C. Raj, *Corporate Financial Management*, (New Delhi: Tata McGraw-Hill Publishing Company Ltd., 1978), p.154.

21. Roy, A.Foulke, *Practical Financial Statement Analysis, Indian* Ed., (New Delhi: Tata McGraw-Hill Publishing Company Ltd., 1978), p. 583.

CHAPTER 5

Empirical Analysis of Profitability

In this chapter an attempt has been made to analyze the profitability of selected South Indian private sector sugar industry during the study period in the following aspects.

A. Size and Profitability

B. Growth and Profitability

C. Liquidity and Profitability

D. Determinants of Profitability

E. Impact of Working Capital on Profitability

F. Assessment of Financial Health

SIZE AND PROFITABILITY

In a perfectly competitive market, profit rates tend to equality. As imperfect markets are taken into account, the size of a firm must be considered as a factor in producing profits. The empirical evidence size-profitability relationship, in general, is quite vast and varied. Baumol (1967)[1] suggested that the larges firm may be in a position to earn a higher rate of return on its investment than the smaller firm because it has all the options of smaller firm open to it and in addition it can undertake projects which are of large scale that are denied to smaller firms. A similar argument had earlier been put forward by Steindl (1944).[2] A counter-argument is that size breads inefficiency and that, accordingly, large firms cannot undertake the options open to a small firm as efficiently as the small firms and hence profitability may decline with size of firms. Benishay (1961)[3] argued that the stock market would tend to favour large firms so that there will be a negative relationship between profitability and equity. Further, studies which reported a negative relationships include Samuels and Smyth (1968),[4] Marcus (1969),[5] Hains (1970),[6] Raidice (1971),[7] Shephered (1972),[8] Smyth, Boyes and Peseau (1975),[9] Whittington (1980),[10] Pamfret and Shaprio (1980),[11] Ravenscraft (1983),[12] Amato and Wilder (1985)[13] and Vishnukanda Prohit (1998).[14] Studies which reported a positive relationship include Alexander (1944),[15] Steklar (1964),[16] Hall and Weisel (1967),[17] Kamerschen (1968)[18] and Vijayakumar (2003).[19] Thus, we find that some theoretical arguments suggest that profitability should increase with firm size, others suggest a negative relationship. It is in view of these contradictory suggestions, that it becomes necessary to study the relationship between size and profitability of firms in selected South Indian private sector Sugar Industry during the study period.

Further, the analysis of this relationship is also important from another angle, i.e., profitability increases on average, with the size of the firm. This will suggest that profitability is not constrained by size; in fact, in this case it is a positive inducement to further growth. If profitability does not vary systematically with size, it will not be a constraint on future growth, but neither will be positive inducement to growth.

One may also be interested in the relationship between profitability and size for other two broad reasons, (1) its likely effect on industrial concentration and (2) its possible implications for returns to scale and monopoly power. A positive relationship between average profitability and size would suggest that industrial concentration is likely to be increased by large firms growing at a faster average rate than the small firms. This will reinforce the tendency for concentration to increase as a result of the inter-firm dispersion of growth. The implications of relationship between profitability and size for economies of scale and monopoly power are ambiguous, because the two effects are not identified separately (though profitability can be expected to be directly related to the monopoly power and increasing returns to scale). Economies of scale will affect the cost structure of firms of different size, whereas monopoly power will affect revenue (through decisions as to price and quantity of output). Monopoly power may also enable a monopolistic firm to operate inefficiently, so that it is not forced towards its production possibility frontier and does not take full advantage of economies of scale. Therefore, clear inferences about either economies of scale or monopoly power from the above relationship cannot be made.

This part is devoted to the testing of Baumol's hypothesis that larger sized firms have more profitability. This is presented with the help of regression analysis.

Regression Analysis

One of the methods of investigating the relationship between size and profitability is the regression analysis of profitability on size. There can be different possibilities (1) certain economic pressures might be supposed to be working in the direction of higher rates of return for larger firm, such as technical and marketing opportunities associated with size, (2) firm size can also be a main source of barriers to entry since firms with large assets will be less hindered by the capital requirements barrier to early, the net effect of size on profitability may be positive, (3) in the opposite direction usually the higher capital intensity in the larger firms should lead, other things being equal, to lower profitability. It is with these possibilities in mind, that a regression model to test the relationship between size structure and profitability has been developed.

Specification of Model

With a view to estimating the relationship between the size and profitability, this study was semi-logarithmic specification.

For this purpose, four different models using varying concepts of size and profitability are considered. This helps in analyzing changes in the results due to different measures of profitability and size.

Two different measures of size are used viz., sales and total assets. Profit is defined in terms of gross profit. The concept of gross profit is employed for calculating profitability as ratio to sales and ratio to total assets. Profitability ratio is calculated in two different ways by using sales as well as profit margin as indicated below.

(*a*) **Profit on Total Assets (PR) :** This concept uses gross profit as a percentage of total assets. Total assets are defined as share capital plus reserves plus borrowings.

(*b*) **Profit Margin (PM) :** This concept follows gross profit as a percentage of sales turnover.

Among the above two concepts, the Profit Margin (PM) is a flow concept while the Profit on total assets (PR), is a stock concept. The profit rate concept has certain constraints that should be kept in mind while analyzing the results.

1. The numerator is a flow variable for each year while denominator is a stock variable and represents the sum of capital formation at different points of time.
2. Investment allowance, subsidy and other incentives given to different sectors affect the levy of tax on profits and hence the rate of return on capital.
3. The depreciation on physical assets is not an economic depreciation. Hence it affects the real rate of return.

Using the above concepts and constraints to investigate the relationship between size and profitability, the following Models are used.

$$PR = b_0 + b_1 \log \text{size}_1 + U_1$$

$$PR = b_0 + b_1 \log \text{size}_2 + U_2$$

$$PM = b_0 + b_1 \log \text{size}_1 + U_3$$

$$PM = b_0 + b_1 \log \text{size}_2 + U_4$$

Where PR = ratio of gross profit to total assets

PM = ratio of gross profit to sales turnover

$Size_1$ = size measured by total assets

$Size_2$ = size measured by sales turnover

U = random disturbance term

b_0, b_1 = parameters.

The results of the regression analysis are presented in the following pages. It is to be noted that figures in parentheses in the regression results indicate 't' values. These values marked with asterisk sign denotes that the results of significant at particular level of significance.

Size and Profitability – Whole Industry

The pooled regression results of the model regressing profit margins with sales and total assets for the selected South Indian private sector sugar industry are presented in the Table 5.1. The overall results presented in the table are encouraging. Co-efficient is statistically significant and goodness of fit of the model is also satisfactory.

The results of regression equation show that degree of explanation of profitability by size is 26 per cent and 30 per cent respectively. The result also shows the positive relationship between the size and profitability. It is evident from the results that one unit increase in sales had resulted in 1.65 units increase in profitability and this is significant at one per cent level. Similarly one unit increase in total assets will lead 1.47 units increase in profitability which is significant at one per cent level. These findings are consistent with the conclusions of Alexander (1944), Steindl (1945), Steklar (1964), Baumal (1967), Hall and Weiss (1967), Kamerschen (1968) and Vijayakumar (2003) who advocate positive relationship between size and profitability. The result is contradictory to the findings of Samuel and Smyth (1968), Marcus (1969), Hains (1970), Raidice (1971), Shephered (1972), Smyth, Boyes and Peseau (1975), Whittington

(1980), Pamfret and Shaprio (1980), Ravenscraft (1983), Amato and Wilder (1985) and Vishnukanda Prohit (1998) who advocate negative relationship between size and profitability.

Table 5.1. Size and Profitability – Regression Results (Whole industry)

(*a*) PM = $b_0 + b_1$ log $size_1$

(*b*) PM = $b_0 + b_1$ log $size_2$

Constant	Co-efficient	R^2	F value	D.W
(*a*) -5.20	1.65 (3.542)*	0.26	10.29	0.87
(*b*) 1.95	1.47 (4.126)*	0.30	18.26	0.89

(*a*) PR = $b_0 + b_1$ log $size_1$

(*b*) PR = $b_0 + b_1$ log $size_2$

Constant	Co-efficient	R^2	F value	D.W
(a) 10.74	2.81 (3.614)*	0.30	10.38	0.73
(b) 15.52	4.07 (3.968)*	0.38	27.42	0.75

PM - Ratio of Gross profit on sales

PR - Ratio of Return on Total Assets

b_0, b_1 - Regression co-efficient

$Size_1$ - log value of sales

$Size_2$ - log value of total assets

DW - Durbin – Watson statistics

Figures within parentheses indicate 't' values

*Significant at 0.01 level

Source: Computed.

The pooled results of the model regressing profit rates (PR) with sales and total assets for the selected South Indian private sector Sugar Industry are presented in Table 5.1. The overall results presented in the table are encouraging, co-efficient statistically significant and goodness of fit of the model is also satisfactory. These results show more or less similar findings to the results of regressing profit margin with sales. However, the explanation of sales and total assets on profit rate is improved in this model. It explains 30 per cent and 38 per cent variation in profit margin respectively. It is evident from the results that one unit increase in the sales has resulted in 2.81 units increase in profitability and this is significant at one per cent level. Similarly one unit increase in total assets will lead to 4.07 units increase in profitability which is also significant at one per cent level.

Size and Profitability – Large-sized Industry

The pooled results of the model regressing profit margin with sales and total assets for large-sized selected South Indian private sector Sugar Industry are presented in Table 5.2. The overall results presented in the table are encouraging. Co-efficient is statistically significant and goodness of the fit of the model is also satisfactory in majority of the industry under this group.

The results of regression equation shows that degree of explanation of profit by sales and total assets are 25 per cent and 26 per cent respectively. The results also show the positive relationship between the size and profitability. It is evident from the results that one unit increase in sales will lead to 1.32 unit increase in profitability which is significant at five per cent level. Similarly, one unit increase in total assets will lead to 2.04 units increase profitability which also significant at five per cent level. These findings are consistent with the conclusions of Alexander (1944), Steklar (1964), Hall and Weiss (1967), Kamerschen (1968) and Vijayakumar (2003).

The results of equation for large-sized selected South Indian private sector Sugar Industry, for which the analysis is attempted for seven selected industry indicated that Bannari Amman Sugars Ltd, EID Parry Ltd and Ugar Sugar Works Ltd are the industry where size and profitability have shown positive significant relationship. In these industry more than 25 per cent of profitability are explained by size. Rests of the firms do not have any significant relationship between size and profitability. However, three firms viz, Rajshree Sugars & Chemicals Ltd, Sakthi Sugars Ltd and Thiru Arooran Sugars Ltd. have negative relationship with profit margin as given in Table 5.2.

The pooled regression results of the model regressing profit rates with sales and total assets are presented in Table 5.3. The overall results presented in the table are encouraging. The co-efficient is statistically significant in four out of seven industries. These results show more or less similar findings to the results of regressing profit margin with the sales and total assets. The explanation capacity of sales and total assets on profit rate are 28 per cent and 26 per cent respectively. It is evident from the results that one unit increase in sales will lead to 12.21 unit increase in profitability which is also significant at five per cent level. Similarly one unit increase in total assets had resulted in 2.18 units increase in profitability and this is significant at five per cent level.

The firm wise analysis indicated that Bannari Amman Sugars Ltd, EID Parry Ltd, and Ugar Sugar Works Ltd have shown positive significant relationship. The rests of the firms do not have any significant relationship between size and profitability. However, Sakthi Sugars Ltd had negative relationship between size and profitability.

Size and Profitability - Medium-sized Industry

The pooled results of model regressing profit margin with sales and total assets (size) for medium-sized selected South Indian private sector Sugar Industry are presented in Table 5.4. The overall results presented in the table are encouraging. The co-efficient is statistically significant and goodness of the fit of the model is also satisfactory in most of the industry under this group.

The results of regression equation show that degree of explanation of profit by size is 20 per cent and 24 per cent respectively. The results also show the positive relationship between the size and profitability. It is evident from the results that one unit of increase in sales will lead to 5.22 units increase in profitability which is significant at five per cent level. Similarly, one unit increase in total assets will lead to 6.80 units increase in profitability which also significant at five per cent level. These findings are consistent with the conclusions of Alexander (1944), Steklar (1964), Hall and Weiss (1967), Kamerschen (1968) and Vijayakumar (2003).

The results of equation for medium-sized selected South Indian private sector sugar industry for which the analysis is attempted for four industry indicated that Sri Sarvaraya Sugars Ltd is the industry where size and profitability have shown positive significant relationship. In this industry 30 per cent of profitability is explained by size. However, Kakatiya Cements Sugar & Industries Ltd has negative significant relationship between size and profitability. In this industry 33 per cent of the profitability is explained by size. Rests of the industry do not have any significant relationship between size and profitability.

The pooled regression results of the model regressing profit rates with sales and total assets are presented in Table 5.5. The overall results presented in the table are encouraging. The co-efficient is statistically significant in one out of four industries. These results show more or less similar findings to the results of regressing profit margin with the sales and total assets. The explanation capacity of sales and total assets on profit is 20 per cent and 28 per cent respectively. It is evident from the results that one unit increase in sales will lead to 6.26 units increase in profitability, which is also significant at five per cent level. Similarly one unit increase in total assets had resulted in 4.18 units increase in profitability and this is significant at five per cent level.

Table 5.2. Size and Profitability – Regression Results (Large-sized industry)

(a) PM = $b_0 + b_1 \log size_1$

Sl.No.	Industry	Constant	Co-efficient	R^2	F value	D.W
1.	Bannari Amman Sugars Ltd	3.26	4.58 (2.161)**	0.26	4.67	0.95
2.	EID Parry Ltd	4.73	1.63 (3.243)*	0.31	6.96	0.47
3.	Jeypore Sugars & Chemicals Ltd	-16.94	1.42 (1.067)	0.08	1.14	1.64
4.	Rajshree Sugars & Chemicals Ltd	26.56	-6.11 (0.761)	0.04	0.58	0.80
5.	Sakthi Sugars Ltd	9.56	-1.94 (0.237)	0.12	0.06	0.94
6.	Thiru Arooran Sugars Ltd	12.95	-0.32 (0.022)	0.16	0.01	2.66
7.	Ugar Sugar Works Ltd	-36.64	18.15 (3.307)*	0.46	10.94	1.14
	Large-sized industry	**5.03**	**1.32 (2.192)****	**0.25**	**4.53**	**1.09**

(*b*) $PM = b_0 + b_1 \log size_2$

Sl.No.	Industry	Constant	Co-efficient	R^2	F value	D.W
1.	Bannari Amman Sugars Ltd	1.93	4.83 (1.969)**	0.23	3.88	0.87
2.	EID Parry Ltd	-4.52	4.89 (4.057)*	0.36	6.12	0.53
3.	Jeypore Sugars & Chemicals Ltd	-18.82	11.09 (0.999)	0.07	1.00	1.49
4.	Rajshree Sugars & Chemicals Ltd	27.61	-6.26 (0.718)	0.04	0.57	0.79
5.	Sakthi Sugars Ltd	33.15	-10.39 (1.686)	0.18	2.84	1.06
6.	Thiru Arooran Sugars Ltd	61.02	-20.26 (3.142)	0.16	2.51	2.99
7.	Ugar Sugar Works Ltd	-36.27	18.29 (4.505)*	0.61	20.29	1.33
	Large-sized industry	**9.44**	**2.04 (2.118)****	**0.26**	**4.12**	**1.52**

PM - Ratio of Gross profit on sales
$Size_1$ - log value of sales
DW - Durbin – Watson statistics
b_0, b_1 - Regression co-efficient
$Size_2$ - log value of total assets

Figures within parentheses indicate 't' values

*Significant at 0.01 level **Significant at 0.05 level

Source: Computed

Table 5.3. Size and Profitability – Regression Results (Large-sized industry)

(a) PR = $b_0 + b_1$ log $size_1$

Sl.No.	Industry	Constant	Co-efficient	R^2	F value	D.W
1.	Bannari Amman Sugars Ltd	-2.15	3.62 (2.169)**	0.27	4.17	1.22
2.	EID Parry Ltd	8.45	1.41 (2.435)**	0.18	3.96	0.91
3.	Jeypore Sugars & Chemicals Ltd	-9.54	5.28 (0.906)	0.06	0.82	1.05
4.	Rajshree Sugars & Chemicals Ltd	15.32	-3.90 (-0.538)	0.02	0.29	1.18
5.	Sakthi Sugars Ltd	17.50	-6.99 (1.929)***	0.22	3.72	1.65
6.	Thiru Arooran Sugars Ltd	17.31	-7.60 (-1.669)	0.18	2.79	1.07
7.	Ugar Sugar Works Ltd	-9.51	4.92 (3.288)**	0.28	4.69	1.61
	Large-sized industry	**10.42**	**12.21 (2.913)****	**0.28**	**4.61**	**1.01**

(b) $PR = b_0 + b_1 \log size_2$

Sl.No.	Industry	Constant	Co-efficient	R^2	F value	D.W
1.	Bannari Amman Sugars Ltd	-0.89	2.87 (2.392)**	0.18	3.94	1.26
2.	EID Parry Ltd	4.06	0.12 (2.652)**	0.16	3.78	0.89
3.	Jeypore Sugars & Chemicals Ltd	-3.47	2.03 (0.330)	0.01	0.11	1.01
4.	Rajshree Sugars & Chemicals Ltd	20.86	-6.34 (-0.819)	0.05	0.67	1.16
5.	Sakthi Sugars Ltd	19.95	-7.27 (-2.638)**	0.35	6.96	1.98
6.	Thiru Arooran Sugars Ltd	28.67	-11.19 (-3.189)*	0.44	10.17	1.21
7.	Ugar Sugar Works Ltd	-3.96	2.50 (3.722)*	0.38	10.42	1.07
	Large-sized industry	**9.46**	**2.18 (2.756)****	**0.26**	**4.68**	**1.01**

PR - Ratio of Return on Total Assets
$Size_1$ - log value of sales
DW - Durbin – Watson statistics
b_0, b_1 - Regression co-efficient
$Size_2$ - log value of total assets

Figures within parentheses indicate 't' values
*Significant at 0.01 level **Significant at 0.05 level ***Significant at 0.10 level

Source: Computed

Table 5.4. Size and Profitability – Regression Results (Medium-sized industry)

(a) PM = $b_0 + b_1$ log size$_1$

Sl.No.	Industry	Constant	Co-efficient	R^2	F value	D.W.
1.	Kothari Sugars & Chemicals Ltd	-101.79	52.72 (0.895)	0.09	0.80	1.15
2.	Sri Chamundeswari Sugars Ltd	22.38	-9.29 (0.588)	0.11	0.35	2.34
3.	Sri Sarvaraya Sugars Ltd	-26.11	16.93 (2.379)**	0.30	5.66	1.68
4.	Kakatiya Cements Sugar & Industries Ltd.	42.35	-13.81 (2.542)**	0.33	6.46	0.78
	Medium-sized Industry	**-4.56**	**5.22 (2.441)****	**0.20**	**4.19**	**1.51**

(b) $PM = b_0 + b_1 \log size_2$

Sl.No.	Industry	Constant	Co-efficient	R^2	F value	D.W.
1.	Kothari Sugars & Chemicals Ltd	186.01	81.10	0.15	2.34	1.14
2.	Sri Chamundeswari Sugars Ltd	15.36	-4.89 (0.371)	0.18	0.14	2.18
3.	Sri Sarvaraya Sugars Ltd	-37.03	22.15 (2.137)***	0.26	4.57	1.64
4.	Kakatiya Cements Sugar & Industries Ltd.	51.25	-16.50 (2.895)**	0.39	8.38	0.77
	Medium-sized industry	**27.08**	**6.80 (2.541)****	**0.24**	**4.5**	**1.54**

PM - Ratio of Gross profit on sales
b_0, b_1 - Regression co-efficient
$Size_1$ - log value of sales
$Size_2$ - log value of total assets
DW - Durbin – Watson statistics
Figures within parentheses indicate 't' values
**Significant at 0.05 level
***Significant at 0.10 level
Source: Computed

Table 5.5. Size and Profitability – Regression Results (Medium-sized industry)

(*a*) PR = $b_0 + b_1 \log size_1$

Sl.No.	Industry	Constant	Co-efficient	R^2	F value	D.W.
1.	Kothari Sugars & Chemicals Ltd	-5.88	1.44 (0.068)	0.10	0.01	1.12
2.	Sri Chamundeswari Sugars Ltd	-7.84	-3.64 (0.400)	0.12	0.16	1.25
3.	Sri Sarvaraya Sugars Ltd	5.56	-0.99 (2.413)	0.26	4.17	1:71
4.	Kakatiya Cements Sugar & Industries Ltd	17.63	-6.12 (2.901)***	0.22	3.61	0.74
	Medium-sized industry	**17.48**	**-6.26 (3.093)****	**0.20**	**4.19**	**0.99**

(*b*) PR = $b_0 + b_1 \log size_2$

Sl.No.	Industry	Constant	Co-efficient	R^2	F value	D.W.
1.	Kothari Sugars & Chemicals Ltd	57.16	-26.62 (-1.427)	0.14	2.04	1.35
2.	Sri Chamundeswari Sugars Ltd	1.62	-1.34 (1.176)	0.12	2.76	1.35
3.	Sri Sarvaraya Sugars Ltd	8.35	-2.36 (2.707)	0.24	3.16	1.74
4.	Kakatiya Cements Sugar & Industries Ltd	24.36	-8.70 (-2.723)**	0.36	7.42	0.76
	Medium-sized industry	**10.12**	**4.18 (-3.893)**	**0.28**	**6.78**	**1.11**

PR - Ratio of Return on Total Assets
b_0,b_1 - Regression co-efficient
$Size_1$ - log value of sales
$Size_2$ - log value of total assets
DW - Durbin – Watson statistics
Figures within parentheses indicate 't' values
**Significant at 0.05 level
***Significant at 0.10 level
Source: Computed

The industry wise analysis indicated that Kakatiya Cements Sugar & Industries Ltd had shown negative significant relationship. The rests of the industry do not have any significant relationship between size and profitability.

Size and Profitability – Small-sized Industry

The pooled results of the model regressing profit margin with sales and total assets for the selected small-sized South Indian private sector sugar industry are presented in Table 5.6. The overall results presented in the table are encouraging. The co-efficient is statistically significant and goodness of the fit of the model is also satisfactory in half of the industry under this group.

The results of regression equation show that degree of explanation of profit by sales and total assets are 21 per cent each respectively. The results also show positive relationship between the size and profitability. It is evident from the results that one per cent increase in sales will lead to 6.15 units increase in profitability, which is significant at five per cent level. Similarly, one unit increase in total assets will lead to 10.48 units increase in profitability which also significant at five per cent level. These findings are consistent with the Alexander (1944), Steindl (1945), Steklar (1964), Baumal (1967), Hall and Weiss (1967), Kamerschen (1968) and Vijayakumar (2003).

The results of equation for small-sized South Indian private sector Sugar Industry, for which the analysis is attempted for four selected industry indicate that Empee Sugars & Chemicals Ltd and India Sugars and Refineries Ltd are the industry where size and profitability have shown positive significant relationship. In these industry more than 20 per cent profitability are explained by sales alone. Rests of the industry do not have any significant relationship between size and profitability. However, two industry Dharani Sugars & Chemicals Ltd and Ponni Sugars Ltd have negative relationship with profit margin as given in Table 5.6.

The pooled regression results of the model regressing profit rates with sales and total assets are presented in Table 5.7. The overall results presented in the table are encouraging. The co-efficient is statistically significant in two out of four industries. These results show more or less similar findings to the results of regressing profit margin with the sales and total assets. The explanation capacity of sales and total assets on profit is 18 per cent and 25 per cent respectively. It is evident from the results that one unit increase in sales will lead to 2.54 units incrcasc in profitability, which is also significant at five per cent level. Similarly, one unit increase in total assets had resulted in 1.68 unit increase in profitability and this is significant at five per cent level.

The firm wise analysis indicated that Empee Sugars & Chemicals Ltd and India Sugars and Refineries Ltd have shown positive significant relationship. The Dharani Sugars & Chemicals Ltd and Ponni Sugars Ltd had negative relationship between size and profitability.

GROWTH AND PROFITABILITY

When the study of growth is undertaken in terms of systematic influences which may affect growth, rather than regarding the growth as a wholly chance phenomenon, then the most important systematic influence on growth, is that of profitability. Thus the relationship between growth and profitability is of considerable interest both from theoretical and practical points of view[20].

As far the theoretical point of view is concerned, the traditional neo-classical theory of the firm is not very helpful in this respect. Under its usual assumption of perfect competition in all markets, given technology, etc., firm may grow only in order to achieve the 'optimum size' at which they maximize profits. Therefore in equilibrium when all firms are at their optimum size, there will be no relationship at all between the profitability and growth of firms, simply

Table 5.6. Size and Profitability – Regression Results (Small-sized industry)

(*a*) $PM = b_0 + b_1 \log size_1$

Sl.No.	Industry	Constant	Co-efficient	R^2	F value	D.W.
1.	Dharani Sugars & Chemicals Ltd	25.23	-10.81 (1.211)	0.10	1.47	1.37
2.	Empee Sugars & Chemicals Ltd	-62.93	43.85 (2.627)**	0.35	6.90	2.39
3.	India Sugars and Refineries Ltd	-59.91	40.45 (1.970)***	0.23	3.88	1.29
4.	Ponni Sugars Ltd	48.41	-24.25 (1.722)	0.19	2.97	0.80
	Small-sized industry	**-11.51**	**6.15 (2.788)****	**0.21**	**4.62**	**1.55**

(*b*) $PM = b_0 + b_1 \log size_2$

Sl.No.	Industry	Constant	Co-efficient	R^2	F value	D.W.
1.	Dharani Sugars & Chemicals Ltd	42.75	-17.65 (2.416)**	0.31	5.84	1.72
2.	Empee Sugars & Chemicals Ltd	-249.42	141.34 (1.697)	0.18	2.88	2.23
3.	India Sugars and Refineries Ltd	-23.92	13.78 (0.568)	0.02	0.32	1.05
4.	Ponni Sugars Ltd	88.90	-13.02 (2.397)**	0.31	5.74	1.28
	Small-sized industry	**-25.14**	**10.48 (2.711)****	**0.21**	**4.03**	**1.56**

PM - Ratio of Gross profit on sales
b_0, b_1 - Regression co-efficient
$Size_1$ - log value of sales
$Size_2$ - log value of total assets
DW - Durbin – Watson statistics
Figures within parentheses indicate 't' values
**Significant at 0.05 level
***Significant at 0.10 level
Source: Computed

Table 5.7. Size and Profitability – Regression Results (Small-sized Industry)

(*a*) PR = $b_0 + b_1$ log size$_1$

Sl.No.	Industry	Constant	Co-efficient	R^2	F value	D.W.
1.	Dharani Sugars & Chemicals Ltd	16.95	-8.21	0.15	2.34	1.22
2.	Empee Sugars & Chemicals Ltd	-25.29	13.27 (1.887)***	0.22	3.56	1.66
3.	India Sugars and Refineries Ltd	-28.42	18.15 (4.076)**	0.31	8.42	1.19
4.	Ponni Sugars Ltd	24.53	-14.52 (-0.929)	0.06	0.86	1.41
	Small-sized industry	**-7.94**	**2.54 (3.435)****	**0.18**	**4.19**	**0.92**

(*b*) PR = $b_0 + b_1$ log $size_2$

Sl.No.	Industry	Constant	Co-efficient	R^2	F value	D.W.
1.	Dharani Sugars & Chemicals Ltd	30.09	-13.32 (-3.334)*	0.41	11.11	1.73
2.	Empee Sugars & Chemicals Ltd	10.19	18.85 (-3.251)**	0.21	6.26	1.63
3.	India Sugars and Refineries Ltd	-22.11	12.71	0.04	0.49	0.96
4.	Ponni Sugars Ltd	33.87	-18.30 (-0.844)	0.05	0.71	1.48
	Small-sized industry	**2.39**	**1.68 (3.435)****	**0.25**	**5.92**	**0.96**

PR - Ratio of Return on Total Assets
b_0, b_1 - Regression co-efficient
$Size_1$ - log value of sales
$Size_2$ - log value of total assets
DW - Durbin – Watson statistics
Figures within parentheses indicate 't' values
*Significant at 0.01 level
**Significant at 0.05 level
***Significant at 0.10 level
Source: Computed

because no firm will grow further. If, for some reason, some or all firms are not in equilibrium at any moment of time, and are assumed to be moving towards equilibrium, there may well emerge some relationship between profitability and growth on a cross section basis.[21]

Other aspects of relationship between growth and profitability; not only does growth depend on profitability, but profitability itself is a function of growth. There are certain costs involved in the growth which increase as the growth rate increases, thereby reducing profitability. The costs of growth arise mainly from the expenses of obtaining a larger share of existing markets and of increasing rates of diversification for growth, because of increasing resistance from the rival firms and partly due to managerial constraints to the growth of the firm. So it is also due to the conflict between profitability and growth that sometime a relatively high growth rate may not be profitable for the firm in the sense of profit maximization because growth means increase in supply which may mean lower price even lower than the price maximization price. Therefore, the relationship between the growth and profitability may be negative beyond certain growth rate; i.e. the higher the growth the lower the level of profitability of the firm. If this negative relationship between the two exists, it is possible in principle that it may be so strong as to completely outweigh the tendency for positive association between growth and profitability.

Further, it is also argued that growth displays a favourable impact on its profitability except for the samples of bigger firms.[22] It might be argued that smaller firms, being more flexible, tend to take chance more readily than their bigger rivals. It may also be that smaller firms can profitably exploit chances by expanding sales at unreduced prices. A firm's rate of growth depends both on its ability to grow and on its willingness to grow. Its ability to finance growth is closely related to its achieved profitability. The higher the level of its profitability, the more it would be in a position to grow from retained profits. Furthermore, a high 'level of achieved profitability' will be taken by potential investors as a strong indication and the further level of profitability will be high, so that the firm will be able to make new issues on favourable terms. This correspondence between a high ability to grow and 'high level of achieved profitability' is particularly close when growth is measured in terms of the long term finance (i.e. net assets) of the business.

However, a firm's willingness to grow does not depend so directly on its profitability. Profitability does provide an incentive for growth, but there are other factors such as the state of competition, the nature of management, the state of demand and the technological opportunities. For example, for the same profitability, a firm operating in an industry with a buoyant demand may be expected to grow more, by retaining profits or raising new issues, than the firm which operates in an industry with less buoyant demand. Similarly, a firm which is run by a growth oriented management may be expected to grow more than a firm, with the same level of profitability, which is run by a profit maximizing owner manager. In the same way it is possible that there are industries in which there is competition amongst the leading firms to increase their relative market shares, so that they have to grow at a faster rate for the same level of profitability than firms in a less competitive industry.

Further, the factors affecting the willingness to grow may be different for large firms as opposed to small firms in the same industry. In particular, a large firm is usually more diversified and may produce a range of products which could be classified as belonging to more than one industry, so that the firm's willingness to grow will probably be influenced by conditions in a range of industries rather than a single industry. Due to these reasons, the nature of the relationship between profitability and growth for these (large) management dominated firms may be different from that for the smaller sized firms.

In an expanding economy, we could expect a positive association between growth and profitability of firms, because profits provide the ability to grow. However, the factors affecting the willingness to grow are such that these are likely to vary between different industries. These are also likely to vary within the same industry at different points of time, e.g. as demand for the product of the industry changes. This means that the magnitude and the precise form of the positive association between profitability and growth will be different in different industries at a particular time and in the same industry at different times.

To sum up, the above considerations suggest that we can expect, in general, a positive or negative association between growth and profitability. Furthermore, the nature and form of this relationship may vary between firms of different sizes, between industries and over time for the same industry. One of the purposes of this part is to examine the extent and significance of these differences for the industries under study.

Growth and Profitability – Empirical Result

In this part of the discussion, the relationship between profitability and growth has been explored by means of regression analysis in the following form.

$$P = a + bG + u$$

Where, P - Profitability

G - growth rate

u - error term

a and b are parameters

For each industry, sector and whole industry, regression equations were estimated, pertaining to alternative measures of profitability and growth. The alternative measures of growth viz., growth rate of total assets, growth rate of fixed assets and growth rate of sales were used. Thus, in all various regression equations were estimated to know how far differences in profit rates could be explained by differences in growth rates. The results of these equations are presented in the Tables 5.8 to 5.10.

Table 5.8 shows the extent to which changes in profitability margin are explained by the changes in the growth of total assets. The co-efficient of determination (R^2) is in the case of whole industry i.e. 0.21, this means that 21 per cent change in profitability margin are explained by growth of total assets. The value of regression co-efficient (b) is 0.12 indicating thereby that one per cent increase in growth rate is associated with 0.12 per cent increase in profitability. This co-efficient is statistically significant at 10 per cent level. It is evident from the table that the percentage change in profit margin are explained by the growth of total assets are 52 per cent, 31 per cent and 7 per cent respectively in large-sized sector, medium-sized sector and small-sized sector during the study period.

The value of regression co-efficient is indicated that one per cent increase in growth rate is associated with 0.12 per cent, 0.10 per cent and 0.08 per cent increase in profitability of Large-sized, medium-sized and Small-sized sectors respectively during the study period. Among the large-sized sector industries except Bannari Amman Sugars Ltd and Jeypore Sugars & Chemicals Ltd showed positive relationship between growth and profitability. Further, values of regression co-efficient are statistically significant only in case of Rajshree Sugars & Chemicals Ltd and Sakthi Sugars Ltd. Similarly, all the selected industries under medium-sized sector and small-sized sector showed positive relationship between growth and profitability. Thus, as expected there is positive relationship between growth rate of total assets and profitability in the selected South Indian private sector sugar industry during the study period.

Table 5.8. Growth and Profitability – Regression Results

$PR = b_0 + b_1 ROG_1$

S.No.	Industry	Constant	Co-efficient	R^2	F value	D.W.
1.	Bannari Amman Sugars Ltd	6.99	-0.04 (-1.623)	0.17	2.64	1.46
2.	EID Parry Ltd	3.91	0.03 (1.171)	0.10	1.37	0.99
3.	Jeypore Sugars & Chemicals Ltd	1.52	-0.03 (-0.29)	0.01	0.08	1.02
4.	Rajshree Sugars & Chemicals Ltd	0.11	0.46 (4.591)*	0.62	21.08	1.74
5.	Sakthi Sugars Ltd	-1.89	0.10 (2.390)**	0.31	5.71	1.10
6.	Thiru Arooran Sugars Ltd	0.51	0.09 (1.604)	0.17	2.57	1.42
7.	Ugar Sugar Works Ltd	1.47	0.01 (0.241)	0.01	0.06	2.00
	Large-sized industry	**1.15**	**0.12 (3.721)***	**0.52**	**13.89**	**1.07**
8.	Kothari Sugars & Chemicals Ltd	6.99	-0.04 (-1.623)	0.17	2.64	1.46
9.	Sri Chamundeswari Sugars Ltd	3.91	0.03 (1.171)	0.10	1.37	0.99
10.	Sri Sarvaraya Sugars Ltd	1.52	-0.03 (-0.29)	0.01	0.08	1.02

11.	Kakatiya Cements Sugar & Industries Ltd	0.11	0.46 (4.591)*	0.62	21.08	1.74
	Medium-sized industry	**-1.89**	**0.10 (2.390)****	**0.31**	**5.71**	**1.10**
12.	Dharani Sugars & Chemicals Ltd	-0.49	0.09 (1.959)***	0.23	3.84	0.81
13.	Empee Sugars & Chemicals Ltd	-6.11	0.03 (0.51)	0.02	0.26	1.46
14.	India Sugars and Refineries Ltd	-.389	0.09 (0.695)	0.04	0.48	0.86
15.	Ponni Sugars Ltd	-3.19	0.09 (0.852)	0.05	0.73	1.49
	Small-sized industry	**-3.55**	**0.08 (0.952)**	**0.07**	**0.91**	**0.87**
	Whole industry	**-0.49**	**0.12 (1.835)*****	**0.21**	**3.37**	**0.82**

PR - Ratio of Return on Total Assets;
b_0, b_1 - Regression co-efficient
ROG_1 - Growth rate of Total Assets
DW - Durbin – Watson statistics
Figures within parentheses indicate 't' values
*Significant at 0.01 level
**Significant at 0.05 level
***Significant at 0.10 level
Source: Computed

Table 5.9. Growth and Profitability – Regression Results

$$PR = b_0 + b_1 ROG_2$$

Sl.No.	Industry	Constant	Co-efficient	R^2	F value	D.W.
1.	Bannari Amman Sugars Ltd	6.76	-0.03 (-1.618)	0.17	2.62	1.33
2.	EID Parry Ltd	3.98	0.02 (0.843)	0.02	0.20	1.00
3.	Jeypore Sugars & Chemicals Ltd	0.65	0.02 (0.447)	0.02	0.20	1.00
4.	Rajshree Sugars & Chemicals Ltd	7.67	0.01 (0.012)	0.01	0.01	1.07
5.	Sakthi Sugars Ltd	-0.51	0.03 (1.02)	0.07	1.04	1.07
6.	Thiru Arooran Sugars Ltd	1.39	0.02 (0.603)	0.03	0.36	0.80
7.	Ugar Sugar Works Ltd	1.44	0.01 (0.231)	0.01	0.05	1.90
	Large-sized Industry	**2.36**	**0.05 (1.089)**	**0.08**	**1.19**	**1.04**
8.	Kothari Sugars & Chemicals Ltd	-2.58	-0.01 (-0.075)	0.01	0.01	1.12
9.	Sri Chamundeswari Sugars Ltd	-2.28	0.09 (0.90)	0.06	0.81	1.08
10.	Sri Sarvaraya Sugars Ltd	2.27	0.10 (1.478)	0.14	2.19	1.60
11.	Kakatiya Cements Sugar & Industries Ltd	6.91	-0.01 (-0.058)	0.01	0.01	0.57

	Medium-sized industry	**1.39**	**0.02 (0.168)**	**0.01**	**0.03**	**0.86**
12.	Dharani Sugars & Chemicals Ltd	1.96	-0.05 (-1.160)	0.09	1.35	0.77
13.	Empee Sugars & Chemicals Ltd	-3.63	-0.01 (-2.485)	0.32	6.18	1.01
14.	India Sugars and Refineries Ltd	-5.99	0.27 (1.008)	0.07	1.02	0.90
15.	Ponni Sugars Ltd	-2.84	0.01 (0.148)	0.01	0.02	1.38
	Small-sized industry	**-2.20**	**-0.01 (-0.466)**	**0.02**	**0.22**	**0.80**
	Whole industry	**1.12**	**0.01 (0.259)**	**0.01**	**0.67**	**0.74**

PR - Ratio of Return on Total Assets; b_0,b_1 - Regression co-efficient
ROG_2 - Growth rate of Gross block
DW - Durbin – Watson statistics
Figures within parentheses indicate 't' values
Source: Computed

Table 5.10. Growth and Profitability – Regression Results

$$PR = b_0 + b_1 ROG_3$$

Sl.No.	Industry	Constant	Co-efficient	R^2	F value	D.W.
1.	Bannari Amman Sugars Ltd	5.86	0.01 (0.228)	0.01	0.05	0.95
2.	EID Parry Ltd	3.76	0.05 (1.792)***	0.20	3.21	0.74
3.	Jeypore Sugars & Chemicals Ltd	1.05	0.01 (0.061)	0.01	0.01	0.99
4.	Rajshree Sugars & Chemicals Ltd	5.85	0.06 (1.657)	0.17	2.74	1.21
5.	Sakthi Sugars Ltd	0.43	-0.01 (-0.470)	0.02	0.22	1.99
6.	Thiru Arooran Sugars Ltd	1.30	0.02 (0.753)	0.04	0.57	0.73
7.	Ugar Sugar Works Ltd	1.12	0.03 (1.024)	0.08	1.05	1.77
	Large-sized industry	**2.01**	**0.06 (2.512)****	**0.33**	**6.31**	**1.42**
8.	Kothari Sugars & Chemicals Ltd	-7.41	0.28 (2.407)**	0.31	5.79	1.82
9.	Sri Chamundeswari Sugars Ltd	-1.68	0.02 (0.752)	0.04	0.57	1.28
10.	Sri Sarvaraya Sugars Ltd	3.37	0.01 (0.461)	0.02	0.21	1.68
11.	Kakatiya Cements Sugar & Industries Ltd	6.27	0.03 (0.493)	0.02	0.24	0.52

	Medium-sized industry	**1.00**	**0.03 (0.586)**	**0.03**	**0.34**	**0.98**
12.	Dharani Sugars & Chemicals Ltd	-0.99	0.06 (2.567)**	0.34	6.59	1.03
13.	Empee Sugars & Chemicals Ltd	-6.49	0.03 (0.72)	0.04	0.52	1.48
14.	India Sugars and Refineries Ltd	-4.12	0.09 (0.928)	0.06	0.86	1.23
15.	Ponni Sugars Ltd	-2.85	0.01 (0.128)	0.01	0.02	1.40
	Small-sized industry	**-5.57**	**0.13 (2.062)**	**0.25**	**4.25**	**1.45**
	Whole industry	**-1.66**	**0.13 (2.978)****	**0.41**	**8.87**	**1.70**

PR - Ratio of Return on Total Assets; b_0, b_1 - Regression co-efficient
ROG_3 - Growth rate of Net Sales
DW - Durbin – Watson statistics
Figures within parentheses indicate 't' values
**Significant at 0.05 level
***Significant at 0.10 level
Source: Computed

Table 5.9 shows the results of regression of profitability margin on growth of fixed assets. Inter-industry differences regarding relationship between profitability and growth rate are evident from the table. In this table co-efficient of determination (R^2) is 0.01 in case of whole industry suggesting that one per cent change in profitability is explained by growth of fixed assets. The value of regression co-efficient is 0.01 indicating thereby that one per cent change in growth rate of fixed assets leads to 0.01 per cent change in profitability in case of these industries. In the cases of large-sized sector, medium-sized sector and small-sized sector, the values of R^2 respectively are 0.08, 0.01 and 0.02 suggesting that 8 per cent change in profitability of large-sized sector, one per cent change in profitability of medium-sized sector and two per cent change in profitability of small-sized sector are explained by the one per cent change in growth rate of fixed assets. None of the regression co-efficient of growth rate of fixed assets is significant during the study period. Bannari Amman Sugars Ltd in large-sized sector, Kothari Sugars & Chemicals Ltd and Kakatiya Cements Sugar & Industries Ltd in medium-sized sector and Dharani Sugars & Chemicals Ltd and Empee Sugars & Chemicals Ltd in small-sized sector showed negative relationship between growth rate of fixed assets and profitability. Thus, as expected there is positive, though weak, relationship between growth rate of fixed assets and profitability in the selected sectors and the sample industry as a whole during the study period.

Table 5.10 depicts the results of regression of profitability on growth of net sales of all firms. Regression co-efficient is statistically significant in EID Parry Ltd (large-sized), Kothari Sugars & Chemicals Ltd (medium-sized) and Dharani Sugars & Chemicals Ltd (small-sized). The highest value of R^2 (i.e. 0.41) in this industry tells that 41 per cent variations in profitability are explained by variation in growth of sales. Further, in the cases of large-sized sector, medium-sized sector and small-sized sector, 33 per cent, 3 per cent and 25 per cent changes in profitability are due to changes in growth of net sales.

The value of regression co-efficient in this industry (i.e.0.13) indicating that one per cent increase in growth rate of sales is associated with 0.13 per cent increase in profitability. It was 0.06 per cent, 0.03 per cent and 0.13 per cent as in the cases of large-sized, medium-sized and small-sized sectors during the study period. It is evident from the result that as expected, there is positive relationship between growth rate of sales and profitability during the study period.

LIQUIDITY AND PROFITABILITY

Liquidity and profitability are two important aspects of corporate business life. Liquidity measures the ability of a company to honour all the maturing obligations. No firm can endure without liquidity. Profitability is the rate of return on company's investment. An unwarranted high investment in current assets would reduce this rate of return. Working capital management has thus, because a basic and broad aspect of adjudicating the performance of a corporate entity. It is, therefore, essential to maintain an adequate degree of liquidity for smooth running of the business operations. The liquidity should be neither excessive nor inadequate. Excessive liquidity indicates accumulation of idle funds which do not earn any profit for the firm and inadequate liquidity not only adversely effects the credit worthiness of the firm but also disrupts the production process and impedes its earning capacity to great extent.

Conventionally, almost all the textbooks pertaining to the financial management and working capital management apparently stress on inverse relationship between liquidity and profitability. The most common measure of liquidity is current ratio and of profitability is return on capital employed. A high current ratio indicates a larger investment in current assets which means a low rate of return on investment for the firm, as excess investment in current asset will not gross enough return. A low current ratio indicates a smaller investment in current assets which means a high rate of return on investment for the firm, as no idle investment is tied up in current assets. However, a low current ratio could also mean interrupted production and sales, because of frequent stock out and inability to pay to creditors in time due to restrictive policy.

Thus, it can be said that the inverse relationship between profitability and liquidity is not forever, rather up to a certain level of liquidity, this theory holds good; beyond that level decline in liquidity will cause decline in profitability. A very poor liquidity position in a firm shall create problems in smooth running of business, thereby obstructing the course of business and causing a decline in profitability. Hence, one should strike a balance between liquidity and profitability. It is felt that there is a need to study the impact of liquidity in profit generating process.

Therefore, in this part an effort has been made to make an empirical study of South Indian private sector sugar industry for assessing the impact of liquidity on profitability during the period of study. The impact of liquidity on profitability has been examined by computing co-efficient of correlation and regression analysis of liquidity ratio and profitability ratio. The objective of this attempt is to measure the extent of relationship between liquidity and profitability by using simple correlation co-efficient and also to test the significance of such correlation co-efficient. Further, to study the impact of liquidity on profitability, regression analysis was done individually for all the industries under study.

Liquidity and Profitability – Correlation Analysis

The correlation co-efficient of current ratio and return on capital employed ratios of fifteen industries under study are mentioned in Table 5.11. It is evident from the result that there was a positive correlation between profitability and liquidity in the South Indian private sector Sugar Industry during the study period. The correlation co-efficient between current ratio and return on capital employed is 0.634 and it is statistically significant at 5 per cent level. Similarly, the correlation co-efficient of large-sized industry and small-sized industry have shown positive correlation between profitability and liquidity and its statistical significance is one per cent and five per cent respectively. Further, the medium-sized sugar industry also showed positive correlation between profitability and liquidity but it was not statistically significant.

Among the large-sized industry group, however, five industries depicted negative correlation between current ratio and return on capital employed. These industries are Bannari Amman Sugars Ltd, EID Parry Ltd, Jeypore Sugars & Chemicals Ltd, Sakthi Sugars Ltd and Ugar Sugar Works Ltd. The two industries viz., Rajshree Sugars & Chemicals Ltd and Thiru Arooran Sugars Ltd showed positive correlation co-efficient between their liquidity and profitability. Among the medium-sized industry, out of four industries two industries viz., Sri Chamundeswari Sugars Ltd and Sri Sarvaraya Sugars Ltd showed negative correlation co-efficient between current ratio and return on capital employed. However, the two industries viz., Kothari Sugars & Chemicals Ltd and Kakatiya Cements Sugar & Industries Ltd showed positive correlation co-efficient between their liquidity and profitability. Among the four industries under small-sized groups except Ponni Sugars Ltd, the remaining three industries viz., Dharani Sugars & Chemicals Ltd, Empee Sugars & Chemicals Ltd and India Sugars and Refineries Ltd showed positive correlation co-efficient between their liquidity and profitability. Except Jeypore Sugars & Chemicals Ltd and Kakatiya Cements Sugar & Industries Ltd none of the industry's correlation co-efficient was found to be statistically significant.

The correlation analysis between liquidity and profitability position of the fifteen industries under study indicated a mix of positive and negative correlation co-efficient. However, eight out of fifteen industries revealed negative correlation and seven out of fifteen industries depicted positive correlation. However, only two industries (Jeypore Sugars & Chemicals Ltd and Kakatiya Cements

Table 5.11. Liquidity and profitability relationship

ROCE = f(CR)

Industry	r	Cons-tant	Co-efficient	R^2	F-value	DW
Bannari Amman Sugars Ltd	-0.136	23.74	-2.94 (-0.494)	0.02	0.24	1.77
EID Parry Ltd	-0.262	28.34	-8.16 (-0.980)	-0.01	0.96	0.65
Jeypore Sugars & Chemicals Ltd	-0.512***	156.37	-133.58 (-2.151)***	0.21	4.63	0.74
Rajshree Sugars & Chemicals Ltd	0.212	15.67	6.90 (0.783)	0.05	0.61	1.34
Sakthi Sugars Ltd	-0.366	25.73	-6.31 (-1.416)	0.13	2.00	1.75
Thiru Arooran Sugars Ltd	0.013	10.61	0.76 (0.047)	0.01	0.01	0.49
Ugar Sugar Works Ltd	-0.409	106.45	-67.31 (-1.614)	0.17	2.60	1.61
Large-sized firms	**0.711***	**-24.37**	**39.11 (3.644)***	**0.51**	**13.28**	**1.45**
Kothari Sugars & Chemicals Ltd	0.312	-46.70	36.05 (1.185)	0.10	1.41	2.96
Sri Chamundeswari Sugars Ltd	-0.031	20.70	-1.46 (-0.112)	0.01	0.01	1.21
Sri Sarvaraya Sugars Ltd	-0.024	26.14	-1.40 (-0.088)	0.01	0.01	1.51
Kakatiya Cements Sugar & Industries Ltd	0.477***	10.80	2.07 (1.956)***	0.17	3.83	1.02

Medium-sized firms	**0.200**	**-0.17**	**10.01 (0.738)**	**0.04**	**0.54**	**2.86**
Dharani Sugars & Chemicals Ltd	0.055	16.26	1.10 (0.197)	0.01	0.04	1.38
Empee Sugars & Chemicals Ltd	0.275	-0.33	8.35 (1.03)	0.08	1.06	1.20
India Sugars and Refineries Ltd	0.426	-33.42	67.61 (1.699)	0.18	2.89	1.24
Ponni Sugars Ltd	-0.271	19.29	-4.21 (-1.01)	0.07	1.03	1.26
Small-sized firms	**0.577****	**-4.84**	**18.42 (2.546)****	**0.33**	**6.48**	**1.02**
Whole Industry	**0.634****	**-12.44**	**24.68 (2.915)****	**0.40**	**8.5**	**2.00**

Note: Figures in brackets indicate t-values of co-efficient.
*Significant at 0.01 level
**Significant at 0.05 level
***Significant at 0.10 level
Source: Computed

Sugar & Industries Ltd) out of fifteen industries depicted significant correlation.

Liquidity and Profitability – Regression Analysis

For performing regression analysis current ratio has been taken as independent variable and return on capital employed as dependent variable. The simple regression has been performed to assess the effect of current ratio on return on capital employed. In this regard the following research hypothesis is tested.

H_0 - There is a significantly negative relationship between liquidity and profitability of South Indian private sector Sugar Industry.

The regression equation to be estimated is:

ROCE = a + bCR + e

Where,

ROCE stands for Return on Capital Employed

'a' denotes intercept of regression equation

'b' denotes co-efficient of independent variable

'CR' stands for current ratio

'e' denotes error term

In Table 5.11 regression co-efficient for 15 industries under study are given along with their co-efficient of determination (R^2). The analysis of data in Table 5.11 indicates that there was a positive relationship between liquidity and profitability in the selected South Indian private sector sugar industry. The regression equation of selected South Indian private sector sugar industry as a whole indicates that an increase of one per cent in current ratio will cause an increase of 24.68 per cent in return on capital employed. Similarly, large-sized industry and small-sized industry showed positive and statistically significant relationship between liquidity and profitability at one per cent and five per cent level respectively.

Out of 15 industries, eight industries indicate negative relationships between liquidity and profitability. However, out of the eight industry only one industry viz., Jeypore Sugars & Chemicals Ltd's co-efficient was found to be statistically significant at 10 per cent level. The remaining industries showed positive relationship between liquidity and profitability. Of these seven industries, none of the industries' co-efficient depicted statistically significant relationship between liquidity and profitability.

Generally, the theories have revealed that there is inverse relationship between liquidity and profitability. But, on the whole, it may be concluded that no established relationship between liquidity and profitability exists for this industry: the various forms of the industries depicted different type of relationship (both negative and positive) between liquidity and profitability during the study period.

DETERMINANTS OF PROFITABILITY

The question of determination of profit is of great importance. The profit of a business may be measured by studying the profitability of investment in it. Profitability is a relative term and its measurement can be achieved by profit and its relation with the other objects by which the profit is effected. It is the test of efficiency, powerful motivational factor and the measure of control in any business. Actually profitability is highly sensitive economic variable which is affected by host of factors operating through a variety of ways. Some of them affect product prices and quantities, some affect the cost of production while others make changes in capital stock, size, market share and growth of the firm. Further, corporate policy relating to various functions will affect profitability. Some of them are relevant in short run while others have impact in the long run. It is doubtful to build a theory of profitability, which accounts for all such factors. Because of these difficulties it is natural to analyze the variation in profitability by taking the partial approach i.e. to find the affect of certain major variables, ignoring the implications of other left out independent variables at a time. In this part an attempt is made to identify the major determinants of profitability in selected South Indian private sector sugar industry with the help of empirical data for the years 1991-92 to 2005-06.

There are a number of cross sectional studies that provide direct evidence about the determinants of profitability. Those studies include Shepherd (1972), Berry (1975), Agarwal (1978), Ramachandran (1980), Chaudhury (1982), Clarkson and Miller (1982), Ravenscraft (1983), Hary and Morris (1979), Narayan (1984), Amato Swilder (1985), Agarwal, (1987), Chandrasekaran (1993), Sidhu and Bhatia (1998), Vijayakumar (2002) and Vijayakumar and Kathirvel (2003). The review of the above empirical works facilitates to understand various structural and non-structural variables that determine profitability. It gives an idea of extensive and diversified works on determinants of profitability.

The objective of this part is to examine determinants of profitability of selected South Indian private sector sugar industry during the period 1991-92 to 2005-06. Determinants of profitability are analyzed using the techniques of ordinary least squares. Based on existing theories and relevant econometric empirical works, variables are selected. The variables occurring in the models and their measurement are described in methodology, while using the regression technique, efforts are made to reduce the problem of multi-collinearity and auto correlation.

Specification of Profitability Model

In order to explain the profitability of selected sectors of South Indian private sector Sugar Industry, the model specified for estimating profitability function is as follows:

$$P = b_0 + b_1S + b_2GRA + b_3L + b_4CR + b_5ITR + b_6\text{OESR} + b_7VI + b_8\text{Age}$$

Where,

S - Size

GRA - Growth Rate of Assets

L - Leverage

CR - Current Ratio

ITR - Inventory Turnover Ratio

OESR - Operating Expense to Sales Ratio

VI - Vertical Integration

Age - Age

The model was estimated using ordinary least square method, while estimating checks were made for model violation such as multi-collinearity.

Analysis of Results

The model described above has been estimated for large-sized sector, medium-sized sector, small-sized sector and the sample industry as a whole. The results are presented in Tables 5.12 to 5.15. It presents beta co-efficient and 't' values of the variables.

Whole Industry

For the sample South Indian private sector Sugar Industry, the model explains 97 per cent of variation in profitability of the firms included in the industry (Table 5.12). The analysis shows that all the variables except growth rate of assets are found to be statistically significant in explaining profitability of South Indian private sector Sugar Industry. It is evident from the results that current ratio is the strongest determinant of profitability followed by size, leverage, inventory turnover ratio, growth rate of assets, operating expenses to sales ratio, vertical integration and age. The size, growth rate of assets and inventory turnover ratio did support hypothesis with expected sign. However, the co-efficient of leverage, current ratio, operating expenses

Table 5.12. Determinants of Profitability in South Indian Private Sector Sugar Industry - Multiple Regression Model (Whole Industry)

[Dependent Variable: Ratio of profit rate on total assets (PR)]
(PR = 16.08 + 8.99S + 0.09GRA + 3.16L + 16.44CR + 1.66 ITR + 0.08 OESR-24.11VI –108.89Age)

Variables		Co-efficient	t-value	Significant/Not Significant
Constant		16.08		
1. Size [S-Total Assets in log.]		8.99	3.11	Significant**
2. Growth Rate of Assets [GRA]		0.09	1.48	Not Significant
3. Leverage [L]		3.16	4.88	Significant*
4. Current Ratio [CR]		16.44	4.82	Significant*
5. Inventory Turnover Ratio [ITR]		1.66	3.64	Significant**
6. Operating Expenses to Sales Ratio [OESR]		0.08	2.50	Significant **
7. Vertical Integration [VI]		-24.11	2.81	Significant**
8. Age		-108.89	-2.30	Significant***
R^2	0.97			
Adjusted R^2	0.92			
F	21.02			
DW	1.87			

*Significant at 0.01 level.
**Significant at 0.05 level.
***Significant at 0.10 level.
Source: Computed

Correlation Matrix – [Whole industry]

Variables	PR	Size	GRA	L	CR	ITR	OER	VI	Age
PR	1	-.273	.454	-.359	.456*	.501**	.246	-.171	-.073
Size		1	-.392*	.415**	-.614**	.240	-.257	-.452	-.537**
GRA			1	-.302*	.390*	-.069	.460**	.541**	.252
L				1	-.226*	-.218	-.015	-.050	.050
CR					1	.174	.336	.232	-.037
ITR						1	-.195	-.202**	-.157
OER							1	.405*	.087
VI								1	.287
Age									1

*Correlation is significant at the 0.01 level (2-tailed).
**Correlation is significant at the 0.05 levei (2-tailed).

to sales ratio, vertical integration and age did not support our hypothesis rather appear with opposite sign.

It is evident from the results that co-efficient of size shows the increase of 8.99 per cent in profitability as a result of one per cent increase in size which is statistically significant at five per cent level. The co-efficient of growth rate of assets indicates that an increase of 0.09 per cent in profitability as a result of one per cent increase in leverage but which is not significant. It is appeared from that value of one per cent increase in leverage resulted in 3.16 per cent increase in profitability, which is significant at one per cent level. The co-efficient of current ratio, inventory turnover ratio and operating expenses to sales ratio shows that 16.44 per cent, 1.66 per cent and 0.08 per cent increases in profitability respectively during the study period. All these co-efficient are statistically significant. It is also apparent from the table that co-efficient of vertical integration and age shows 24.11 per cent and 108.89 per cent respectively decrease in profitability as a result of one per cent increase which is also statistically significant.

The overall explanatory power of the regression appears to be good. This may be inferred from the co-efficient of determination (R^2) which is the measure of extent of movement in the dependent variable and that is explained by the independent variables. It is 97 per cent and adjusted explanation is around 92 per cent.

Determinants of Profitability - Large-sized Sector

For the large-sized sector the model explains 93 per cent of variation in profitability of firms included in the sector (Table 5.13). The analysis shows that all the selected independent variables except leverage and operating expense to sales ratio are found to be statistically significant in explaining profitability of large-sized sector of selected South Indian private sector sugar industry. It is evident from the results that age is the strongest determinant of profitability followed by current ratio, size, leverage, operating expenses to

Table 5.13. Determinants of Profitability in South Indian Private Sector Sugar Industry - Multiple Regression Model (Large-sized sector)

[Dependent Variable: Ratio of profit rate on total assets (PR)]

(PR = –21.00 + 3.24S + 0.12GRA + 2.61L + 11.07CR + 0.06ITR + 0.13OESR-21.47VI + 28.60Age)

Variables		Co-efficient	t-value	Significant/Not Significant
Constant		-21.00		
1. Size [S- Total Assets in log]		3.24	3.91	Significant*
2. Growth Rate of Assets [GRA]		0.12	2.87	Significant**
3. Leverage [L]		2.61	0.66	Not Significant
4. Current Ratio [CR]		11.07	1.97	Significant***
5. Inventory Turnover Ratio [ITR]		0.06	2.93	Significant*
6. Operating Expenses to Sales Ratio [OESR]		0.13	0.80	Not Significant
7. Vertical Integration [VI]		-21.47	2.33	Significant**
8. Age		28.60	2.92	Significant**
R^2	0.93			
Adjusted R^2	0.83			
F	9.76			
DW	1.95			

*Significant at 0.01 level
**Significant at 0.05 level
***Significant at 0.10 level
Source: Computed

Correlation Matrix of selected sugar industry [Large-sized sector]

Variables	PR	Size	GRA	L	CR	ITR	OER	VI	Age
PR	1	-.313	.519*	.103	.548*	.534**	-.039	-.153	.183
Size		1	-.381*	-.603*	-.248	.164	-.397	-.458	-.342*
GRA			1	.332	.573**	.043	.481	.423	.380
L				1	-.046	.082	.152	.250	.438*
CR					1	.503	-.001	-.096	.071
ITR						1	-.525**	-.573**	-.105
OESR							1	.471*	.278
VI								1	.345
Age									1

* Correlation is significant at the 0.01 level (2-tailed).
** Correlation is significant at the 0.05 level (2-tailed).

sales ratio, growth rate of assets, inventory turnover ratio and vertical integration. The size, growth rate of assets, inventory turnover ratio and age did support our hypothesis with the expected sign. However, the co-efficient of leverage, current ratio, operating expense to sales ratio and vertical integration did not support our hypothesis rather these appear with opposite sign.

It is evident from the results that co-efficient of size shows that the increase of 3.24 per cent in profitability as a result of one per cent increase in size which is statistically significant at one per cent level. Further, one per cent increase in growth rate of assets, leverage, current ratio, inventory turnover ratio and operating expense to sales ratio shows 0.12 per cent, 2.61 per cent, 11.07 per cent, 0.06 per cent and 0.13 per cent increase in profitability respectively during the study period. All these co-efficient are statistically significant except the co-efficient of leverage and operating expense to sales ratio. The co-efficient of vertical integration shows the decrease of 21.47 per cent in profitability as a result of one per cent increase in vertical integration, which is statistically significant at 5 per cent level. The co-efficient of age is also shows an increase of 28.60 per cent in profitability as a result of one per cent increases in age that is also significant at five per cent level.

The overall explanatory power of regression appears to be good. This may be inferred from the co-efficient of determination (R^2) which is the measure of extent of movement in the dependent variable that is explained by the independent variables. It is 93 per cent and adjusted explanation is around 83 per cent.

Determinants of Profitability – Medium-sized Sector

For the medium-sized sector, model explains 69 per cent of variation in profitability of firms included in the sector (Table 5.14). The analysis shows that all the variables except leverage are found to be statistically significant in explaining the profitability of medium-sized sector. It is evident from

Table 5.14. Determinants of Profitability in South Indian Private Sector Sugar Industry - Multiple Regression Model (Medium-sized sector)

[Dependent Variable: Ratio of profit rate on total assets (PR)]
(PR= 50.40 + 8.76S + 0.15GRA-1.39L-7.84CR + 0.75ITR-0.05OESR-21.41VI-51.50 Age)

Variables		Co-efficient	t-value	Significant/Not Significant
Constant		50.40		
1. Size [S-Total Assets in log]		8.76	3.96	Significant*
2. Growth Rate of Assets [GRA]		0.15	2.77	Significant**
3. Leverage [L]		-1.39	0.66	Not Significant
4. Current Ratio [CR]		-7.84	3.75	Significant*
5. Inventory Turnover Ratio [ITR]		0.75	2.54	Significant**
6. Operating Expenses to Sales Ratio [OESR]		-0.05	3.33	Significant*
7. Vertical Integration [VI]		-21.41	2.81	Significant**
8. Age		-51.50	2.51	Significant**
R^2	0.69			
Adjusted R^2	0.52			
F	1.69			
DW	2.15			

*Significant at 0.01 level
**Significant at 0.05 level
Source: Computed.

Correlation Matrix of selected sugar industry [Medium-sized sector]

Variables	PR	Size	GRA	L	CR	ITR	OER	VI	Age
PR	1	-.496	.433	-.358*	.331**	.460	.316	-.145	-.339
Size		1	-.476*	.482*	-.561**	.197	.209	-.271	-.029
GRA			1	-.593**	.498	-.186	-.027	.578**	-.078
L				1	-.502*	-.232	.091	.076	.216
CR					1	.321	-.006	-.288	-.402
ITR						1	.554*	-.413	-.223
OESR							1	-.003	-.102
VI								1	.422
Age								.	1

*Correlation is Significant at the 0.01 level (2-tailed).
**Correlation is Significant at the 0.05 level (2-tailed).

the result that size is the strongest determinant of profitability followed by inventory turnover ratio, growth rate of assets, operating expenses to sales ratio, leverage, current ratio, vertical integration and age. As expected size, growth rate of assets, leverage, current ratio and inventory turnover ratio did support our hypothesis with the expected sign. However, the co-efficient of operating expense to sales ratio, vertical integration and age did not support our hypothesis rather these appear with opposite sign.

It is evident from the result that co-efficient of size shows the increase of 8.76 per cent in profitability as a result of one per cent increases in size which is statistically significant at one per cent level. Further, one per cent increase in growth rate of assets and inventory turnover ratio shows 0.15 per cent and 0.75 per cent per cent increase in profitability respectively during the study period. All these co-efficient are statistically significant. It is also evident from the result that value of one per cent increase in leverage, current ratio, vertical integration and age shows 1.39 per cent, 7.84 per cent, 21.41 per cent and 51.50 per cent decrease in profitability respectively during the study period. All these co-efficient except leverage are statistically significant.

The overall explanatory power of the regression was not much encouraging. This may be inferred from the co-efficient of determination (R^2) which is the measure of extent of movement in the dependent variable that is explained by the independent variables. It is 69 per cent and adjusted explanatory is around 52 per cent.

Determinants of Profitability – Small-sized Sector

For the small-sized sector, model explains 94 per cent of variation in profitability of firms included in the sector (Table 5.15). The analysis shows that all the selected independent variables are found to be statistically significant in explaining profitability of small-sized sector. It is evident from the result that inventory turnover ratio is the strongest determinant

Table 5.15. Determinants of Profitability in South Indian Private Sector Sugar Industry - Multiple Regression Model (Small-sized sector)

[Dependent Variable: Ratio of profit rate on total assets (PR)]
(PR = -8.56 + 5.08S + 0.15GRA + 0.46L-2.27CR + 7.70ITR + 1.46OESR-138.65VI-484.74Age)

Variables		Co-efficient	t-value	Significant/Not Significant
Constant		-8.56		
1. Size [S-Total Assets in log.]		5.08	3.50	Significant*
2. Growth Rate of Assets [GRA]		0.15	2.68	Significant**
3. Leverage [L]		0.46	3.09	Significant*
4. Current Ratio [CR]		-2.27	2.68	Significant**
5. Inventory Turnover Ratio [ITR]		7.70	8.96	Significant*
6. Operating Expenses to Sales Ratio [OESR]		1.46	4.42	Significant*
7. Vertical Integration [VI]		-138.65	-4.09	Significant*
8. Age		-484.74	-3.27	Significant**
R^2	0.94			
Adjusted R^2	0.86			
F	12.11			
DW	2.00			

*Significant at 0.01 level
**Significant at 0.05 level
Source: Computed

Correlation Matrix of selected sugar industry [Small-sized sector]

Variables	PR	Size	GRA	L	CR	ITR	OER	VI	Age
SPR	1	-.191	.255	-.057	.242	.327**	.105	.043	-.113
Size		1	-.453*	.306	-.584**	.052	.083	.132	-.327
GRA			1	-.440**	.508**	-.239	.362	.363	-.120
L				1	-.518**	.000	-.005	-.059	.037
CR					1	-.152	.138	.091	-.234
ITR						1	-.404	-.358	.295
OESR							1	.566*	-.354
VI								1	-.427
Age									1

* Correlation is significant at the 0.01 level (2-tailed).
** Correlation is significant at the 0.05 level (2-tailed).

of profitability followed by size, operating expenses to sales ratio, leverage, growth rate of assets, current ratio, vertical integration and age. As expected size, growth rate of assets, current ratio and inventory turnover ratio did support our hypothesis with the expected sign. However, the co-efficient of leverage, operating expenses to sales ratio, vertical integration and age did not support our hypothesis rather these appear with opposite sign.

It is evident from the result that co-efficient of size shows increases of 5.08 per cent in profitability as a result of one per cent increase in size which is statistically significant at one per cent level. It is apparent from the result that an increase of 0.15 per cent, 0.46 per cent, 7.70 per cent and 1.46 per cent in profitability as a result of one per cent increase in growth rate of assets, leverage, inventory turnover ratio and operating expense to sales ratio. All these co-efficient are statistically significant. Further one per cent increase in current ratio, vertical integration and age shows 2.27 per cent, 138.65 per cent and 484.74 per cent decrease in profitability respectively during the study period. All these co-efficient are also statistically significant.

The overall explanatory power of regression appears to be good. This may be inferred from the co-efficient of determination (R^2) which is the measure of extent of movement in the dependent variable that is explained by the independent variables. It is 94 per cent and adjusted explanation is around 86 per cent.

IMPACT OF WORKING CAPITAL ON PROFITABILITY – AN EMPIRICAL ANALYSIS

In conventional production function approach for determination of relationship between output and profit fixed capital is taken into account as explanatory variable amongst others; the role of working capital is ignored. It is therefore felt necessary to study the vital role of working capital in profit generating process. Sarkar and Saha (1987)[23] have aptly observed the management of working capital has an important bearing on the profitability of an enterprise. Generally, the higher the working capital, the less the rate of return on capital employed while a lower value of working capital yields a higher rate of return. Hence, in this study, an attempt is made to study the association of profitability with working capital. The impact of working capital on profitability has been examined by regression between profitability ratio and working capital ratios, viz., Current Ratio (CR), Liquidity Ratio (LR), Working Capital Turnover Ratio (WTR), Inventory Turnover Ratio (ITR), Cash Turnover Ratio (CTR) and Receivables Turnover Ratio (RTR).

Multiple Regression Analysis

For the purpose of establishing definite relationships between working capital ratios and profitability ratio, Karl Pearson, correlation co-efficient can be applied. It implies the interdependence of the set of variables upon each other in such a way that changes in the one are in sympathy with changes in the other. In order to identify influence on profitability, a linear multiple regression model was used. In the analysis, working capital ratios, such as current ratio, liquidity ratio, working capital ratio, inventory turnover ratio, receivables turnover ratio and cash turnover ratio are taken as independent variables and profit before tax to total assets ratio is used as dependent variable.

For the purpose of selection of variables for the model, the co-efficient of correlation between the independent variables are computed and presented. It is evident from the table that there is a high degree of correlation between current ratio and liquidity ratio (0.703). Therefore, current ratio was omitted for the analysis.

Whole Industry

The pooled regression results of the model showing impact of working capital ratios on profitability for the selected South Indian private sector Sugar Industry are presented in Table 5.16.

The table indicates that the impact of liquidity ratio, working capital ratio, inventory turnover ratio, receivables turnover ratio and cash turnover ratio were statistically significant as seen from the values of regression co-efficient. For a unit increase in liquidity ratio profitability decreased by 21.45 units, which was statistically significant at one per cent level. When working capital turnover ratio increased by one unit, profitability increased by 0.27 unit, which was statistically significant at one per cent level of significance. When inventory turnover ratio and receivables turnover ratio increased by one unit, profitability increased by 0.46 unit and 0.01 unit respectively which were statistically significant at 10 per cent level of significance. For a unit increase in cash turnover ratio, the profitability decreased by 0.02 unit, which was significant at one per cent level. The five independent variables contribute 86 per cent of the variation in the profitability of selected South Indian private sector Sugar Industry. Thus, the overall results presented in the table are encouraging. The signs of all co-efficient are as expected and also statistically significant.

Table 5.16. Estimated regression results on the impact of working capital on profitability (Whole Industry)

$[PBT/TA = b_0 + b_1LR + b_2WTR + b_3ITR + b_4RTR + b_5CTR]$

Variables		Beta Co-efficient	t-value	Significant/Not Significant
Constant		-2.34		
Liquidity Ratio (LR)		-21.45	3.46	Significant*
Working capital Turnover Ratio(WTR)		0.27	3.87	Significant*
Inventory Turnover Ratio(ITR)		0.46	2.03	Significant***
Receivables Turnover Ratio(RTR)		0.01	2.10	Significant***
Cash Turnover Ratio(CTR)		-0.02	1.47	Significant*
R^2	0.86			
Adjusted R^2	0.78			
F	11.14			
Durbin-Watson	1.67			

*Significant at 0.01 level;
***Significant at 0.10 level
Source: Computed

Large-sized Sector

The pooled regression results of the model showing impact of working capital ratios on profitability for the selected large-sized South Indian private sector Sugar Industry are presented in Table 5.17.

The table indicates that the impact of liquidity ratio, working capital ratio, inventory turnover ratio, receivables turnover ratio and cash turnover ratio on profitability were statistically significant as seen from the values of regression co-efficient. For a unit increase in liquidity ratio, profitability decreased by 24.90 units, which was statistically significant at one per cent level. When working capital turnover ratio increased by one unit, profitability increased by 0.15 unit, which was statistically significant at one per cent level of significance. When inventory turnover ratio increased by one unit, profitability increased by 0.47 unit, which was statistically significant at five per cent level of significance. When cash turnover ratio increased by one unit, profitability decreased by 0.02 per cent, which was statistically significant at five per cent level of significance. But, when there is increase in receivables turnover ratio, profitability decreased by 0.02 unit, which was insignificant. The five independent variables contribute 80 per cent of the variation in the profitability of selected of South Indian private sector Sugar Industry. Thus, the overall results presented in the table are encouraging. The signs of all the co-efficient are as expected. The co-efficient are also statistically significant except for receivables turnover ratio.

Medium-sized Sector

The pooled regression results of the model showing impact of working capital ratios on profitability for the selected South Indian private sector Sugar Industry are presented in Table 5.18. The table indicates that the impact of liquidity ratio, working capital ratio, receivables turnover ratio and cash turnover ratio on profitability co-efficient. For a unit increase inwere statistically significant as seen from the values of

Table 5.17. Estimated regression results on the impact of working capital on profitability (Large-sized sector)

$$[PBT/TA = b_0 + b_1 LR + b_2 WTR + b_3 ITR + b_4 RTR + b_5 CTR]$$

Variables		Beta Co-efficient	t-value	Significant/Not Significant
Constant		-0.54		
Liquidity Ratio (LR)		-24.90	3.68	Significant*
Working Capital Turnover Ratio(WTR)		0.15	4.22	Significant*
Inventory Turnover Ratio(ITR)		0.47	2.33	Significant**
Receivables Turnover Ratio(RTR)		-0.02	1.14	Not significant
Cash Turnover Ratio(CTR)		-0.02	2.78	Significant**
R^2	0.80			
Adjusted R^2	0.65			
F	8.76			
Durbin-Watson	1.78			

* Significant at the 0.01 level;
** Significant at the 0.05 level
Source: Computed

Table 5.18. Estimated regression results of impact of working capital on profitability (Medium-sized sector)

$$[PBT/TA = b_0 + b_1 LR + b_2 WTR + b_3 ITR + b_4 RTR + b_5 CTR]$$

Variables		Beta Co-efficient	t-value	Significant/Not Significant
Constant		10.12		
Liquidity Ratio(LR)		-5.85	2.75	Significant*
Working Capital Turnover Ratio(WTR)		0.16	3.87	Significant*
Inventory Turnover Ratio(ITR)		0.37	1.17	Not significant
Receivables Turnover Ratio(RTR)		-0.39	-2.13	Significant***
Cash Turnover Ratio(CTR)		-0.03	-3.50	Significant ***
R^2	0.84			
Adjusted R^2	0.76			
F	9.72			
Durbin-Watson	2.03			

*Significant at 0.01 level; **Significant at 0.05 level; ***Significant at 0.10 level
Source: Computed

regression liquidity ratio, profitability decreased by 5.85 units, which was statistically significant at one per cent level of significance. When working capital turnover ratio increased by one unit, profitability increased by 0.16 unit, which was statistically significant at one per cent level of significance. When receivables turnover ratio and cash turnover ratio increased by one unit, profitability decreased by 0.39 unit and 0.03 unit respectively which were statistically significant at ten per cent level of significance. The impact of inventory turnover ratio on profitability was insignificant. The five independent variables contribute 84 per cent of the variation in the profitability of the selected South Indian private sector Sugar Industry. Thus, the overall results presented in the table are encouraging. The signs of all co-efficient are as expected and also statistically significant except the receivables turnover ratio.

Small-sized Sector

The pooled regression results of the model showing the impact of working capital ratios on profitability for the selected South Indian private sector Sugar Industry are presented in Table 5.19.

The table indicates that the impact of liquidity ratio, working capital ratio, inventory turnover ratio and cash turnover ratio on profitability were statistically significant as seen from the values of regression co-efficient. For a unit increase in liquidity ratio, profitability decreased by 6.60 units, which was statistically significant at one per cent level of significance. When working capital turnover ratio increased by one unit, profitability increased by 0.34 unit, which was statistically significant at one per cent level of significance. When inventory turnover ratio increased by one unit, profitability increased by 0.11 unit, which was statistically significant at 10 per cent level of significance. For a unit increase in cash turnover ratio, profitability decreased by 0.01 unit, which was significant at five per dent level of significance. The receivables turnover ratio had insignificant impact on the profitability. The five independent

Table 5.19. Estimated regression results on the impact of working capital on profitability (Small-sized sector)

$[PBT/TA = b_0 + b_1LR + b_2WTR + b_3ITR + b_4RTR + b_5CTR]$

Variables		Beta Co-efficient	t-value	Significant/Not Significant
Constant		-1.92		
Liquidity Ratio (LR)		-6.60	4.16	Significant*
Working Capital Turnover Ratio (WTR)		0.34	3.45	Significant*
Inventory Turnover Ratio(ITR)		0.11	2.38	Significant***
Receivables Turnover Ratio (RTR)		0.05	0.52	Not significant
Cash Turnover Ratio (CTR)		-0.01	-2.11	Significant**
R^2	0.89			
Adjusted R^2	0.78			
F	9.45			
Durbin-Watson	1.50			

*Significant at 0.01 level; **Significant at 0.05 level; ***Significant at 0.10 level

Source: Computed

variables contribute 89 per cent of the variation in the profitability of the selected South Indian private sector Sugar Industry. Thus, the overall results presented in the table are encouraging. The signs of all co-efficient are as expected and also statistically significant, except the receivables turnover ratio.

Assessment of Financial Health of Selected South Indian Private Sector Sugar Industry – Altman's Z Score Analysis

In this part, an attempt has been made to have an insight into the financial stability and operational health of the selected South Indian private sector Sugar Industry during the post liberalisation period. Altman's 'Z' score analysis has been applied by Financial Analysts to evaluate the general trend in the financial health of an enterprise over a period. Some of the individual accounting ratios used frequently to predict the financial performance of an enterprise may only provide warnings when it is too late to take a corrective action. Further single ratio does not convey much of the sense. There is no internationally accepted standard for financial ratio against which the results can be compared. Therefore, Altman (1968)[24] combined a number of accounting ratios (liquidity, leverage, activity and profitability) to form an index of the profitability, which are effective indicators of corporate performance in predicting bankruptcy well over a year or two in advance. In this direction a variety of studies have been conducted, over the period, by applying Multiple Discriminate Analysis (MDA) to predict the corporate failure, as for instance, Bevar (1966),[25] John (1976),[26] Gupta (1979),[27] Ohlson (1980),[28] Etebari (1987),[29] Makridakis (1991)[30] and Sastry (1994).[31]

One of the objectives of this study is to predict the financial health and viability of the selected South Indian private sector sugar industry during the post liberalisation period to improve its operational efficiency and effectiveness, productivity and profitability. The data collected are first analysed with the help of five accounting ratios. These different ratios are combined into a single measure 'Z' score analysis with the help of Multiple Discriminate Analysis (MDA). The formula used to evaluate the 'Z' score analysis as established by Altman is:

$$Z = 1.2X_1 + 1.4X_2 + 3.3X_3 + 0.6X_4 + 0.999X_5$$

Where 'Z' is the overall index

X_1 - ratio of working capital to total assets (WC/TA)

X_2 - ratio of net operating profit to net sales (NOP/S)

X_3 - ratio of earnings before interest and tax to total assets (EBIT/TA)

X_4 - ratio of market value of equity to book value of debt (MVE/BVD)

X_5 - ratio of sales to total assets (S/TA)

Variables Used in Z-score Analysis

The following accounting ratios are used as variables to combine them into a single measure (Index), which is efficient in predicting bankruptcy.

X_1 - The ratio of working capital to total assets. It is the measure of the net liquid assets of concern to the total capitalization.

X_2 - The ratio of net operating profit to net sales. It indicates the efficiency of the management in manufacturing, sales, administration and other activities.

X_3 - The ratio of earnings before interest and tax to total assets. It is a measure of productivity of assets employed in an enterprise. The ultimate existence of an enterprise is based on the earning power.

X_4 - The ratio of market value of equity to book value debt. It is reciprocal of the familiar debt – equity ratio. This measure shows how much assets of an enterprise can decline in value before the liabilities exceed the assets and the concern becomes insolvent.

X_5 - The ratio of sales to total assets. The capital turnover ratio is standard financial measure for illustrating the sales generating capacity of the assets.

Measurement of Financial Health

According to Altman (1968), the following three situations are considered for studying financial health of selected South Indian private sector Sugar Industry (see Table 5.20).

I. The 'Z' score below 1.8 unit is considered to be bankruptcy zone. Failure is certain and extremely likely and would occur probable of two years.

II. If a unit's 'Z' score is1.8 or above but less than 3.0, its financial viability is considered to be healthy. The failure in this situation is uncertain to predict.

III. The 'Z' score 3.0 and above indicates too healthy zone. Its financial health is very viable and not to fall.

Table 5.20. Altman's Z-score

Category	'Z' score	Zone	Situation
I	Below 1.8	Bankruptcy zone	Certain to fall
II	1.8 to 2.99	Healthy zone	Uncertain to predict
III	3.0 and above	Too healthy zone	Not to fall

Whole Industry

The 'Z' scores with respect to the selected South Indian private sector Sugar Industry have been computed and presented in Table 5.21. Further, the scores obtained over the period have been represented graphically in Fig. 5.1. It is imperative from the analysis that the 'Z' scores for the sugar industry are less than 3.0 during the entire period of post liberalisation. It implies that the selected industry was not in the too healthy zone during post liberalisation period. However, the industry as a whole had a healthy financial position during the first phase (initial) of five years and the second half of third phase (maturity) as the 'Z' scores are between 1.8 and 3.0. This may be due to under trading, excess working capital, negative operating profit, poor ratio of turnover etc,. It is also found the worst financial health in 1996-97. The industry was remained bankruptcy zone during the period from 1995-96 to 2003-04. A significant improvement in the financial soundness was noticed at the tail end of the study period.

Large-sized Sector

In order to ascertain the financial health of the large-sized sector of the selected South Indian private sector Sugar Industry 'Z' scores have been computed and presented in Table 5.22. The general trend in the financial health of the industry has been depicted graphically in Fig. 5.2. It is evident from the table that the 'Z' scores of the large-sized industry witness the good financial health during the first (phase) of the study as the scores between 1.8 and 3.0.

Table 5.21. 'Z' Score of selected South Indian private sector Sugar Industry [Whole Industry]

Year	X_1	X_2	X_3	X_4	X_5	Z Score
1991-92	0.28	0.13	0.10	0.46	0.72	1.84
1992-93	0.31	0.14	0.10	0.29	0.76	1.83
1993-94	0.33	0.15	0.13	0.47	0.73	2.05
1994-95	0.40	0.13	0.11	0.33	0.65	1.88
1995-96	0.31	0.13	0.12	0.17	0.71	1.76
1996-97	0.31	0.10	0.06	0.10	0.57	1.35
1997-98	0.31	0.11	0.09	0.08	0.74	1.60
1998-99	0.32	0.10	0.07	0.06	0.64	1.42
1999-00	0.34	0.10	0.07	0.07	0.67	1.50
2000-01	0.34	0.12	0.09	0.05	0.67	1.58
2001-02	0.32	0.11	0.09	0.05	0.67	1.51
2002-03	0.25	0.11	0.07	0.05	0.70	1.40
2003-04	0.28	0.12	0.08	0.12	0.75	1.57
2004-05	0.21	0.22	0.19	0.50	0.90	2.38
2005-06	0.23	0.19	0.16	0.75	1.09	2.62

X_1 : Working capital to total assets; X_2 : Net operating profit to net sales X_3 : Earnings before interest and taxes to total assets X_4 : Market value of equity to book value of debt; X_5 : Sales to total assets

Source : Computed

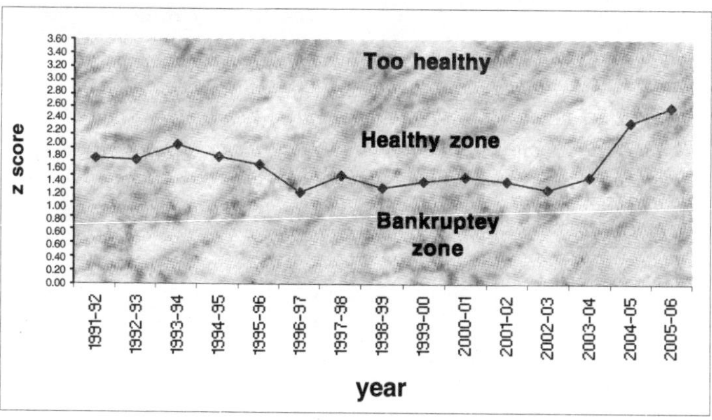

Fig. 5.1. 'Z Score of selected South Indian private sector Sugar Industry (Whole Industry)

Table 5.22. 'Z' Score of selected large-sized South Indian private sector Sugar Industry

Year	X_1	X_2	X_3	X_4	X_5	Z Score
1991-92	0.27	0.15	0.10	0.56	0.95	2.15
1992-93	0.30	0.16	0.12	0.39	0.83	2.05
1993-94	0.32	0.14	0.12	0.73	0.76	2.16
1994-95	0.37	0.15	0.13	0.39	0.78	2.09
1995-96	0.32	0.15	0.13	0.24	0.81	1.96
1996-97	0.30	0.11	0.09	0.15	0.76	1.66
1997-98	0.27	0.14	0.11	0.11	0.75	1.69
1998-99	0.33	0.12	0.09	0.12	0.67	1.61
1999-00	0.37	0.15	0.12	0.12	0.68	1.79
2000-01	0.34	0.14	0.11	0.09	0.74	1.77
2001-02	0.30	0.12	0.09	0.11	0.74	1.62
2002-03	0.23	0.09	0.06	0.09	0.69	1.33
2003-04	0.24	0.10	0.07	0.22	0.61	1.40
2004-05	0.20	0.15	0.11	0.53	0.78	1.92
2005-06	0.21	0.17	0.14	1.16	0.82	2.47

X_1 : Working capital to total assets; X_2 : Net operating profit to net sales X_3 : Earnings before interest and taxes to total assets; X_4 : Market value of equity to book value of debt; X_5 : Sales to total assets

Source: Computed

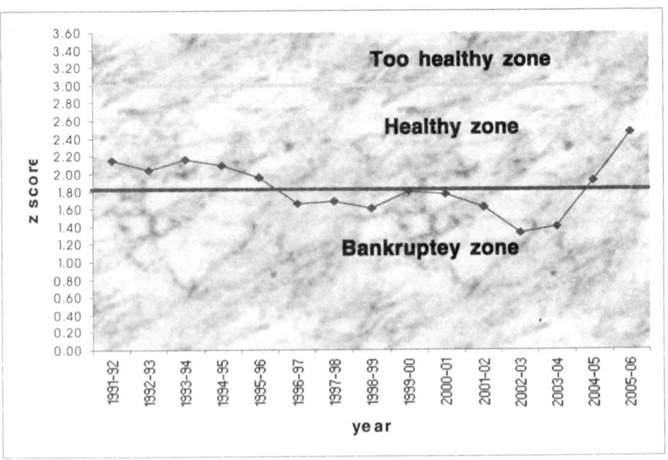

Fig. 5.2. 'Z' Score of selected large-sized South Indian private sector Sugar Industry

The selected large-sized South Indian private sector Sugar Industry had never enjoyed too healthy financial position in any year of the post liberalisation period as the z scores obtained are below the 3.0 over the period. The industry was remained in the bankruptcy zone (or) "Distress" zone from 1996-97 to 2003-04 as it had below 1.8 scores. During the last two years of the study period the financial health slightly improved and entered the healthy zone. The highest 'Z' score obtained at 2005-06 and the lowest score was 1.33 in 2002-03. It may be inferred from the figure that the industry after enjoying sound financial health at the initial phase, a sharp decline was faced during the midway and started picking up at the end of the study period.

Medium-sized Sector

The 'Z' scores with respect to the selected medium-sized sector of the selected South Indian private sector Sugar Industry for the period from 1991-92 to 2005-06 have been computed and presented in Table 5.23. Further, using the data points, the scores obtained over the period have been plotted through a graph in Fig. 5.3. It is imperative from the analysis that the 'Z' scores for the medium-sized industry are less than 3.0 during the entire period of study. It disclosed that the financial health of the medium-sized industry was never in the too healthy zone in any year of the study period. This is attributable to under trading owing to the excess working capital, failure to achieve the adequate sales, under utilisation of capacity etc.,. It is also witnessed from the table that the 'Z' scores for the selected medium-sized industry are more than 1.8 in the years 1992-93, 1993-94, 1994-95, 2004-05 and 2005-06. It is noticed from the table that there was a sudden improvement in the financial soundness of the industry from the bankruptcy zone in 2003-04 to the healthy zone in 2004-05. This improvement may be attributed to the positive changes in the net operating profit resulted from the increased sales volume and market capitalisation of the equity in the year 2004-05.

Table 5.23. 'Z' Score of selected medium-sized South Indian private sector Sugar Industry

Year	X_1	X_2	X_3	X_4	X_5	Z Score
1991-92	0.28	0.12	0.10	0.33	0.55	1.57
1992-93	0.32	0.17	0.14	0.09	0.73	1.86
1993-94	0.34	0.16	0.15	0.28	0.76	2.06
1994-95	0.39	0.14	0.12	0.37	0.69	1.99
1995-96	0.27	0.12	0.11	0.17	0.74	1.68
1996-97	0.26	0.11	0.10	0.08	0.48	1.31
1997-98	0.30	0.09	0.06	0.05	0.63	1.34
1998-99	0.29	0.10	0.07	0.04	0.67	1.39
1999-00	0.28	0.10	0.07	0.04	0.57	1.29
2000-01	0.32	0.12	0.09	0.03	0.67	1.53
2001-02	0.25	0.10	0.07	0.02	0.63	1.33
2002-03	0.23	0.14	0.07	0.02	0.67	1.38
2003-04	0.26	0.17	0.09	0.04	0.84	1.72
2004-05	0.25	0.33	0.29	0.32	0.86	2.76
2005-06	0.25	0.17	0.15	0.47	0.94	2.26

X_1 : Working capital to total assets; X_2 : Net operating profit to net sales
X_3 : Earnings before interest and taxes to total assets; X_4 : Market value of equity to book value of debt; X_5 : Sales to total assets
Source: Computed

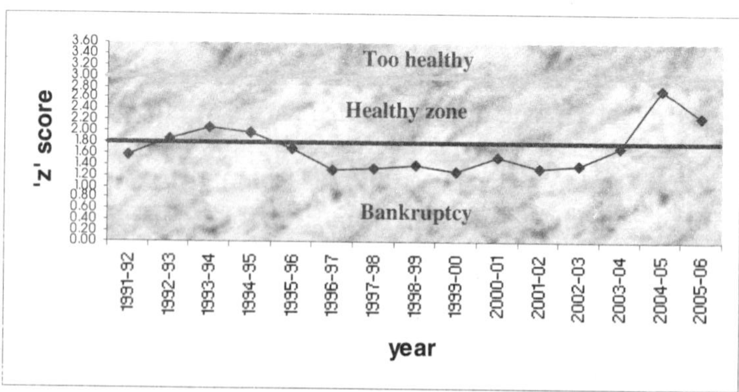

Fig. 5.3. 'Z' Score of selected medium-sized South Indian private sector

Table 5.24. 'Z' Score of selected small-sized South Indian private sector Sugar Industry

Year	X_1	X_2	X_3	X_4	X_5	Z Score
1991-92	0.30	0.12	0.09	0.50	0.66	1.79
1992-93	0.30	0.09	0.05	0.39	0.72	1.59
1993-94	0.32	0.15	0.13	0.41	0.67	1.93
1994-95	0.42	0.10	0.08	0.24	0.50	1.55
1995-96	0.35	0.13	0.12	0.11	0.58	1.63
1996-97	0.36	0.07	0.01	0.08	0.48	1.08
1997-98	0.36	0.11	0.09	0.07	0.83	1.77
1998-99	0.34	0.07	0.05	0.03	0.58	1.26
1999-00	0.38	0.05	0.03	0.04	0.77	1.42
2000-01	0.36	0.10	0.08	0.03	0.61	1.44
2001-02	0.40	0.12	0.09	0.01	0.64	1.59
2002-03	0.28	0.10	0.08	0.03	0.74	1.50
2003-04	0.32	0.10	0.07	0.09	0.79	1.59
2004-05	0.17	0.19	0.16	0.66	1.05	2.46
2005-06	0.22	0.24	0.21	0.62	1.49	3.13

X_1 : Working capital to total assets; X_2 : Net operating profit to net sales
X_3 : Earnings before interest and taxes to total assets; X_4 : Market value of equity to book value of debt; X_5 : Sales to total assets
Source: Computed

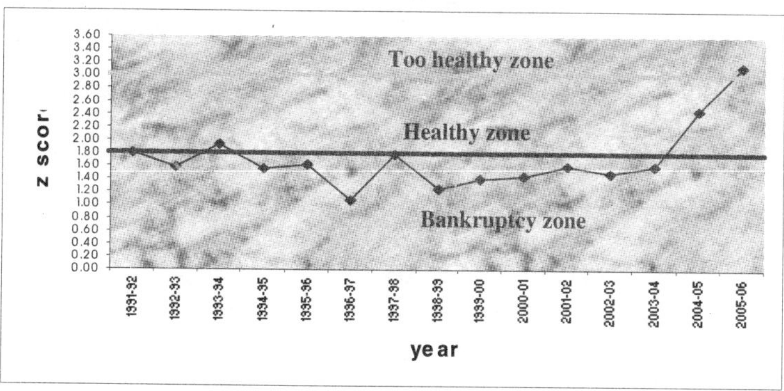

Fig. 5.4. 'Z' Score of selected small-sized Indian private sector Sugar Industry

Small-sized Sector

The 'Z' scores with respect to the selected small-sized sector of the selected South Indian private sector Sugar Industry for the study period are presented in Table 5.24. Further, using data points, the scores obtained over the period have been plotted through a graph in Figure 5.4. It is imperative from the analysis that the 'Z' scores for the selected small-sized industry are less then 3.0 during the entire study period except in the year 2005-06. It has also disclosed that the financial health of the small-sized industry was never in the too healthy zone in the post liberalisation period except in the year 2005-06. This is attributable to poor turnover, excess working capital, under attestation of the capitals, poor market capitalisation, over non-operating expenses, etc.,. It is also witnessed from the table that the 'Z'scores for the small-sized industry are more than 1.8 in 1993-94, 2004-05 and 2005-06. The 'Z'scores for the study period range from 1.08 in 1996-97 to 2.46 in 2004-05. The industry has got enough scope to improve its financial health further more in the years to come as it is seen abrupt improvements at the tail end of the study period.

NOTES

1. Baumol, W.J. (1967), Business, Behaviour, Values and Growth (Revised Ed.), New York Hardcount Brace and World, New York, pp. 67-72.
2. Steindl, J. (1944), Small and Big Business: Economic Problems of the size of Firms. Oxford University Press, pp. 33-35.
3. Benishay, Haskel. (1961), Variability in Earnings – Price Ratios of Corporate Equities, American Economy Review, Vol. 51, pp. 81-94.
4. Samuel Smyth (1968), *op. cite,* p. 130.
5. Marcus (1969), *op. cite,* p. 105.
6. Hains Walter W "The Profitability of Large-size Firms", rivista Internazionale di Scienze Economiche e Commerciali, April 1970, 17, pp. 321-351.
7. Raidice, H.K, "Control Type, Profitability and Growth in Large Firms", Economic Journal, September 1971, 81, pp. 547-562.

8. Shephered William G, "The Elements of Market Structure," Review of Economics and Statistics, February 1972, 54, pp. 25-37.
9. Smyth David J, Boyes William J and peseau Dennis E, Size, Growth, Profits and Executive Compensation in the LargeCorporation: A study of the 500 Largest United Kingdom and United states of Industrial corporations, London: Macmillan Press, 1975.
10. Whittington (1980), *op.cite.,* p. 336.
11. Pamfret, R, and Shapiro, D, "Firm Size, Diversification and Profitability of Large Corporation in Canada", Journal of Economic Studies, 1980, 7(3) pp.140-150.
12. Ravencraft David J, "Structure Profit Relationships at the Line of Business and Industry Level," The Review of Economic and Statistics, February 1983, 65, pp. 23-31.
13. Amato Louis and Wilder Ronald P "The Effects of Firm Size on Profit Rates in US Manufacturing", Southern Economic Journal, July 1985, 52, pp. 181-190.
14. Vishnukanda Prohit (1998), *op.cite.,* p. 12.
15. Alexander S.S, "The Effect of Size of Manufacturing Corporations on the Distribution of the Rate of Return", Review of Economics and Statistics, August 1949, pp. 229-235.
16. Steklar (1964), *op.cite.,* p. 1184.
17. Hall Marshall and Weiss Leanard. "Firm Size and Profitability", Review of Economics and Statistics, August 1967, 49, pp.319-331.
18. Kamerschen D R, "The influence of Ownership and Control on Profit Rates", American Economic Review, June 1968, 58, pp. 432-437.
19. Vijayakumar.A (2003), *op. cite.,* p. 816.
20. Singh, Ajit and Whittington, G. Growth (1968), Profitability and Valuation, Cambridge University Press, Cambridge.
21. *Ibid.*
22. Hannah, L. and Kay, J. A. (1977), Concentration in modern industry. Theory, measurement and the UK experience, Macmillan, Londan.
23. Sarkar and Saha, (1987), "Profitability crises and working capital management in the public sector in India", The Management Accountant, p.329.
24. Edwin I Altman (1968), Financial Ratios—Discriminate analysis and prediction of corporate bankruptcy, Journal of Financ, Vol. 9, pp. 589-609.
25. Bevar. W.R. (1966), Financial ratios as prediction of failure, Juornal of Accounting Research, pp. 71-110.

26. Argenti John (1976), Corporate collapse – the causes and symptoms, (New york: Mc.Graw Hill), p.91.
27. Gupta, L.O (1979), Financial ratios as forwarding predicators of sickness, ICICI, Bombay, pp. 65-69.
28. Ohlson, S. (1980), Financial ratios and the prediction of bankruptcy, Journal of Accounting Research, pp. 109-131.
29. Etebari, A. (1987), Financial ratio criteria: A hypotheesis and empirical test, Working paper, University of New Hareschrie, pp. 27-32.
30. Sastry, K.S. (1994), Uses of 'Z' score of selective privatization marrtioused note, Indian Journal of Finance and Research, Nw Delhi, pp. 85-88.

CHAPTER 6

Findings and Conclusion

The corporate sector is the backbone of the Indian economy so far, as it provides a vital, effective and organized system for the growth of industrial as well as non-industrial sectors of the economy. The rapid growth of corporate sector in India and the increasing scale of its operations and investments have turned it into the most dominant form of economic organization. The ever-increasing importance of the corporate sector in the economic growth of the country has attracted several academicians, professional institutions, researchers and administrators. There is a need to study industry's profitability performance which ultimately determine the overall industrial development in future. The present study is a small endeavor in this direction.

The study in general aimed at making profitability performance of South Indian private sector Sugar Industry after liberalisation. The study specifically aimed at assessing the trends in the profits, analysing profitability position from the view point of financial management, shareholders and utilisation of assets, the relationship of profitability with size, growth, liquidity and working capital and determinants of profitability of South Indian private sector Sugar Industry. Further, an attempt has also been made to assess the financial health of selected sugar industry using Altman Z-Score Model.

This study covers three sectors of South Indian private sector sugar industry, namely, large-sized sector, medium-sized sector and small-sized sector. The sectoral classification was made on the bases of sugarcane crushing capacity per day. The selected sectors include 95 industries. Out of 95 industries, 15 years data are available only for 15 industries. Therefore, all the 15 industries are included in the sample which accounts for 15.79 per cent of the total industries available in the South Indian private sector Sugar Industry. The period covered under the study extends over 15 years from 1991-92 to 2005-06. The data for the study were taken from "Capitaline" and "PROWESS" databases, which are the most reliable on the empowered corporate databases of Bombay Stock Exchange and Centre for Monitoring Indian Economy (CMIE) respectively. The important statistical techniques used in the study are correlation, multiple regression, analysis of variance, t-test, F-test, mean, co-efficient of variation and compound annual growth rate besides simple percentages, ratios and graphs.

This chapter being the concluding part of the study is an endeavour to present a summarized version of the findings of the present study. The summary of the major findings is given below.

Profitability Analysis

In an era where there is a need for inclusive growth, the sugar industry is amongst the few industries that have successfully contributed to the country economy. The sector supports over 50 million farmers and their families and delivers value addition at the farm side. The sector also has a significant standing in the global sugar space. The Indian domestic sugar market is one of the largest markets in the world, in volume terms. India is also the second largest sugar producing geography. India remains a key growth driver for world sugar, growing above the Asian and world consumption growth average. Such business needs profits not only for its existence but also for expansion. The profitability performance of South Indian private sector sugar industry under review has been studied by computing various ratios relating to profitability. The profitability ratios have been determined on the basis of sales and investment. The profitability analysis has been made from the point of view of financial management, shareholders and utilisation of assets. The findings observed from the analysis made from the financial management point of view are detailed as follows.

Profitability Analysis from the View Point of Financial Management

The profitability measured through operating profit margin ratio is satisfactory in all the three sectors of South Indian private sector sugar industry and found adequate to cover the fixed charges and dividend reserve during the study period. The mean operating profit margin ratio was the highest in medium-sized industry (20.35%) followed by large-sized industry (19.2%) and small-sized (16.11%). The overall fluctuating trend of this ratio in all the sectors can be attributed to the factors like variation in operating expenses, market condition, operation problem, change in demand of sugar and government policy. The analysis of variance showed that there are significant differences in the operating profit margin between the sectors. The analysis of operating profit margin between different phases of liberalisation reveals that declining trend during growth phase which could be attributed to the lower production of sugarcane due to lower rainfall which resulted poor performance of small and medium-sized industry. But during maturity phase, all the selected sectors and whole industry registered an increasing trend in operating profit margin because of change in levy-free sugar ratio (from 40:60 to 10:90 in 1997-98), improved market condition, upward revision of sales price and reduction in the cost of sales with the help of modernisation and expansion. The study also point out that there were no significant differences in operating profit margin of selected South Indian private sector sugar industry between phases.

The industry-wise analysis reveals that Bannari Amman Sugars Ltd, Jeypore Sugars & Chemicals Ltd, Rajshree Sugars & Chemicals Ltd, Sakthi Sugars Ltd and Thiru Arooran Sugars Ltd under large-sized, Kothari Sugars & Chemicals Ltd and Kakatiya Cements Sugar & Industries Ltd under medium-sized and Dharani Sugars & Chemicals Ltd under small-sized sector showed better performance regarding operating profit margin. The operating profit margin ratio was significant in between the industry only under large-sized sector. In all the remaining cases there were insignificant differences in between the years and industry. Thus, the overall analysis of profitability measured through operating profit margin ratio was satisfactory during the study period.

The overall analysis of gross profit-margin ratio shows the ability of the selected industry to withstand competition and adverse condition during the study period. The average gross profit margin was higher than the industry average in large-sized and medium-sized sectors. The overall gross profit margin was 6.92 per cent for the whole industry during the study period. The analysis of variance reveals that there were significant differences in the gross profit margin ratios between the years and sectors. The analysis of gross profit margin between the three phases of liberalisation reveals that a declining trend during growth phase, which could be attributed to the poor performance of small, and medium seized sugar industry. There was a significant difference between initial phase and growth phase in medium-sized industry and also between initial phase and maturity phase in small-sized industry. But, there was no significant difference in the gross profit margin ratio between the years and industry during the study period.

The overall analysis of return on capital employed ratio showed that this ratio has improved significantly during the study period which was on account of considerable increase in profit margin as well as assets turnover. In fine, it can be inferred that the operating efficiency of selected South Indian private sector sugar industry was satisfactory and the management generally succeeded in investing capital funds. The analysis of return on capital employed also reveals that this ratio varied significantly between the three different phases. This was due to wide fluctuation in the growth rate of earnings before interest and capital employed in the South Indian private sector Sugar Industry during the study period.

It is concluded from the analysis of interest coverage ratio of the selected sectors of South Indian private sector sugar industry measured through the interest coverage, the ratio is satisfactory subject to the variation in the coverage. The earnings before interest and tax of all the sample industries is adequate to cover the financial charges of debt and credit facilities. Industry-wise analysis of interest coverage ratio showed that EID Parry Ltd among large-sized and Kothari Sugars and Chemicals Ltd among medium-sized sugar industry are not taking the advantages of 'trading on equity' and are very conservative in using debt and credit facilities as its interest coverage ratios were too high. It is also noticed that Empee Sugars Ltd under small-sized sector signifies a danger signal as the firm was highly dependent on borrowed funds since the interest coverage ratio was very low.

From the analysis of interest coverage ratio of the selected sectors of South Indian private sector sugar industry, it is concluded that overall interest coverage ratio is satisfactory inspite of variation in the coverage. The earnings before interest and tax of all the sample industries are adequate to cover the financial charges of debt and credit facilities.

Hence, the overall analysis of profitability of selected sectors of South Indian private sector sugar industry during the period under review highlighted the better performance and prospects from the point of view of financial management.

Profitability Analysis from the View Point of Shareholders

The analysis of net profit margin ratio reveals that on an average, South Indian private sector Sugar Industry had an overall negative net profit margin ratio due to the poor performance of medium-sized and small-sized sugar industry during the period of study. The average net profit margin ratio varied from sector to sector, the highest average was 3.14 per cent in large-sized sugar industry. Whereas the average of small-sized industry was –6.06 per cent followed by –0.46 per cent in medium-sized industry over the period of study. The analysis of net profit margin was continued to be negative during the initial phase and growth phase of liberalisation. The industries slowly recovered and climb up to the profit zone during the maturity phase. Further, large-sized sugar industries were able to sustain its net profit margin during the study period but at declined rate. The comparison of gross profit margin with net profit margin revealed that the operating expenses relating to sales have been increasing during the three phases of liberalisation. The analysis of variance indicated that there are significant differences in net profit margin ratio between the sectors.

Industry wise analysis of net profit margin reveals that performance of Bannari Amman Sugars Ltd, EID Parry Ltd, Ugar Sugar Works Ltd and Jeypore Sugars & Chemicals Ltd under large-sized sector is satisfactory because its average net profit margin ratios were better than the industry average. In this circumstance, the industries under small-sized sector failed to achieve satisfactory return on shareholders funds and these could not withstand competition and adverse condition during the study period. But positive sign was observed during the maturity phase giving good hope for the shareholders in the years to come.

The analysis of return on total assets ratio depicts that operating assets were effectively utilised in profitable manner by the selected sectors of South Indian private sector Sugar

Industry during the study period except small-sized sector. The overall fluctuating trend of return on total assets ratio could be attributed to the differences in the growth rates of profit after tax and total assets because of the excess investment in assets, under utilisation of assets due to seasonal factor in getting sugarcane. The analysis of variance reveals that the return on total assets ratios were significantly differs between the years and sectors during the study period. The efficiency in generating profit on its assets was better in Rajshree Sugars & Chemicals Ltd, Bannari Amman Sugars Ltd and EID Parry Ltd under large-sized sector and Kakatiya Cements Sugar & Industries Ltd and Sri Sarvaraya Sugars Ltd under medium-sized sector. It was observed that no small-sized sector industries were operated efficiently in utlising its assets for generating profit on its assets. This poor performance may be attributed to the under utilisation of assets and over stocking.

The analysis of return on shareholders fund also reveals that owners funds was utilised profitably by all the selected sectors during the study period except small-sized sector. The average return on shareholders fund is 9.83 per cent during initial phase and it has declined to negative average return during the growth phase and reached a positive average return of 13.63 per cent in the maturity phase. This wide fluctuation was caused by the differences in the rates of small-sized and medium-sized sector during the growth phase. The analysis of return on shareholders fund during the three different phases of liberalisation reveals that Rajshree Sugars & Chemicals Ltd, Bannari Amman Sugars Ltd, EID Parry Ltd and Ugar Sugar Works Ltd under large-sized sector and Sri Sarvaraya Sugars Ltd, Kakatiya Cements Sugar & Industries Ltd and Kothari Sugars & Chemicals Ltd under medium-sized sector have performed well in generating adequate return for the capital invested by the owners and the industries utilised the resources of owners well. No industry under small-sized sector failed to attain adequate return for their shareholders during the study period. The overall returns among three sectors over the period are fluctuating and denote unstable return in the whole industry, wide fluctuating trend in small-sized sector, upward fluctuation trend in the medium-sized sector and low deviation in large-sized sector.

It is significant to note that the position regarding earnings per share and dividend pay-out ratio in all the selected sectors of South Indian private sector sugar industry during the period under review shows the better performance and prospects from the view point of shareholders. However, the fluctuating trend of the ratio can be attributed to the factors like profitability position, fluctuation in the market price and dividend policy.

To sum up the above, the analysis of profitability of selected sectors of South Indian private sector sugar industry except small-sized sector during the period under review highlighted the better performance and prospects from the point of view of owners.

Analysis of Profitability from the View Point of Utilisation of Assets

Turnover ratio reflects how efficiently the companies managing its resources. Turnover ratios affect the overall profitability of a company to a larger extend. A study of turnover of various assets reveals the following observations.

The total assets turnover, which indicates the effectiveness of utilisation of assets, registered a fluctuating trend in almost all the sectors under study. The average ratio was always nearing one time throughout the study period. This shows that the additions to investment in various assets could result in proportionate increase in sales. The highest average total assets turnover ratio is 0.94 times which was recorded in small-sized sector followed by 0.87 times in large-sized and 0.80 times in medium-sized sector. The analysis of variance reveals that there is no significant difference in the mean percentage of assets turnover between the years and sectors. Similarly, there was a significant difference in this ratio between the three phases of liberalisation. The industry wise analysis reveals that the assets turnover of EID Parry Ltd and Ugar Sugar Works Ltd under large-sized sector, Sri Sarvaraya Sugars Ltd under medium-sized sector and India Sugars and Refineries Ltd and Ponni Sugars Ltd under small-sized sector was satisfactory. The utilisation efficiency of assets in Thiru Arooran Sugars Ltd under large-sized sector was very poor among the selected South Indian private sector sugar industry during the study period for the reason that its average ratio was the least among the industry and below the industry average.

The analysis of fixed assets turnover ratio and current assets turnover ratio indicate a mixed trend in almost all the selected industries under study during the period under review. The analysis of the turnover ratios suggest that all the selected industries were able to utilise the fixed assets and current assets properly in generating sales. The average ratio is more than one throughout the study period. Thus, the addition to investment in fixed assets and current assets could result in proportionate increase in sales.

The inventory turnover ratio represents a fluctuating trend during the study period. On an average, the South Indian private sector sugar industry had overall inventory turnover ratio of 2.79 times. The overall turnover ratio varied from sector to sector, the highest average was 4.07 times in medium-sized sugar industry followed by 2.89 times in large-sized and 2.11 times in small-sized sectors. Such fluctuations could be attributed to the differences in the growth rates of inventories and sales because of the factors such as market conditions, rise in sugarcane price and upward revision of selling price. The analysis of variance of inventory turnover ratio indicates that there are significant differences in inventory turnover ratio between the years and sectors. A notable point in analysis of inventory turnover ratio was that small-sized sugar industry failed to maintain its inventory turnover on par with the industry average.

All the assets turnover ratios of selected South Indian private sector sugar industry showed a declining trend during the growth phase. Such a declining trend could be attributed mainly to the poor performance of medium-sized and small-sized sugar industry. But during maturity phase the entire selected sectors and whole industry registered an increasing trend in its assets turnover ratios. This shows that good hope for further development in the years to come. The overall analysis of asset turnover reveals the different assets were utilised effectively by the selected industry of South Indian private sector Sugar Industry during the study period.

Profitability Trend

The analysis of profitability trend reveals that linear models of time trend of profitability has proved to be good fit in case of eight out of fifteen industries (53.33%) examined. The results showed that Sakthi Sugars Ltd, Thiru Arooran Sugars Ltd, Ugar Sugar Works Ltd (large-sized), Kothari Sugars & Chemicals Ltd and Sri Chamundeswari Sugars Ltd (medium-sized) and India Sugars and Refineries Ltd (small-sized) experienced a strong tendency in profitability to decline over the study period. The falling tendency of profit rate of these industries is the proof of adverse effect of various controls on process, output, expansion, investment, distribution etc, excerpted by government on these industries over time. Only in case of two industries viz., Jeypore Sugars & Chemicals Ltd (large-sized) and Ponni Sugars Ltd (small-sized), the time trend co-efficient of profit rate is positive, implying a tendency of profit rate of rise over time. The sector wise time trend regression results reveal that all the three sectors and the whole industry had a strong tendency for profit rate to fall over the study period. Further, variation in value of R^2 implies that time explain profitability variations of different industries in different degrees over the time. The industry wise dispersion in rate of profit of South Indian private sector Sugar Industry over the study period showed that Ugar Sugar Works Ltd experienced highest rate of profit over the study period. Another observation made is that mean rate of profit for South Indian private sector Sugar Industry varied greatly irrespective of the sector to which they belong. The relative dispersion in the series of profit rate is captured by the value of co-efficient of variation. It is observed that five out of fifteen industries experienced erratically fluctuating variation in profit rate series. Further, four out of fifteen industries experienced highly fluctuating variance, five out of fifteen industries have moderately fluctuating variation and one industry (Bannari Amman Sugars Ltd) experienced relatively stable variation in profit rate series.

Size and Profitability

The pooled regression results of the model regressing profit rate with size measured by sales showed that degrees of explanation of profitability by size are 26 per cent in whole industry, 25 per cent in large-sized industry, 20 per cent in medium-sized industry and 21 per cent in small-sized industry. The results also showed the positive relationship between size and profitability in all the three sectors and the whole industry which support the findings of Baumol (1967), Hall and Weiss (1967) and Vijayakumar (2003) who advocate positive relationship. It is also evident from the results that negative relationship between size and profitability reported in Rajshree Sugars & Chemicals Ltd, Sakthi Sugars Ltd and Thiru Arooran Sugars Ltd (large-sized), Sri Chamundeswari Sugars Ltd (medium-sized) and Dharani Sugars & Chemicals Ltd and Ponni Sugars Ltd (small-sized) which support the findings of Samuls and Smyth (1968), Marcus (1969), Whittington (1985) and Vishnu Kanta Purohit (1998) who advocated negative relationship between size and profitability. The co-efficient of size is also statistically significant and goodness of fit of the model is also satisfactory.

The pooled regression results of the model regressing profit margin with size measured by total assets shows more or less similar findings to the results of regressing profit rate with sales. The co-efficient is also statistically significant and goodness of fit of the model is also satisfactory. It can be concluded from the analysis that size and profit have positive relationship in all the three sectors and whole industry.

Growth and Profitability

The relationship between profit and growth has been explored by means of regression analysis. The pooled regression results of the model regressing profit rate with growth measured by growth rate of total assets shows that degree of explanation of profitability by growth is 21 per cent in whole industry, 52 per cent in large-sized industry, 31 per cent in medium-sized industry and seven per cent in small-sized industry. The results also showed the positive relationship between growth and profitability in all the sectors and whole industry. It is also evident from the results that negative relationship between the growth and profitability reported in Bannari Amman Sugars Ltd and Rajshree Sugars & Chemicals Ltd (large-sized) and Kothari Sugars & Chemicals Ltd and Sri Sarvaraya Sugars Ltd (medium-sized).

The pooled regression results of the model regressing profit margin with growth measured by rate of gross block and rate of sales shows more or less similar findings to the results of regressing profit margin with growth rate of total assets. However, the explanatory capacity of growth rate of gross block and growth rate of net sales on profit rate has not improved in this model. It can be concluded from the analysis that growth and profit have positive relationship in all the sectors and whole industry.

Liquidity and Profitability

The relationship between liquidity and profitability has been examined through correlation and regression analysis. It is evident from the results that there is positive correlation between profitability and liquidity in all the three sectors and whole industry during the study period. But, the correlation analysis between liquidity and profitability position of the 15 industries under study indicated a mix of positive and negative correlation. Eight out of fifteen industries reveal negative correlation and the remaining industry depicted positive correlation. The regression analysis also showed that there is a positive relationship between liquidity and profitability in all the three sectors and whole industry.

Generally, the theories have revealed that there is inverse relationship between liquidity and profitability. But in the whole, it may be concluded that no established relationship between liquidity and profitability exists for these industries. The various forms of the industries depicted different type of relationship (both negative and positive) between liquidity and profitability during the study period.

Determinants of Profitability

Determinants of profitability are analysed using the technique of ordinary least square. In South Indian private sector Sugar Industry, the model explain 97 per cent of variation in profitability of firms included in the industry. The analysis reveals that current ratio is the strongest determinant of the profitability followed by size, leverage, inventory turnover ratio, vertical integration and age in the South Indian private sector sugar industry.

In large-sized sector, model explains 93 per cent of variation in profitability of firms included in the sector. Among the variables age is the strongest determinant of profitability followed by current ratio, size, leverage, operating expenses to sales ratio, growth rate of assets, inventory turnover ratio and vertical integration. The selected variables explain 69 per cent on the variation in profitability of firms included in the medium-sized sector. It is evident from the results that size is the strongest determinant followed by inventory turnover ratio, growth rate assets, operating expenses to sales, leverage, current ratio, vertical integration and age. In small-sized sector, the selected variables explain 94 per cent of the variation in profitability of firms included in the sector. Among the variables inventory turnover ratio is the strongest determinant of profitability followed by size, operating expenses to sales ratio, leverage growth rate of assets, current ratio, vertical integration and age.

The overall explanatory power of regression appears to be good in all the three sectors of South Indian private sector Sugar Industry. This may be inferred from the co-efficient of determination (R^2), which is the measure of the extent of movement in the dependent variable that is explained by the independent variables.

Impact of Working Capital on Profitability

The study of the impact of working capital ratio on profitability of South Indian private sector sugar industry showed both negative and positive impact. Two out of six working capital ratios namely, liquidity ratio and cash turnover have shown negative association and remaining ratios have shown positive association with profitability. In the large-sized sector, liquidity ratio, receivables turnover ratio and cash turnover ratio have shown negative association, in medium-sized industry liquidity ratio, receivables turnover ratio, current turnover ratio and in small-sized industry liquidity ratio and cash turnover ratio have shown negative association with profitability. The pooled regression results of the model showing the impact of working capital ratios on profitability for South Indian private sector Sugar Industry as a whole are encouraging. The selected independent variables contribute 85 per cent of the variation in the profitability of selected South Indian private sector Sugar Industry. The selected variables also contribute 80 per cent in large-sized sector, 84 per cent in medium-sized sector and 89 per cent in small-sized sector of the variation in their profitability.

Assessment of Financial Health

The assessment of financial health of South Indian private sector sugar industry has been made by using Altman's Z score. The analysis shows that the financial health of South Indian private sector Sugar Industry during the study period was lying in bankruptcy zone. This shows the poor financial performance of South Indian private sector Sugar Industry. This was due to excessive use of working capital, failure to achieve adequate sales and poor inventory turnover of industry. It is also obvious from the analysis that the financial health of South Indian private sector sugar industry has been improved at the terminal years of the study period. This showed a good scope for improvement of its financial health in the future.

Suggestions

Keeping in view the observations relating to the study the following measures are suggested which would go a long way to improve the performance of South Indian private sector sugar industry.

1. It has been suggested that government should take measures for providing of infrastructure facilities to the industry, which in turn will increase the production performance of the industry and thereby improving their profitability. An effective and integrated policy of the government as regards restrictions on the import and export of sugar and low excise duty may further enhance the production performance of the industry. Application of latest technology, which makes the industry relationship cordial and congenial to increase the capacity utilisation ratio, more fast in research and development are suggested for further improvement in the production performance.
2. It is suggested that still there is a need for sugar industry to adopt better market strategy and by

reducing cost enhance their volume of profit so as to go ahead in the era of competition.

3. The profitability trend of selected South Indian private sector Sugar Industry experienced a strong tendency in profitability to decline over the study period. Therefore, it is suggested that all the selected industry should undertake cost control measures further so that profit margin of the industry may enhance the earning power ratios.
4. It is suggested that the standards for each component of cost of production should be fixed by the industry. It should make inter-firm comparison study and each unit should try to stick to the standards. An analysis of deviation, if any, should be made periodically. Materials management plays an effective role in controlling the cost of production and its reduction. A special emphasis and attention, therefore, should be given to sound and efficient materials management. Cost reduction and control techniques like budgetary control, standard costing, control ratios and value analysis should be adopted.
5. Cost accounting and cost audit should be made mandatory in sugar industry and they should be called to prepare cost sheet along with their annual financial statements.
6. A systematic, prompt and regular flow of information and its analysis is important for improving productivity, efficiency and profitability. A suitable management information system needs to be evolved which will take care of the data requirement of administrative offices as well as other units like factory etc., for internal management and control. Appropriate organisational management should be made for the successful implementation of management information system in South Indian private sector sugar industry.

7. At present, in India, the financial statements are presented on historical cost basis. As such these statements do not exhibit the correct realisable value of the assets on the date of the financial statements. Thus, the true profitability can not be ascertained on the basis of figures given in the financial statements on historical cost basis. It is, therefore, suggested that a supplementary statement should be included in the annual reports showing the figures of incomes, expenses, assets and liabilities on the basis of current values.
8. At present, the profit and loss account of multi-product industry is disclosed in a consolidated form, which can not measure and judge the profitability of each activity. Hence, the profit and loss account should be prepared on departmental activity basis by such multi-product industries.
9. It is also suggested that EVA has been used as a performance evaluation tool of an industry. The cost drivers of EVA like sales growth, operating profit margin, cost of capital etc., should be measured based on the improvement made in this value drivers. It appears to be useful in spotting changes in a industry's on going performance that are hidden in EPS.
10. Studies such as this could help us to find the factors responsible for poor profitability performance certain industries and guide the formation among industries. The government should not make uniform policy for all the industries. For example, the agro-based industry like sugar industry is the most vulnerable to the monsoon. The policy should contain special provisions to provide to such industry protection and incentives in the form of tax holdings, subsidies and/ or the like. It is also suggested that the rates of excise duty, power tariff and such other sales tax to be

reduced to a reasonable level to boost the sugar industry. Further, corporate tax should be abolished gradually to encourage the capital market for the sugar industries.

11. The unfavourable impact of leverage on profitability in certain industry can be avoided by reducing the dependability on debt capital, particularly when the business does not produce a rate of return at least equivalent rate of interest to be paid on borrowed capital.

12. It is essential to have objectivity performance appraisal criteria for every industry. For this purpose, the best way will be to introduce performance audit and revise the performance indicators. Commercial performance must take care of all the objectives and goals. For this purpose, a suitable system of financial and non-financial objectives must be developed. Policymaking should be a realistic assessment of cost.

13. The regulatory framework should enable all industry within the sector to compete effectively without any distortions either in cane supply or in sugar marketing. The distortions may be due to state level policy variations or due to conflicts between the regulatory provisions at the Central and State levels. These could be because of policies related to cane pricing, incentive schemes for capacity addition or restrictions on movement of byproducts like molasses, amongst others. Distortions may also be present in the form of restrictive barriers to entry or exit for players.

14. The farmer-industry relationship would be a key driver for the future growth of the sector and the regulatory framework would need to protect and incentivize this relationship. Given the small landholdings in South India, this relationship would need to be basis for inclusive growth for farmers and industry.

15. The regulatory framework would need to continue to ensure that the social objectives of farmers, industry sustainability and consumer protection are adequately addressed in the course of implementation of the business roadmap.
16. The existing regulatory framework in India for sugar is composed of five major regulations. Further alterations in these would need to be evaluated for developing the regulatory system. These regulations are reservation of cane area, cane pricing, monthly release mechanism, international trade regulations and levy sugar. Apart from these regulations, policy imperatives identified as part of the business roadmap, such as byproduct policy and resolution of central and state policy conflicts would also need to be addressed.
17. International markets have a high strategic value for India for managing the surplus and deficits that cannot be managed in the domestic market. The regulatory framework is needed to enable and incentivize greater participation in international trade by the South Indian private sector Sugar Industry.

Finally, in the light of above mentioned implications two precautionary points must be stated precisely. First the findings of the study cannot be taken as conclusive because profitability performance is a complex phenomenon and it is influenced by a number of factors. Here only some of these have been taken into consideration in this thesis. Second, the estimation results might be sensitive to data sample. It has been witnessed that when results were taken with the data sample, changes occurred with regard to the intensity of co-efficient and explanatory power of the model. This suggests that underlying data might be the root of disagreement in empirical results taken by different researchers through using very similar model specifications.

Practical Utility of the Study

The present study is mostly an analytical research on trend and pattern of profitability in South Indian private sector sugar industry during 1991-92 to 2005-06. The concepts of profit and profitability have been minutely discussed. The study has also given an overall idea of profitability of the selected industries. Further, the study compared the profitability of the South Indian private sector sugar industry based on initial, growth and maturity phases of liberalisation. The study also tests some hypotheses concerning the profitability of the South Indian private sector Sugar Industry with the help of theoretical model. It is hoped that the study will be useful to the corporate sector in India in general, and entrepreneurs, financial managers, financial institutions, investors, policy-makers and researchers in particular, for evaluating the profitability of any industry. The sick unit in the corporate sector can use of these findings for improving the financial as well as operational efficiency in future. The government can also use the findings of the study while formulating the industrial and investment policies for better industrial climate in South Indian private sector sugar industry in particular and for the country in general. Finally, South Indian private sector sugar industry can make the best use of the findings of the study for better financial management.

Scope for Further Research

Any research study can explore only a limited field of knowledge. There are many aspects that need to be researched further. In the present case also there is a considerable scope for further research. In spite of every attempt to make this study more intensive there are quite many fields remained unveiled owing to constrains of time and resources. Financial study, specially, has numerous dimensions. Each component of the financial statement has got scope for an extensive study. An analysis of the social profitability of the South Indian private sector sugar industry with the help of value added and the other techniques can provide an ample scope for further research. A considerable scope for further research also exists in the area of diversification, mergers and takeover. Another interesting theme would be to identify sick and healthy units separately in the South Indian private sector Sugar Industry and find out discriminating characteristic of each group with respect to performance. A study can also be undertaken in the area of performance appraisal comparing private sector and public sector.

The findings of the study may not have universal applicability since the study is confined to a definite period and to a definite scheme of corporate sector in India. Hence, to arrive at any general conclusion, the hypothesis need further testing by way of additional research in the same field in different periods and even in different fields in the same period. Last but not least one can make a comparative study of corporate performance in the pre liberalisation and the post liberalisation period. Therefore, research work in the above mentioned area would be of great practical significance and would throw more light on the operations of South Indian private sector sugar industry.

Conclusion

India ranks first in sugar consumption and second in sugar production in the world. From being one of the world leaders in sugar production, along with Brazil, the Indian sugar industry has imperiled itself due to government policies and inherent rigid factors. A new transformation is to be taken place in the South Indian private sector sugar industry as the industries can exhibit a Darwininan ability to adapt, morph and survive by exploring different product mixes and alternate sources of revenue. The profitability of South Indian private sector Sugar Industry has proved to be a volatile with regular boom and bust cycles. The sugar is not the only sweetener for sugar industry. Revenues from renewable (ethanol and power from bagasse) can be generated. The demand for ethanol and power in India is likely to grow in the next few years. The way forward is a balanced portfolio of sugar, alcohol and power, which will enable industries to be profitable and pay farmers a remunerative price. To survive a glut in cane crop, the sugar industry should diversify for producing ethanol and power.

Bibliography

Books

Agarwal, A.N. *Corporate Performance Evaluation*,(Jaipur: Pointer Publishers, 1991).

Agarwal, N.P. *Analysis of Financial Statements: A case study of Aluminium Industry in India* (New Delhi : National Publishing House, 1981).

Anthony, R.N. and Reece J.S. *Management Accounting - Principles* (Homewood, Illinois, Richard D. Irwin, Inc., 1975) 245.

Argenti, John. *Corporate collapse - the causes and symptoms* (New York: McGraw Hill 1976) 91.

Aziz, A. *Performance Appraisal - Accounting and Quantitative Approaches* (Jaipur: Pointer Publishers, 2003) 22.

Basant, C Raj, *A Corporate Financial Management* (New Delhi: Tata McGraw-Hill Publishing Company Ltd., 1978) 154.

Baumol, W.J. *Business Behaviour, Value and Growth* (New York: Harcourt Brace & World, 1967)

Bhayani, Sanjay J. *Practical Financial Statements Analysis* (Jaipur: Raj Book Enterprises, 2004).

Borck, Horace R. *et al. Financial Accounting - Principles and Applications*, 5th ed. (New York : McGraw-Hill Book Company, 1986).

Bradley, J.P. *Administrative Financial Management* (New York: Holt Rinechart and Winston, Inc., 1968) 173.

Das Mohapatra, A.K. *Corporate Financial Management* (New Delhi: Discovery Publishing House, 1999).

Drucker, Peter F., *The Practice of Management* (Allied Publishers, New Delhi, 1970) 46-47.

Duck R.E.V. and Jervis, F.R.J. *Management Accounting* (George G. Har & Company, 1964) 98.

ENO Transportation Foundation Inc. (Lansdowne : Transportation in America, VA, 1996).

Fitzsimmons, J.R, Steffens, P.R. and Douglas, E.J *Growth and Profitability in Small and medium sized Australian Firms* (Melbourne: AGSE Entrepreneurship Exchange, 2005)

Govindan Rao, D. and Mohana Rao, P. *Impact of working capital on profitability in cement industry - A correlation analysis* (New Delhi: Deep and Deep Publications, 1999).

Gupta, M.C. *Profitability Analysis* (Jeypore: Pointer Publishers, 1989) 36.

Gupta, S. P. *Statistical Methods* (New Delhi : Sultan Chand & Sons, 1996).

Guthman, H.G. and H.E. Dougall. *Corporate Financial Policy* (New Delhi : Prentice-Hall, 1982) 61.

Howard and Upton. *Introduction to Business Finance* (New York: McGraw-Hill, 1953), 147.

Hunt, Willian and Donaldson. *Basic Business Finance* (Illinois : Richard D. Jrwinm, 1965).

James, C. Van Horne. *Fundamentals of Financial Management* (New Delhi: Prentice-Hall, 1981) 155.

John, Sizer. *An insight into the Management Accounting* (London: Pitman,1979)170.

Joshi, N.C. *Management - Concept and Analysis* (New Delhi: Vivek Publishing Co., 1977) 50.

Kennedy, Ralph and Steward. Y. *Financial Statements - Forms, Analysis and Interpretation* , 5th ed. (Illinois; Richard D. Irwin Inc, 1968) 215-216.

Khan, M.Y and Jain, P.K. *Financial Management* (New Delhi : Tata McGraw-Hill Publishing Co., Ltd, 1996) 139.

Kulshrestha, N.K., *Theory and Practice of Management Accounting* (Aligarh: Novman Prakashan, 1976) 265.

Lawrence, J. Gitman. *Principles of Management Finance* (New York : Herper & Row Publishers, 1982) 204.

McTaggart, James *et al. The Value Imperative* (New York: Free Press, 1994) 4-6.

Most Knneth, S., *Accounting Theory*, (Columbus, Ohio: Grid Publishing Inc.,1982) P.207.

Panda, J. Patnaik, L.M. *Corporate Profitability* (India: RBSA Publishers, 2005).

Panda, Jagannath and Sradhananda Das. *Corporate Financial Structure* (Jaipur: RBSA Publishers, 2005).

Pandey, I.M. *Financial Management* (New Delhi: Vikas Publishing House Private Ltd., 1996) 449.

Parmar, S.J. *Financial Efficiency Modern Methods, Tools and Techniques* (Jaipur: Raj Book Enterprises, 2004).

Penerose, E.T. *The Theory of Growth of Firm,* (London: Basil Black Well, 1980) 25-36.

Pillai, R.S.N. and Bahavathi. *Management Accounting,* (New Delhi: S.Chand and Company Ltd).

Purohit, Vishnu Kanta. *Profitability in Indian Industries* (New Delhi : Gayatri Publications,1998).

Ralph, D.Kennedy, and M.Stewart. *Financial Statement* (Homewood III; Richard D.Irwin, Inc, 1968) 404.

Ray, Saon, *Economic Reforms and Efficiency of firms: the Indian manufacturing sector during the nineties* (New Delhi: University of Delhi Enclave, 2003)

Rede, Lata Arun. *Profitability Trends and Business Cycle* (New Delhi: Discovery Publishing House, 1998).

Richard, M.S. Wilson and Gerard Metugh. *Financial Analysis: A managerial introduction* (London: Cassell Educational Limited, 1987) 5.

Roy, A.Foulke, *Practical Financial Statement Analysis* (New Delhi: Tata McGraw-Hill Publishing Company Ltd., 1978) 583.

Satyanarayana, J. *State Government Enterprises in Andhra Pradesh: An Overview,* In: Rao Y. Saraswathy (eds.), *Public Enterprises (A State Level Perspective),* (Delhi: B.R. Publishing Corporation, 1986).

Sharma, R.K and Gupta, Shashi. K. *Management Accounting – Principles and Practice,* (New Delhi: Kalyani Publishers, 1986) 150.

Sherlekar, S.A., *Industrial Organisation and Management* (Bombay: Himalaya Publishing House, 1998) 375.

Singh, Ajit and Whittington, G., *Growth, Profitability and Valuation* (Cambridge: Cambridge University Press, 1968)

Slavin, A, *et al. Basic Accounting for Management and Financial Control* (New York : Holt, Rinshart and Winsron, Inc,1968) 173.

Smyth, David J, Boyes William J and Peseua Dennis E *Size, Growth, Profits and Executive compensation in the Large Corporation: A study of the 500 Largest United Kingdom and United States of Industrial Corporations,* (London: Macmillan Press, 1975)

Steindl, J. *Small and big Business* (London: Oxford University press, 1944) 33-35

Varshney, R.L and Maheswari, K.L., *Managerial Economics.* (New Delhi: Sultan Chand and Sons, 1977) 297.

Vijayakumar, A. *Financial Appraisal of Salem Co-operative Sugar Mills Ltd., Mohanur, in the book Research studies in Commerce and Management* (Delhi: Classical Publishing Company, 2002) 51-65.

Vijayakumar, A. *Research Studies in Commerce and Management* (New Delhi : Classical Publishing Company, 2002).

Vijayakumar, A. *Working Capital Management: A Comparative Study* (New Delhi: Northen Book Centre, 2004).

Walker and Boughn. *Financial Planning and Policy* (Harper International Student Edition Reprint, 1984) 151.

Waston, J.F and Brigham E.F. *Managerial Finance*, 6th ed. (Illinois: The Dryden Press, Hinsdale, 1978) 148.

Westons, J.F., and Eugen F. Brigham. *Essentials of Managerial Finance*, 9th ed. (Illinois: The Dryden Press 1984).

Articles

Agarwal, R.N. (1999). Profitability and Growth in Indian Automobile Manufacturing Industry, *Indian Economic Review*, Vol.26, No.1, pp. 81.

Aggarwal, N and Singla, S.K. (2001). How to develop a single index for financial performance, *Indian Management*, Vol. 12, No. 5, pp. 59-62.

Agiomirgianakis, G., Voulgaris, F. and Papadogonas, T. (2006). Financial factors affecting profitability and employment growth: the case, of Greek manufacturing, *International Journal of Financial Service Management,* Vol. 1, Nos. 2/3, pp.232-242.

Ahuja, Gautam and Sumit K. Majumdar (1998). An Assessment of the Performance of Indian State-owned Enterprises, *Jouranl of Productivity Analysis*, Vol. 9, No. 2, pp.113-132.

Altman, Edwin I. (1968). Financial Ratios-Discriminate Analysis and prediction of corporate bankruptcy, *Journal of Finance*, Vol. 9, pp. 589-609.

Anand, *et al.,* (1999). Economic Value Added: Business performance measure of shareholder value, *The Management Accountant*, pp. 351-356.

Bacidore, J.M, Boquist, J.A, Miboum, T.T., and Thakor, A.V. (1997). The Search for the Best Financial Performance Measure, *Financial Analysts Journal*, pp.11-20.

Banerjee and Ashok, (1997). Economic Value Added (EVA): a better performance measure, *The Management Accountant*, pp.86-88.

Banerjee and Ashok, (2000). Linkage between Economic Value Added and Market Value : An Analysis, *Vikalpa,* Vol. 25, No. 3, pp. 23-36.

Bao, B.H. and Bao, D.H., (1999). The Association between firm Value and Economic Value Added, *Indian Accounting Review*, Vol.3, No.2, pp. 161-64.

Bardia, S.C. (2002). Economic Value Added: Overall Consideration, *Economic Challenger*, pp. 1-7.

Barthwal, R.R. (1976). The Determinants of profitability in Indian Textile Industry, *Economica,* Vol. 43, pp. 267-274.

Bevar, W.R. (1966). Financial ratios as prediction of failure, *Journal of Accounting Research,* pp. 71-110.

Bhanu, V. (2005). Merged Companies - their profitability performance, *Indian Journal of Accounting*, Vol.XXXV (2), pp. 19-38.

Bharatwaj, Sunder, G., Varadarajan, Rajan, P., and Szymanski David, M. (1993). An Analysis of Market Share and profitability relationship, *Journal of Marketing*, Vol, pp. 1-18.

Bhata and Dayal Bhat Nagar, (2003). Economic Value Added for comparison among companies of different industries, *The ICFAI Journal of Applied Finance*, No. 3, Vol. XXII, pp. 36-42.

Bothwell, Cooley and Hall (1982). A New View of Market Structure-Performance Debate, *The Journal of Industrial Economics and Statistics,* Vol. 64, pp. 635-645.

Burkette, G. Hedley, T. (1997). The truth about economic value added, *The CPA Journal*, No. 7, p. 46(4).

Burthwal, Nagarajan (1990). Profitability and Structure: A Firm Level Study of Indian Pharmaceutical Industry, *The Indian Economic Journal*, No. 2, Vol. 38, pp. 70-84.

Chalam, G.V. and Dakshinamurthy, D. (1985). Performance of Public Enterprises in India: Impact of Heavy External Financing, *Public Enterprises*, Vol. 6, No. 2, pp. 16-20.

Chander, Subhash and Priyanka Aggarwal (2007). Determinants of Corporate Growth: An Empirical Study of Indian Drugs and Pharmaceutical Industry, *The Journal of Management Research*, Vol. VI, No. 10, pp. 50-70.

Chandrasekaran, N. (1993). Determinants of profitability in Cement Industry, *Decision*, Vol. 20, No. 4, pp. 235-244.

Chattopadhayay, P. (1989). Central Government Enterprises: An Eighteen Years Profile, *Facts for You*, Vol. 10, No. 9, pp. 11-19.

Chawola, Deepak (1986). An empirical analysis of the profitability of the Indian man-made fibres industry, *Decision*, pp. 106-115.

Cleveland and Frederick, W. (1993). Profitability, Uncertainty and Firm Size, *Small Business Economics*, Vol. 5, pp. 87-100.

Conyon, N. and Machin, S. (1991). The Determinants of Profit Margins in U.K. Manufacturing, *The Journal of Economics*, Vol.34, No.4, pp. 369-382.

Costigan, M.H. and Lovata Linda, (2002). Empirical Analysis Adopters of Economic Value Added, *Management Accounting Research*, Vol. 13, No. 2, pp. 40-46.

D'Souza, Juliet and William Megginson, L. (1999). Financial and operating performance of privatized firms during the 1990s, *The Journal of Finance*, Vol. LIV, No. 4, pp. 1397-1434.

Dhankar, Raj S. (1998). A new look at the criteria of performance measurement for business enterprises in India-A study of public sector undertakings, *Finance India*, Vol. II, No. 1, pp. 17-28.

Dodd, James, L, Chen, Shimine, (1997). EVA: A new panacea?, *Business and Economic Review*, Vol. 42, pp. 26-28.

Dutta, Soumyendra Kishore, (1999). An Analysis of Profitability trend in the Indian Cotton Mill Industry, *Asian Economic Review*, Vol. 41, No. 2, pp. 294-307.

Eisenberg, Theodore and Stefan Sundgren. (1993). Profitability, Uncertainty and Firm Size, *Small Business Economics*, Vol. 55, pp. 87-100.

Ethiraj and Govindaraj (1998). The EVA feather in the market cap, *The Economic Times*, p. 1.

Ferri, Michael, G., and Jones, Wesley H. (1979). Determination of Financial Structure: A New Methodological Approach, *The Journal of Finance*, Vol. XXXIV, No. 3, pp. 631-344.

Fu, Tze-Wei, Mei-Chiu ke and Yen-Sheng Huang (2002). Capital Growth, financing source and profitability of Small Business: Evidence from Taiwan Small Enterprises, *Small Business Economics,* Vol. 18, No. 4, pp. 257-267.

Gale, B.T. (1972), "Market Share and Rate of Return", *Review of Economics and Statistics*, Vol. 54, pp. 412-423.

Gangadhar, V. (1982). Cement Industry-Some Aspects of Profitability, *The Management Accountant*, p. 477.

Ghosh, Arindam (2007). Working Capital Management practices in some selected industries in India, *The Management Accountant*, pp. 60.68.

Ghosh, Santany Kumar and Santi Gopal Maji (2003). Utilisation of current assets and operating profitability: An empirical study on cement and tea industries in India, *Indian Journal of Accounting,* Vol. XXXIV, pp. 52-60.

Glancey, K. (1998). Determinants of growth and profitability in small entrepreneurial firms, *International Journal of Entrepreneurial Behaviour and Research,* Vol. 4, No. 1, pp. 18-27.

Grant, J. (1996). Foundation of EVA for investment managers: Just in time, EVA, *Journal of Financial Management*, Vol. 23, No. 1, p. 41(8).

Gupta, L.O. (1979). Financial ratios as forwarding predicators of sickness, *ICICI,* Bombay, pp. 65-69.

Hall, M. and Weiss, L. (1967). Firm size and profitability, *Review of Economics and Statistics*, Vol. 49, pp. 319-331.

Hamsalakshmi and Manickam (2005). Financial performance analysis of selected software companies. *Finance India*, Vol.xix, No. 3, pp. 915-935.

Harihar, T.S. (1999). EVA prorating Myths, *Chartered Finance Analyst*, pp. 8-9.

Islam, Mohammed Rafiqul (2000). Profitability of Fertilizer Industry in Bangladesh, *The Management Accountant*, pp. 338-345.

Jagan Mohan Rao, P. (1993). Financial Appraisal of Indian Automotive Tyre Industry, *Finance India*, Vol. VII, No. 3, pp. 683-685.

John, Steer Peter and Cable. (1978). Internal Organisation and Profit: An Empirical Analysis of Large U.K. Companies, *The Journal of Industrial Economics,* Vol. 27, pp. 13-26.

Kallu Rao, P. (1993). Inter Company Financial Analysis of Tea Industry-Retrospect and Prospect, *Finance India*, Vol. VII, No. 3, pp. 587-602.

Kaur, Kuldip (1998). Size, Growth and Profitability of Firms in India-an Empirical Investigation, *Finance India*, Vol. XII, No. 2, pp. 455-457.

Khustrokhan, H.R, (2002). Tata Tea Ropes in Stern Stewart & Company to Better EVA, *Business Standard*, p. 7.

Kim and Kunchul, (1996). Profitability, Growth and Risk (Optimisation), *Australian Economic Papers*, Vol. 33, pp.65-88.

KPMG-BS. (1998). Corporate India: An Economic Value Score board, *The Strategy*, pp. 22-25.

Krishnaveni, (1991). Profitability and growth in Indian Automobile manufacturing industry, *Indian of Economic Growth*, Vol. 26, pp. 81-97.

Kumar, P. (1985). Corporate growth and Profitability of firms in India, *Margin,* pp. 32-36.

Luber, R. B. (1996). Who are the real wealth creators. *Fortune*, pp. 2-3.

Luthra, Renu, Vaishampayan and Dheeraj Misra (2006). Profitability and Size: A study of small-scale industries in Uttar Pradesh, *The ICFAIN Jouranl of Management Research,* pp. 28-37.

Mallick, Amit and Debasish Sur, (1998). Working Capital and Profitability: A Case Study in Interrelation, *The Management Accountant*, pp. 805-809.

Mallik and Debasish Mukherjee (2006). Performance of leasing industry in West Bengal, *The Management Accountant*, pp. 393-398.

Manasan, Rosario G., Junaita Amatong and Gil Beltran, (1988). The public enterprise sector in the Philippines: economic contribution and performance: 1975-1984, *Public Enterprise*, Vol. 8, No. 4, pp. 339-351.

Mancke, R.B. (1974). Causes of Inter Firm Profit Differences: A New Interpretation of the Evidence, *Quarterly Journal of Economics*, Vol. 83, pp. 181-193.

Mangala, Deepa and Joura Simpy, (2002). Linkage between Economic Value Added and Market Value: An Analysis in Indian context, *Indian Management Studies Journal*, pp. 55-56.

Manor Selvi, A. and Vijayakumar, A. (2007). Structure of profit rates in Indian Automobile industries – A comparison, *The Management Accountant*, Vol. 10, pp. 784-789.

Marcos, A.M., Lima and Marcelo Resende, (2004). Profit margins and business cycles in the Brazilian industry: a panel data study, *Taylor and Francis Journal in Applied Economics*, pp. 923-930.

Marcus, M. (1969). Profitability and Size of firm: some further evidence, *Review of Economics and Statistics*, Vol. 51, pp. 104-107.

Mishra, R.K. (1988). Performance Evaluation of Public Enterprises in India, *Journal of Institute of Public Enterprises*, Vol. 6, No. 2, pp. 3-23.

Mulla, Mansur A. (2002). Use of 'Z' score analysis for evaluation of financial health of textile mills-a case study, *Abhigyan*, Vol. XIX, No. 4, pp. 37-40.

Nakicenovic, N.(1991). Diffusion of Pervasive System: A case of Transport Infrastructures, *Technological Forecasting and Social Change*, p. 39.

Neumann, Bobel and Haid (1979). Profitability, Risk and Market Structure in West German industries, *The Journal of Industrial Economics*, Vol. 28, pp. 227-242.

Nugent, Jim (1998). Corporate profitability in Ireland; Overview and Determinants, *Jouranl of the statistical and social inquiry, Society of Ireland*, Vol. XXVIII, Part-I, pp. 35-70.

Ochsner (1995). Welcome to the new world of economic value added, *Compensation and Benefits*, Vol. 27, No. 2, p. 30(3).

Ohlson, S. (1980). Financial ratios and the prediction of bankruptcy, *Journal of Accounting Research*, pp. 109-131.

Pai V.S, Vadivel.V and Kamala K.H. (1995). Diversified companies and financial performance: A study, *Finance India*, Vol. IX, No. 4, pp. 977-988.

Pandey, I.M. (1980). Concept of Earning Power, *Accounting Journal*, Vol.W, p. 46.

Pant, L.W. (1991). An Investigation of Industry and Firm Structural characteristics in Corporate Turnaround, *Journal of Management Studies*, Vol. 28, No. 12, pp. 623-643.

Parasuram, N.R. (2000). Economic Value Added: Its Computation and Impact on Selected Banking Companies, *The ICFAI Journal of Applied Finance*, Vol. 6, No. 4, pp. 171-178.

Patel, D.M. (200). Profit and Profitability – A case study of Colour-Chem Limited, *ACCST Research Jouranl*, Vol. II, No. 2, pp. 89-95.

Patra, Santimoy (2005). Liquidity Vs. Profitability, *Indian Journal of Accounting,* Vol.XXXV(2), pp. 39-43.

Paul, A. Geroski, Stephen Machin and Christopher F. Walters (1997). A study on Financial Performance of diversified companies, *Journal of Industrial Economics,* Vol. 45, No. 2, pp. 171-189.

Paul, George (1985). Financial performance of Diversified Companies in India: A comparative study of diversified and non-diversified companies, *Vikalpa,* Vol. 10, No. 2, pp. 179-188.

Putnam and Bulford (1997). EVA Analysis predicts tough time in US markets, *Global Investor*, pp. 42-44.

Raghunatha Reddy, D. and Padma, S. (2005). Pre and Post Merger financial performance of selected companies, *Indian Journal of Accounting*, Vol. XXXV (2), pp. 29-38.

Raghunathan, V. and Prabina Das (1999). Corporate Performance: Post- Liberalization, *The ICFAI Journal of Applied Finance*, Vol. 5, No. 2, pp. 6-29.

Raja and Suresh kumar, A. (2006). Is Age or Size Influences Corporate Performance, *PSG Journal of Management*, Vol. 1, No.4, pp.51-62.

Rajeswari, (2000). Liquidity Management of Tamil Nadu Cement Corporation Ltd, Alangulam- A Case Study, *The Management Accountant*, Vol. II, No. 2, pp. 377-378.

Rao, M.P. (1985). Impact of Debt Equity Ratio on Profitability-An Exploratory Study of Engineering Industry, *Lok Udyog,* Vol. 19 (5), pp. 29-34.

RBI Bulletin (1995). Financial performance of private corporate business sector, *Finance India*, Vol. IX, No. 4, pp. 901-908.

RBI Corporate Studies Division, (2003). Performance of corporate business sector during the first half of 2002-2003, *Finance India*, Vol. XVII, No. 3, pp. 987-1002.

Rei, Debashish and Debashish Sur, (2001). Profitability Analysis of Indian Food Products Industry: A case study of Cadbury India Ltd, *The Management Accountant*, Vol. 36, No. 6, pp. 407-412.

Remmers, L., Stonetill, A., Wright, R., and Beakhusen, T., Industry and size as Debt-ratio determinants in manufactuirng internationally, *Financial Managmenet*, Vol. III, Spring, pp. 2975.

Remmers, Lee, Stonenill, Arthur, Wright, Richard and Bekhuisen, (1974). Industry and size as Debt Ratio Determinants in Manufacturing Internationally, *Financial Management*, pp. 24-32.

Rutledge, J. (1993), De-jargoning EVA, *Forbes*, Vol. 152, No. 10, p. 148(1).

Sahu, S.K. (2000). Analysis of corporate profitability: a multivariate approach, *The Management Accountant,* Vol. 35, No. 8, pp. 571-577.

Sam Luther, C.T. (2007). Liquidity, Risk and Profitability analysis – A case study of Madras Cements Ltd, *The Management Accountant*, Vol. 42, No. 10, pp. 784-789.

Samuels, J.M. and Smyth, D.J. (1968). Profits, Variability of Profits and Firm size, *Economica,* Vol. 35, pp. 127-139.

Sanjay, J. and Bhayani (2006). A study on sales trend and cost structure of Indian Cement Industry, *The Management Accountant*, Vol.41, No. 1, pp. 66-72.

Sankar, T.L. Mishra, R.K. and Nandagopal, R.N. (1990). State Level Public Enterprises in India: An Overview, *Economic and Political Weekly*, Bombay, pp. 1-37.

Sastry, K.S. (1994). Uses of 'Z' score of selective privatization marrtioused note, *Indian Journal of Finance and Research*, New Delhi, pp. 85-88.

Scott, David, F. (1972). Evidence on the importance of Financial Structure, *Financial Management*, Summer, pp. 45-50.

Scott, David, F. and Martin, John, D. (1975). Industry influence on Financial structure, *Financial Management*, Vol. 4, Spring, pp. 67-75.

Sengupta, Key (1998). An empirical exploration of the performance of Fertilizers Industry in India: An econometric analysis, *Artha Vijnana*, Vol. XL, No. 3, pp. 252-262.

Shanmugam, K.R. and Bhaduri Saumitra N. (2002). Size, Age and Firm Growth in the Indian Manufacturing Sector, *Applied Economics Letters*, Vol. XI, pp. 607-613.

Shweta, Jani (2003). Godrej Retools for Value , *Business Standard*, p. 6.

Sidhu, H.S. and Bhatia G. (1993). Factors affecting profitability in Indian Textile Industry, *The Indian Economic Journal*, Vol. 41, No. 2, pp. 137-143.

Sidhu, H.S. and Gurpreet Bhatia, (1998). Factors Affecting in Indian Textile Industry, *The Indian Economic Journal*, pp. 137-143.

Singh, S.P. (2007). Performance of sugar mills in Uttar Pradesh by Ownership, size and location, *Pranjana*, Vol. XXXV, No. 4, pp. 233-259.

Stekler, H.O. (1964). The Variability of Profitability with Size of Firms 1947-1958, *Journal of American Statistical Association*, Vol. 59, pp. 1183-1193.

Stern and Joel (1990). One way to build value in your firm, Executive compensation, *Financial Executive*, pp. 51-54.

Steward, G. and Bennet (1994). EVATM Fact and Fantasy, *Journal of Applied Corporate Finance*, pp. 71-84.

Sudarsana Reddy, G. (2003). Financial Performance of Paper industry in A.P, *Finance India*, Vol. XVII, No. 3, pp. 1027-1033.

Sur, Debasish, (1999). Working Capital Profitability; A case study in inter-relation, *The Management Accountant*, Vol. 33, No. 1, pp. 805-809.

Sur, Debasish, (2001). Liquidity Management: An overview of four companies in Indian Power Sector, *The Management Accountant*, pp. 407-412.

Sur, Debasish, Joydeep Biswas and Prasenjit Ganguly, (2001). Liquidity Management in Indian Private Sector Enterprises-A case study of Indian Primary Aluminum industry, *Indian Journal of Accounting*, Vol. XXXII, pp. 8-14.

Thampy, A. and Beheli, R. (2001). Economic Value Added in Banks, *The ICFAI Journal of Applied Finance*, Vol. 7, No. 1, pp. 180-189.

Thenmozhie, M. (1999). Economic value added as a measure of corporate performance, *The Indian Journal of Commerce*, Vol. 52, No. 4, pp. 72-85.

Thirumavalavan, P. (2006). Determinants of Earnings Before Interest and Taxation (EBIT) of Aluminium Companies, *PSG Jouranl of Management Research*, Vol. 1, No. 2, pp. 33-37.

Tully and Shawn, (1997). Adding value, *Business Today*, pp. 68-73.

Vijayakumar A. and Kadirvel S. (2003a). Determinants of profitability in Indian Public Sector Manufacturing Industries –An Econometric Analysis, *The Journal of Institute of Public Enterprises*, Vol. 26, pp. 1-2.

Vijayakumar, A and Kadirvel, S. (2003b). Profitability and Size of the firm in Indian Minerals and Metals industry, *The Management Accountant*, pp. 816-821.

Vijayakumar, A. (1996). Assessment of Corporate Liquidity-A Discriminant Analysis approach, *The Management Accountant*, Vol. 31, No. 8, pp. 589-591.

Vijayakumar, A. (1998). Determinants of corporate size, growth and profitability, *Management Accountant*, Vol. X, No. 4, pp. 925-932.

Vijayakumar, A. (2002). Assessment of liquidity – A Discriminant Analysis approach, *The Management Accountant*, Vol. 14, pp. 50-62.

VijayaKumar, A. (2002). Determinants of Profitability-A Firm Level study of the Sugar Industry of Tamil Nadu, *The Management Accountant*, pp. 458-465.

Vijayakumar, A. and Venkatachalam, A. (1995). Working Capital and Profitability-An Empirical Analysis, *The Management Accountant*, Vol. 15, No. 3, pp. 748-750.

Vishnani, Sushma and Bhupesh Kr Shah (2006). Liquidity Vs profitability – A detailed study in perspective of Indian consumer electronics industry, *Pranjana*, Vol. 9, No. 2, pp. 13-20.

Wei, Zuobao, Oscar Varela, Juliet D'Souza and Kabir Hassan. M. (2003). The financial and operating performance of China's newly privatized firms, *Financial Management*, Vol. 32, No. 2, pp. 107-126.

Whittington, G. (1980). The Profitability and Size of United Kingdom Companies 1960-1964, *The Journal of Industrial Economics*, Vol. 28, pp. 335-342.

Yucel, Tulay, Kurt and Guluzar, (2002). Cash Conversion Cycle, Cash Management and Profitability in: An empirical study on the ISE Traded companies, *Istanbul Stock Exchange Review*, Vol. 6, No. 2, pp. 1-15.

Working Papers

Bosworth, Derek and Joanne Loundes, (2002). The Dynamic Performance of Australian Enterprises, Working paper No. 03/2002, Melbourne Institute of Applied Economic and Social Research, The University of Melbourne.

Chhibber, Pradeep K. and Sumit K.Majumdhar (1997). Foreign Ownership and Profitability: Property Rights, Strategic Control and Corporate Performance in Indian Industry, Working Paper No.6, The William Davidson Institute of Michigan Business School.

Etebari, A. (1987). Financial ratio criteria: A hypothesis and empirical test, University of New Harcshrie, Working paper, pp. 27-32.

Feeny, Simon (2000). Determinants of profitability: an empirical investigation using Australian tax entities, Melbourne Institute of Applied Economic and Social Research, Working paper No:19, The University of Melbourne.

Feeny, Simon and Mark Rogers, (1998). Profitability in Australian Enterprises, Melbourne Institute of Applied Economic and Social Research, Working paper No: 21/98, The University of Melbourne.

Feeny, Simon and Mark Rogers, (1999). Market Share, Concentration and Diversification in Firm Profitability, Melbourne Institute of Applied Economic and Social Research, Working paper No: 20, The University of Melbourne.

Fred, Kaen, R and Baumann Hans (2003). Firm Size, Employees and Profitability in US Manufacturing Industries.

Glen, Jack, Kevin Lee and Ajit Singh, (2002). Corporate profitability and the dynamics of competition in emerging markets. A time services analysis, ESRC Center for Business Research, Working paper No. 248/2002, University of Cambridge.

Kakani, Ram Kumar, Biswatosh Saha and Reddy V.N. (2003). Determinants of financial performance of Indian corporate sector in the post- liberalization era; An exploratory study, NSE Research Initiative, Paper No: 5, National Stock Exchange of India Limited, pp. 1-38.

Leahy, Arthur S. (2004). The determinants of profitability in the Liquor Industry, Briefing Notes in Economics, No. 61, pp. 1-6.

Liu Wan-Chun and Hsu, Chan-Min (2004). Financial Structure, Corporate Finance and Growth of Taiwan's manufacturing firms.

Loundes, Joanne (1998). Performance of Australian Government Trading Enterprises: An overview, Working paper No .22/98, Melbourne Institute of Applied Economic and Social Research, The University of Melbourne.

Loundes, Joanne (2001). The Financial Performance of Australian Government Trading Enterprises pre-and post–reform, Melbourne Institute of Applied Economic and Social Research, Working paper No:5./2001, The University of Melbourne,

McDonald, James Ted (1997). The Determinants of Firm Profitability in Australian Manufacturing, Melbourne Institute of Applied Economic and Social Research, Working paper No. 17/97, The University of Melbourne.

Nitsure, Rupa Rege and Mathew Joseph, (1999). Liberalisation and the Behavior of Indian Industry, ABAS International Conference on "Globalisation and Emerging Economics" at Barcelona, Spain, No. 14.

Pandey, I.M and Bhat, R. (1998). Financial Ratio patterns in Indian Manufacturing Companies: A multivariate Analysis, Working Papers No. 764, Ahmedabad: Indian Institute of Management.

Riceman, S.S. and Cahan, S.F. (2002). Do Managers Perform Better under EVA Bonus Schemes, Social Science Research Network Electronic Paper Collection.

Rogers, Mark, (2001). The Effect of Diversification on Firm Performance, Melbourne Institute of Applied Economic and Social Research, Working paper No.02/2001, The University of Melbourne.

Singh, A., and Hamid J. Corporate financial structure in Developing Countries, IFC technical paper, No.1 The World Bank, Washington, D.C.

Topalova, Petia (2004). Overview of the Indian corporate sector: 1989-2002, IMF working paper No: wp/04/64, Asia and Pacific Department, pp. 1-41.

Weill, Laurent (2004). Leverage and corporate performance-9 frontier efficiency, University Robert Schuman, instituted detudes politiques, 47 avenue de la Foret-Noire, 67082 Strasbourg cedex, France. e-mail: Laurent. Weill @ urs.G-strasbg.fr.

Unpublished Thesis

Jain, Asha (1981). Price- Cost Margin in Indian Manufacturing Industries: An Econometric Analysis, Ph.D thesis, IIT, Kanpur.

Kadirvelu, S. (2002). Profitability Analysis of Selected Indian Public Sector Manufacturing Enterprises-before and after Liberalisation, Unpublished thesis,Bharathiar University, Coimbatore.

Krishnaveni, M. (2004). Performance Appraisal of an Indian Chemical Industry after Liberalisation (1991-92 to 2001-02), Unpublished thesis, Bharathiar University, Coimbatore.

Kulshreshtha, R.S. (1973). Profitability in India's Steel Industry-During the decade 1960-70 (A thesis submitted for the degree of Ph.D., Dept. of E.A.F.M. University of Rajashthan), p. 83.

Sarkaia, Maninder S., Shergil U.S. (2004). Market Structure and Financial Performance-An Indian Evidence with Enhanced Controls, Ph.D Thesis Submitted to the Guru Nanak Dev University.

Wolfgang Aussenegg and Ranko Jelic, (2002). Operating performance of privatized companies in transition economies- the case of Poland, Hungary and the Czech republic, Research abstract, source: www.ssrn.com.

Reports

- *Annual Reports of the South Indian private sector Sugar Industry.*
- *Basic statistics relating to Indian Economy*, Centre for Monitoring Indian Economy, Mumbai, Sep. 1994.
- Government of India, *Annual Survey of Industries* (Series), Central Statistical Organization.
- *Kothari's Industrial Directory of India.*
- *RBI Bulletin*, RBI, Mumbai.

Select on-line Newspapers

- Business Line
- Business Standard
- Business-Standard.com
- Deccan Chronicle
- Deccan Herald.com
- Express India.com
- Financial Express
- Hindustan Times Online
- India Today
- India Daily.com
- India Direct.com
- India Express.com
- India Infoline.com
- India Press.org
- NewsIndia-Times.com
- PatrikaOnline.com
- The Economic Times
- The Hindu
- The Times of India

Select Business Magazines

- Banking & Finance - Bi-monthly magazine on banking & finance.
- Business Barons - Bi-monthly business magazine.
- Business Today - A fortnightly business magazine.
- Business Weekly News - International weekly business reports.
- Capital Market - A business magazine focused on the stock market.
- Dhan - An online business & financial news magazine.
- Domex Information - Fortnightly industrial & business bulletin.
- Fortune - A financial magazine from pathfinder.
- India Investors - Weekly newsletter on stock markets.
- India Times - Online business magazine.
- Industrial Economist - Online business magazine.
- Industrial Magazine Online - Industry news, events, press releases, etc.
- Outlook Profit - A fortnight business magazine.

Index

R

S

T